T0245529

DK EYEWITNESS

unforgettable journeys

THE AMERICAS

unforgettable journeys

THE AMERICAS

DISCOVER THE JOYS OF SLOW TRAVEL

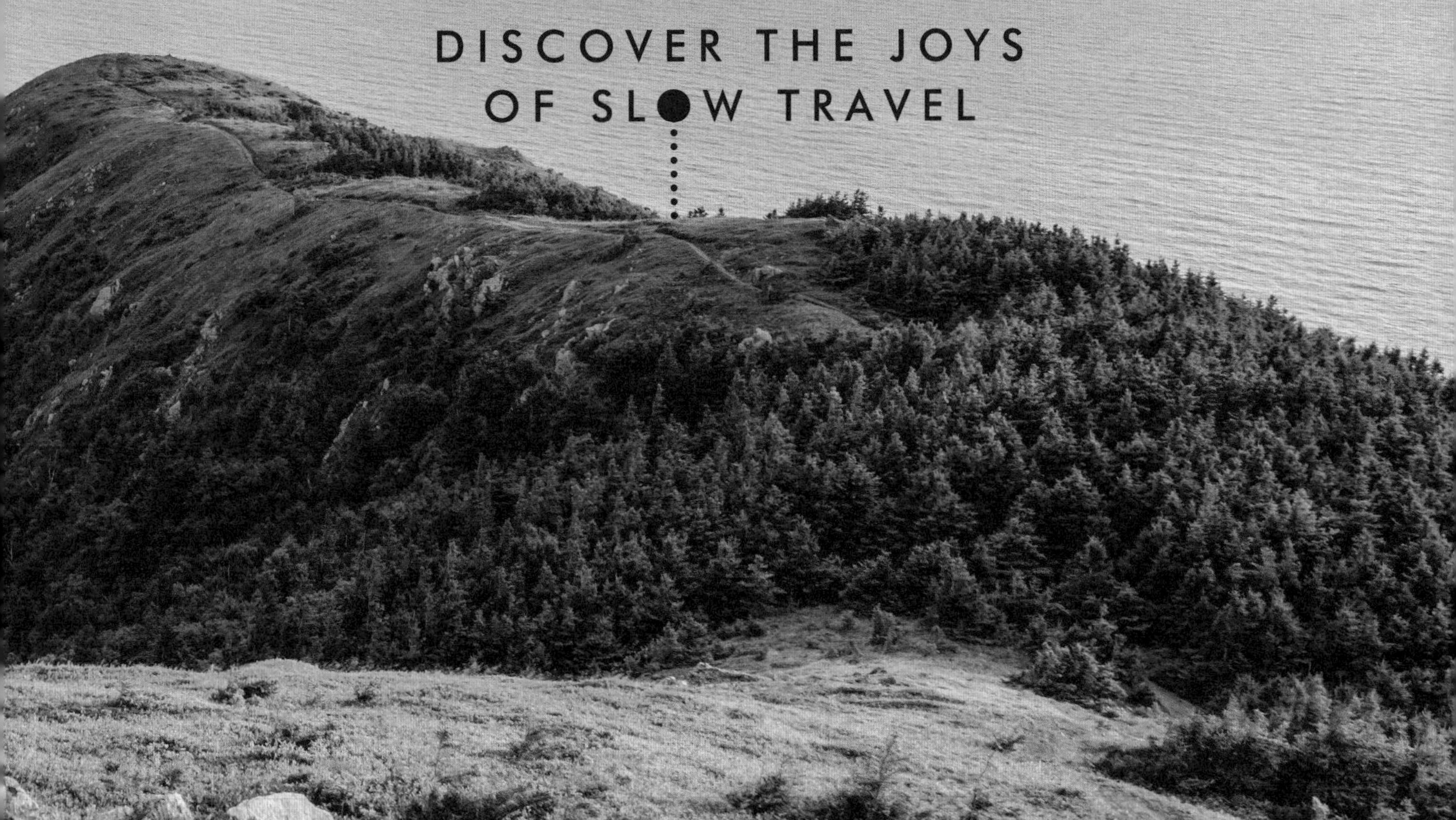

Contents

Previous page *The Skyline Trail look-off in Cape Breton, Nova Scotia, Canada*

Camping under the Northern Lights in the Yukon, Canada

Introduction

Lush misty forests, icy waterways, mind-bending canyons, and pristine paradisiacal islands: the Americas are home to some of the world's most immense landscapes. This is a region of epic proportions, where the planet's biggest salt flat shares the same landmass as ancient smoldering volcanoes.

You could spend a lifetime exploring the staggering expanses of these two continents, but how best to do it? Taking the scenic route, of course. Drift Peru's mighty Amazon on a boat and float past old-growth rainforest, where woolly monkeys swing in the trees. Hop in a car to take the mother of all road trips along the US's Pacific Coast Highway, letting the ocean breeze guide you from arid hills to palm-lined beaches. Or take a train from coast to coast in Canada and trundle past epic river canyons, the snowy Rockies, and soaring skyscrapers in one trip. It's only when you slow down do you truly see the wonders of this world—and within these two continents, the wonders are infinite.

To get you on your way, we've picked out the continents' most inspirational adventures. In *Unforgettable Journeys The Americas*, you'll trundle to the tip of South America, explore the far reaches of Canada, drive from the east to west coast in the United States, and hike across Caribbean rainforest. We've organized the book by modes of transportation, so whether you're an avid hiker or cyclist, or you like nothing better than hitting the open road, riding the rails, or cruising down a river, you'll find plenty to inspire you. But flicking through this book should be only the starting point—after all, who knows where the journey will take you.

ON FOOT

Pioneers, adventurers, hunter-gatherers—the first people to explore the Americas did so on foot, from Lewis and Clark's odyssey across the Pacific Northwest to Ernest Shackleton's arduous journey through South Georgia. Pull on a pack and follow in their footsteps, whether you want to trek along the east coast of Canada or hike up Argentina's highest peak.

KEY TO MAP

Previous page *Cape Spear Lighthouse, a section of the East Coast Trail*

AT A GLANCE

ON FOOT

1

Appalachian Trail

LOCATION US **START/FINISH** Springer Mountain/Mount Katahdin **DISTANCE** 2,192 miles (3,528 km) **TIME** 5–7 months **DIFFICULTY** Challenging; mountainous terrain **INFORMATION** www.appalachiantrail.org

Linking the soaring peaks and misty valleys of the South with the vast forests and clapboard villages of New England, the Appalachian Trail is a mammoth challenge for only the hardiest of hikers.

Few long-distance trails set the imagination ablaze like the Appalachian. Conceived in 1921 by conservationist Benton MacKaye, this multi-seasonal experience—the pinnacle of American wilderness routes—was completed in 1937. Today, around three million people take to the Appalachian Trail each year, although only around a tenth of those hardy hikers attempt to tackle it in one go. To join them requires lots of training and a bottomless supply of inner grit.

Few long-distance trails set the imagination ablaze like the Appalachian

Most thru-hikers start in Georgia's rugged Blue Ridge Mountains in March or April, following the warm weather as it creeps north to reach Mount Katahdin in Maine before mid-October, when the leaves start to erupt in fall color. One of the most popular sections of the trail navigates the Great Smoky Mountains, the country's most visited national park, on the border between North Carolina and Tennessee. Wispy fog explains their "smoky" epithet and veils herds of elk, fire lookout towers, and the Appalachian's highest peak, Clingmans Dome. As spring matures, thru-hikers cross the mountains into Tennessee, where clumps of delicate wildflowers shadow the trail. In Virginia, everything suddenly

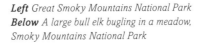

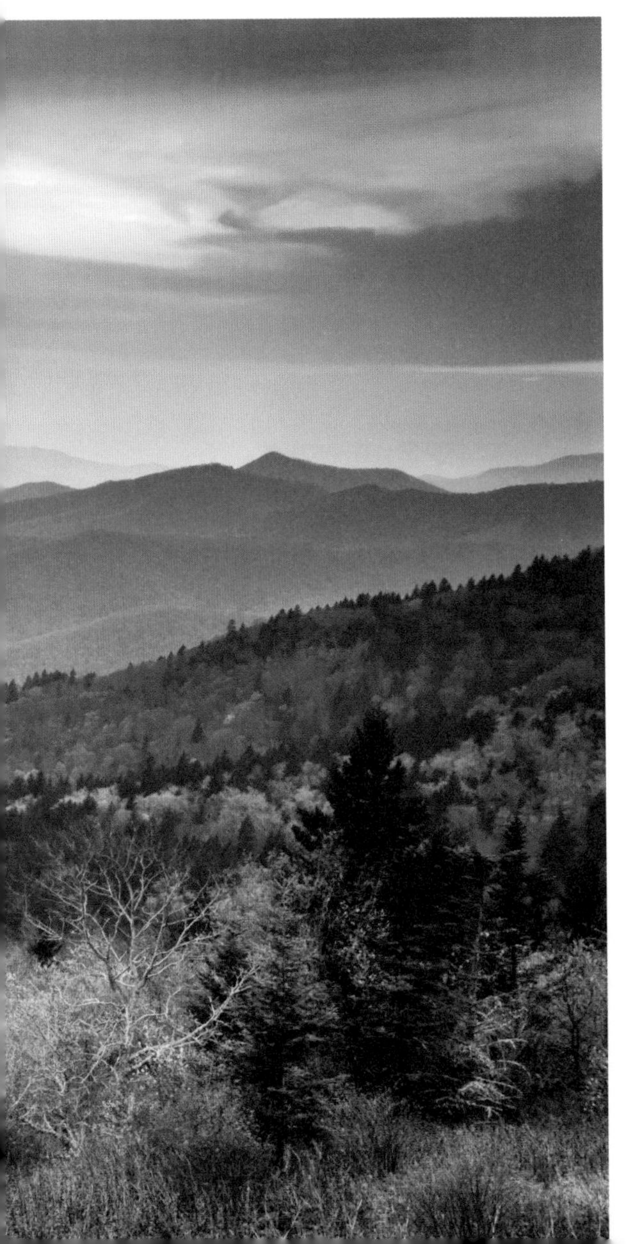

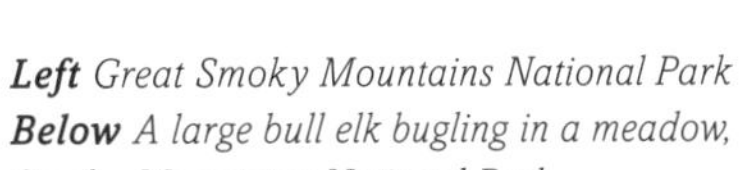

Left *Great Smoky Mountains National Park*
Below *A large bull elk bugling in a meadow, Smoky Mountains National Park*

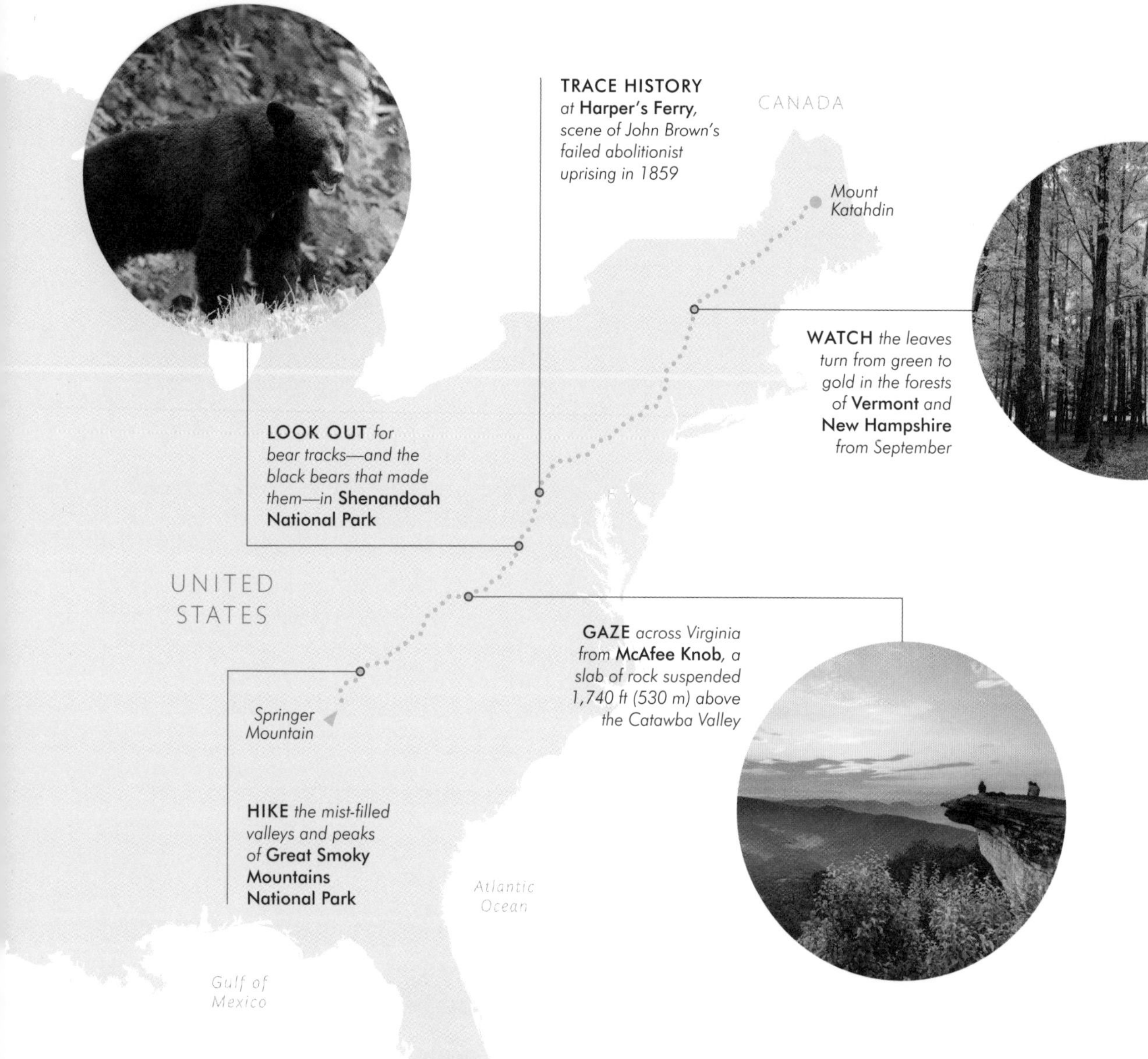

TRACE HISTORY *at* **Harper's Ferry,** *scene of John Brown's failed abolitionist uprising in 1859*

CANADA

Mount Katahdin

WATCH *the leaves turn from green to gold in the forests of* **Vermont** *and* **New Hampshire** *from September*

LOOK OUT *for bear tracks—and the black bears that made them—in* **Shenandoah National Park**

UNITED STATES

GAZE *across Virginia from* **McAfee Knob,** *a slab of rock suspended 1,740 ft (530 m) above the Catawba Valley*

Springer Mountain

HIKE *the mist-filled valleys and peaks of* **Great Smoky Mountains National Park**

Atlantic Ocean

Gulf of Mexico

changes—overlooks, such as McAfee Knob, reveal more pastoral scenes of gentle farmland and rolling hills.

The weather turns hot and humid as you pass into the mid-Atlantic states in midsummer. Maryland features some of the trail's gentlest terrain, while Pennsylvania lives up to its "Rocksylvania" nickname, with its boulder-strewn sections. In New York's Harriman State Park, slip through the "Lemon Squeezer," a narrow crack between giant rocks, before crossing the spectacular Bear Mountain Bridge over the Hudson River.

Temperatures turn milder by the time the trail leads into New England. At Falls Village, watch the Housatonic River tumble over a 50 ft (15 m) high pile of granite slabs; from the top of Mount Greylock, see densely forested hills stretch out in all directions. During the fall foliage season, Vermont and New Hampshire's oceans of maple, birch, and beech turn red, gold,

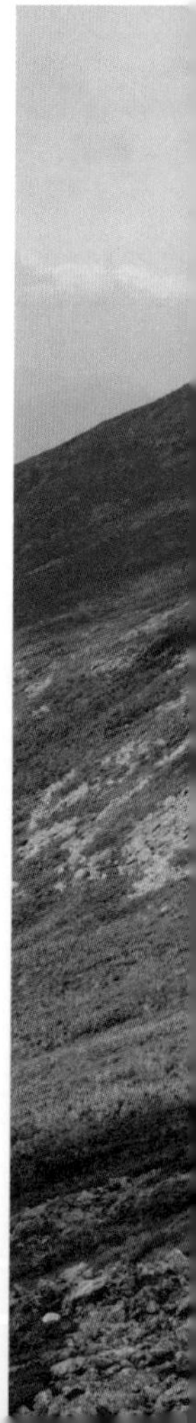

another way

Travelers with only a few days to spare should head straight for the Roan Highlands, a 19-mile (31 km) ridge-top section in Tennessee with the largest natural rhododendron garden in the world. It's ideal for hikers wanting a scenic (albeit still strenuous) stretch of the trail.

and amber. Here, the weather cools again and the way becomes rougher and steeper, with true alpine conditions on the White Mountain tops. Maine presents the most challenging terrain of all. In Mahoosuc Notch, giant boulders block the path and there are countless unbridged streams—although, thankfully, the dangerous crossing over the Kennebec River has a free canoe ferry service during hiking season. Then, finally, Mount Katahdin looms on the horizon. It's a steep, grueling climb to the top, where a simple, weather-beaten sign proclaims the trail's northern terminus. Take in your achievement and absorb the view—nothing else will have seemed quite so beautiful.

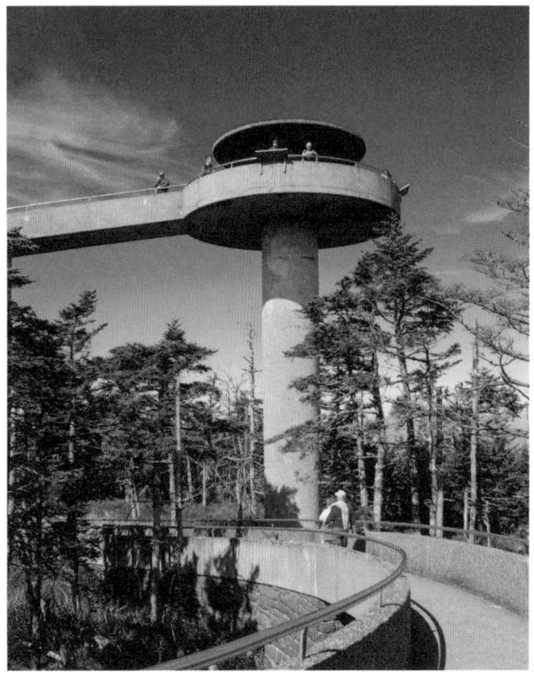

Right *Observation towers, like this one on Clingmans Dome, can be found along the trail*
Below *Pausing to admire the view in New Hampshire's White Mountains*

Early morning mist enshrouding the Berkshire County town of Tyringham

(2) High Road

LOCATION US **START/FINISH** Pittsfield/Lenox **DISTANCE** 8 miles (13 km) **TIME** 1 day **DIFFICULTY** Easy **INFORMATION** www.bnrc.org

Set within the rolling hills of Massachusetts's thickly wooded Berkshires, the High Road will, when completed, weave through pockets of rural conservation lands, connecting charming little communities together. The trail's first segment to open, the Yokun Ridge, is a full day's worth of wandering through a natural corridor of forest between the towns of Pittsfield and Lenox. Benches along the way offer panoramic views of the bucolic landscape—one of the most relaxing ways, surely, of experiencing the vivid golds and fiery reds of a New England fall. At times, you'll walk along former carriage roads, the crumbling remnants of pioneer homesteads peeking out from under the brush. At others, you'll pass pretty farm pastures, deep-blue ponds, and trickling creeks that are wafted with refreshing breezes. The Yokun Ridge ends in the historic town of Lenox, home to several gilded-age mansions that have been converted to elegant inns, the perfect place to retreat under a duvet after a lovely fall walk.

(3) Cliff Walk

LOCATION US **START/FINISH** Memorial Boulevard/Bellevue Avenue **DISTANCE** 3.5 miles (5.5 km) **TIME** 2 hours **DIFFICULTY** Easy to moderate **INFORMATION** www.cliffwalk.com

The cliff-edge walk along Newport's southeastern tip offers a fascinating insight into how the other half once lived. On one side, walkers are gifted views of Atlantic waves crashing into the Rhode Island coastline; on the other, they can catch glimpses of the former homes of some of America's wealthiest families, among them the gorgeous 19th-century The Breakers and Rosecliff, which appeared in the 1974 movie adaptation of *The Great Gatsby*.

Imposing homes aside, this short stretch of coastal path is famous around these parts for the rather peculiar Forty Steps, built in 1880 to lead down to, well, nowhere. The stairway has become a tourist attraction in its own right. Few walkers attempt the final third of the Cliff Walk, which involves a scramble along crags; those that do are greeted by the vast sands and surging shores of private beach club Bailey's Beach and the comically named northeastern Rejects' Beach, open to the public.

another way

Short on time? You can follow a flat 25-minute section of the Cliff Walk from Memorial Boulevard to Ruggles Avenue, passing the famed Forty Steps en route and ending at the grandiose Vanderbilt mansion, The Breakers, which is now a museum.

4

Unicoi Turnpike Trail

LOCATION US **START/FINISH** Coker Creek (return) **DISTANCE** 2.5 miles (4 km) **TIME** 1 hour 30 minutes **DIFFICULTY** Easy **INFORMATION** www.fs.usda.gov

The history of this ancient route exists in layers. The Cherokee peoples built the pathway to move between their "overhill" settlements in the mist-cloaked Southern Appalachian mountains, and it was later used as a turnpike, or toll road, by fur trappers, prospectors, and settlers trading goods in South Carolina.

Now a section of the trail routes through Tennessee's Cherokee National Forest at Coker Creek, where you can hike among wildflower-scattered woodland, following the original roadbed as it cuts a deep groove in the landscape. Keep an eye out for an abandoned gold mine; you might also spot boar and wild turkey.

It all feels a world away from the pathway's poignant past: the Unicoi Turnpike also represents the first leg of the harrowing Trail of Tears. The Cherokee walked this route in the late 1830s on their long and arduous journey to Oklahoma, after being forcibly displaced to so-called Indian Territory west of the Mississippi.

The Unicoi Turnpike also represents the first leg of the harrowing Trail of Tears

5

Whitaker Point Trail

LOCATION US **START/FINISH** Near Kingston (return) **DISTANCE** 3 miles (5 km) **TIME** 2 hours **DIFFICULTY** Easy to moderate **INFORMATION** www.fs.usda.gov

Arkansas is thoroughly deserving of its "Natural State" moniker, thanks, in part, to this woodland odyssey. Whitaker Point shoots into the Upper Buffalo Wilderness in Ozark National Forest, which swallows more than one million green acres in the northwest corner of the state.

This is forest bathing at its finest. Rugged and root-knotted, the path wends its way through clustered oak and ash trees and past a string of small waterfalls. Eventually, the trail's climax reveals itself: Whitaker Point (also known as Hawksbill Crag, for its beaklike shape), a dramatic tongue of sandstone that juts out of the woods, soaring above the thickly forested valley below. In fall, that valley is a blaze of burnt amber and butter yellow; in summer, it's green velvet. Unsurprisingly, the soaring bluff has become a popular spot for proposals. It would be difficult to say "no" amid such natural beauty.

Sunrise at Hawksbill Crag, the climax of the Whitaker Point Trail

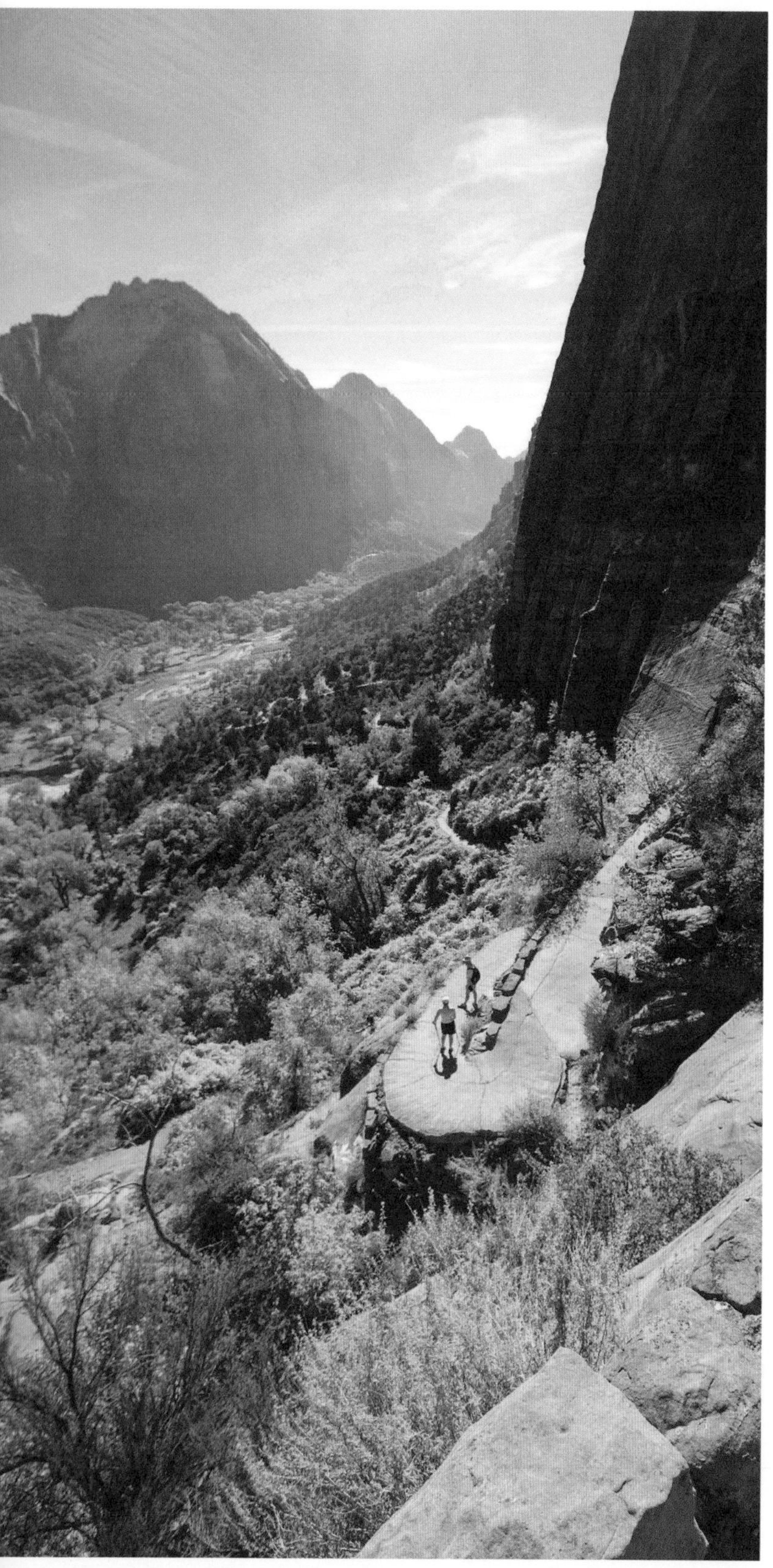

6

Angel's Landing

LOCATION US **START/FINISH** Grotto shuttle stop (return) **DISTANCE** 5 miles (8 km) **TIME** 5 hours **DIFFICULTY** Moderate to challenging **INFORMATION** www.nps.gov; free shuttles run to the trailhead (Apr–Oct)

Zion's very own Stairway to Heaven is a celestial stomp up to Angel's Landing on a gravity-defying, nerve-shattering hike.

Despite being less than a day long, this heart-pumping hike up to a 1,488 ft (454 m) plug of rock in southwest Utah easily ranks among the most spectacular—and scary—in the US.

The trail eases you in gently, but don't be fooled; soon the steep, exposed, shadeless ascent begins (it's murder on a blistering hot summer's day). The leafy cool of Refrigerator Canyon provides some respite, before the seemingly relentless Walter's Wiggles—27 switchbacks hacked into the cliff face. But the effort is worth it—emerging on high at Scout Lookout, you're rewarded with immense views. Rest at this spot with your picnic or join the fearless lot tiptoeing across the knife-edge, cable-secured ridge to the summit of Angel's Landing itself for gasp-out-loud views of Zion Canyon and Big Bend below. It will—almost literally—blow you away.

Join the fearless lot tiptoeing across the knife-edge, cable-secured ridge

Hikers navigating the winding rock path of Angel's Landing

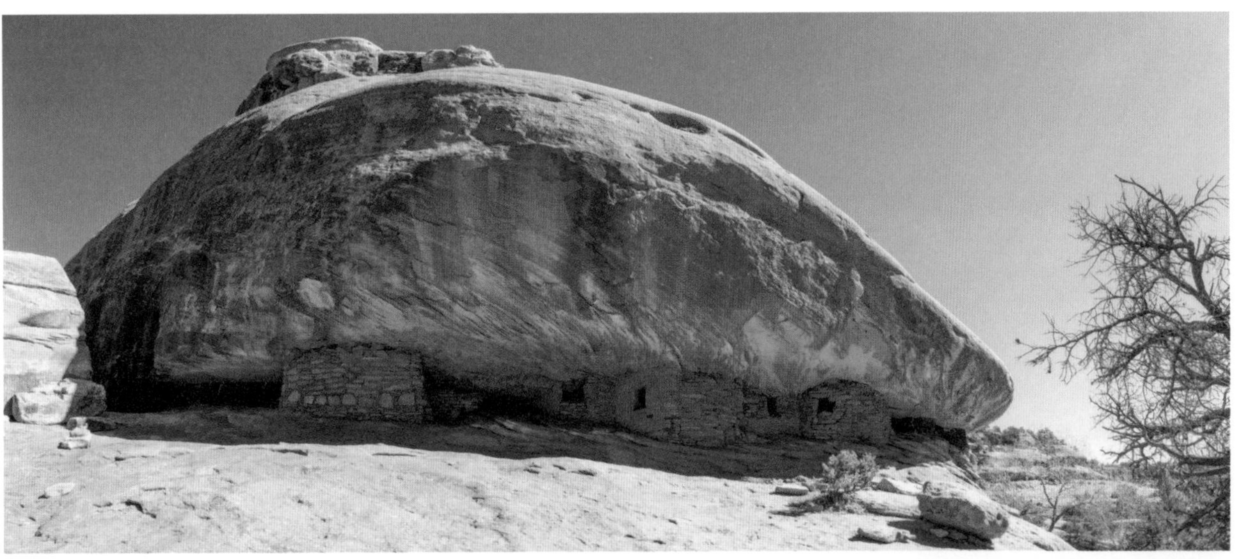

7

House on Fire Trail

LOCATION US **START/FINISH** Mule Canyon (return) **DISTANCE** 2 miles (3 km) **TIME** 35 minutes **DIFFICULTY** Easy to moderate **INFORMATION** www.blm.gov; www.visitutah.com; day-hiking pass required

This short hike through Bear Ears National Monument reveals a hidden-away Ancient Puebloan ruin that seems to burn in sunlight.

Eons before settlers made footprints on Utah's Mule Canyon, Ancestral Puebloans called this rugged land home. These Indigenous Anasazi created intricate rock-hewn dwellings, and although they are thought to have left the area around 700 years ago, precious vestiges of their ancient culture remain. These relics reveal themselves on a short hike within Utah's Bear Ears National Monument, which is stark, sunbaked, and gloriously secluded. The House on Fire Trail enters a world of twisted, burnt-orange rock and scattered juniper, zigzagging over a creek bed and pushing toward a slab of slickrock. This hunk of wind-smoothed rock (which requires a scramble) is the last thing that stands between you and the trail's pièce-de-résistance: the House on Fire Ruin. The Puebloan home is hunkered into the sandstone, its overhanging ceiling beset with intricate ridges. When it's washed with sunshine, it appears as though the whole thing has burst into flames.

Top *House on Fire, hunkered under a slab of sandstone* ***Below*** *Anasazi handprints*

another way

The Cliff Palace in Colorado's Mesa Verde National Park is one of the finest Ancestral Puebloan ruins in the nation. Ranger-guided hikes exploring the ruin cover just 0.5 miles (1 km) but involve steep ladder climbs.

The sensational view from the top of Hunts Mesa

8

Hunts Mesa

LOCATION US **START/FINISH** Big Hogan (return) **DISTANCE** 5 miles (8 km) **TIME** 18 hours (return) **DIFFICULTY** Easy **INFORMATION** www.navajonationparks.org; backcountry permit and official Navajo guide required (book through www.monumentvalleysafari.com or www.navajospirittours.com)

Join a Navajo guide on this unforgettable hike up Monument Valley's majestic Hunts Mesa, a towering red sandstone plateau with some of the finest views in all of Arizona.

When it comes to small hikes with big rewards, this route up to the plateau of Hunts Mesa takes some beating. It's a mere six-hour hike to the tabletop base camp, across a rust-red landscape of chiseled rock formations that is sacred to the Navajo people. What better way of seeing it all than through the eyes of a local Navajo guide.

The trail proper starts near Big Hogan, a natural sandstone arch, and heads over lofty dunes and up a simple rope ladder to the top of the mesa, one of the highest plateaus in Arizona. Here, you'll set up camp for the night around 1,600 ft (490 m) above the valley floor. Settle in under the stars while your Navajo guide shares stories of folklore around a crackling fire.

Sunrise next morning brings stellar views of jutting red sandstone buttes and soaring mesas—it's easy to see why Monument Valley is one of the world's most photographed spots and has been featured in more than 100 movies. Soak it all in and then head back the way you came, stopping off at ancient Anasazi dwellings along the way.

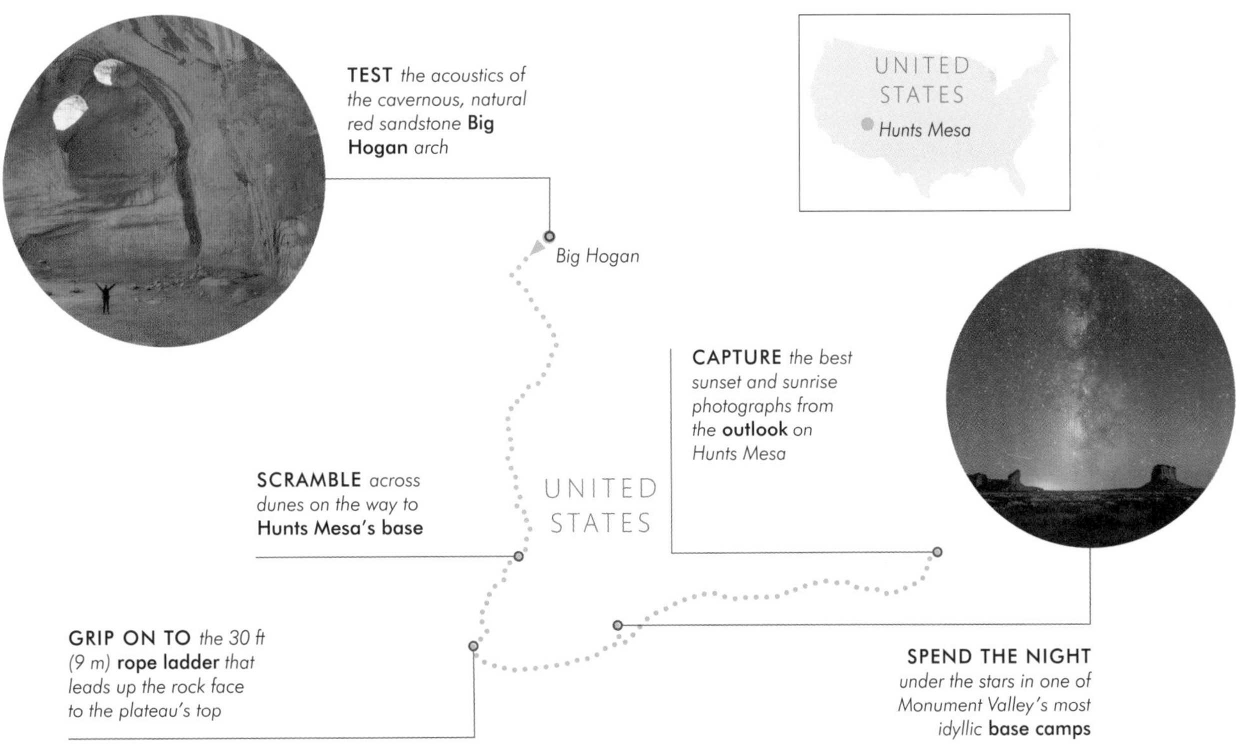
TEST *the acoustics of the cavernous, natural red sandstone* **Big Hogan** *arch*
UNITED STATES
Hunts Mesa
Big Hogan
CAPTURE *the best sunset and sunrise photographs from the* **outlook** *on Hunts Mesa*
SCRAMBLE *across dunes on the way to* **Hunts Mesa's base**
UNITED STATES
GRIP ON TO *the 30 ft (9 m)* **rope ladder** *that leads up the rock face to the plateau's top*
SPEND THE NIGHT *under the stars in one of Monument Valley's most idyllic* **base camps**

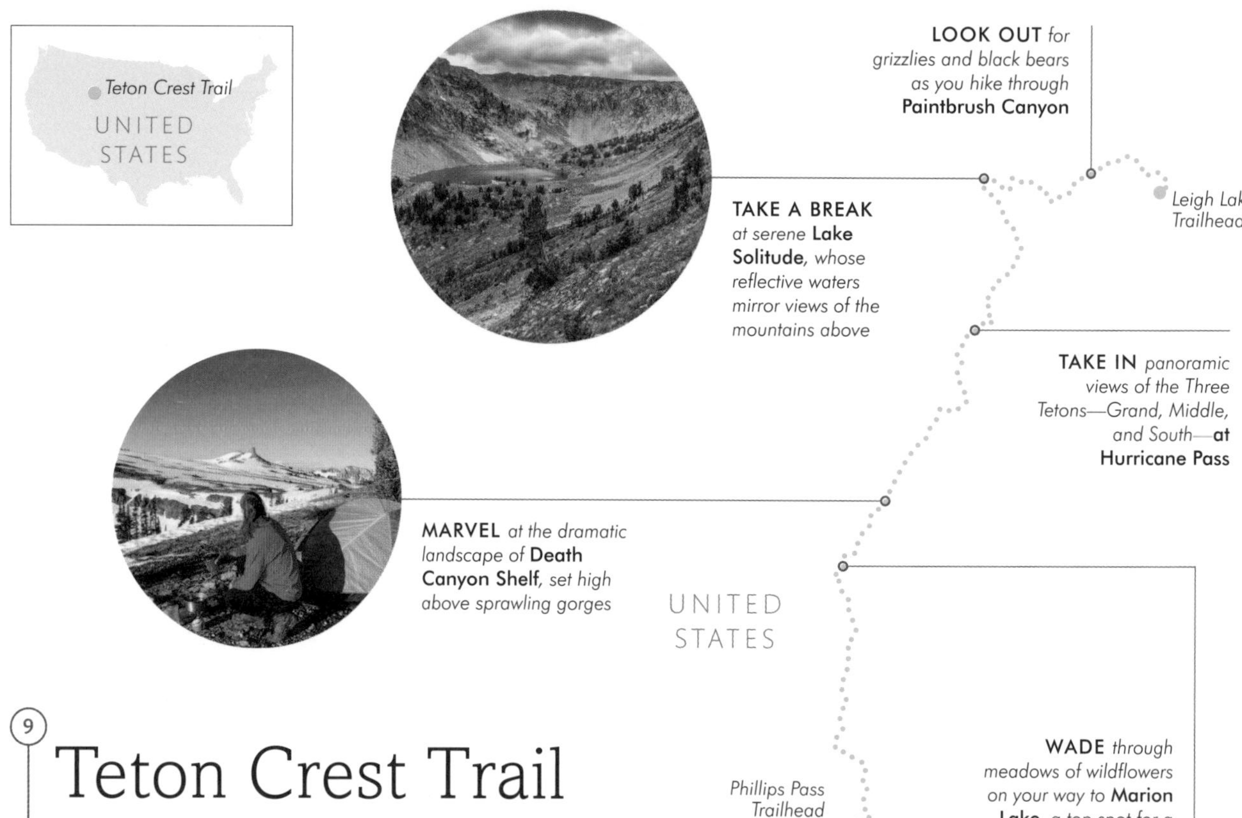
Teton Crest Trail
UNITED STATES
LOOK OUT for grizzlies and black bears as you hike through Paintbrush Canyon
Leigh Lake Trailhead
TAKE A BREAK at serene Lake Solitude, whose reflective waters mirror views of the mountains above
TAKE IN panoramic views of the Three Tetons—Grand, Middle, and South—at Hurricane Pass
MARVEL at the dramatic landscape of Death Canyon Shelf, set high above sprawling gorges
UNITED STATES
Phillips Pass Trailhead
WADE through meadows of wildflowers on your way to Marion Lake, a top spot for a lakeside stroll

9

Teton Crest Trail

LOCATION US **START/FINISH** Phillips Pass Trailhead/Leigh Lake Trailhead **DISTANCE** 40 miles (65 km) **TIME** 4–5 days **DIFFICULTY** Challenging **INFORMATION** www.nps.gov/grte

The Teton Crest Trail is high-alpine heaven, an esteemed hike alongside mighty mountains that winds up among the towering granite peaks of northwest Wyoming.

Nestled among the dramatic peaks of the Teton Range, the Teton Crest Trail, or TCT, holds best-of-the-best status among seasoned backpackers. Its rugged landscape will push your body and mind as you navigate ultra-steep trails at elevations above 8,000 ft (2,435 m) for almost the entire journey.

While the TCT doesn't require technical climbing equipment, it is difficult and takes some planning–you'll need to prebook campsites and negotiate backcountry challenges such as securing water. The payoff is walking among sculpted mountain spires, sprawling meadows, and turquoise lakes, all while towering high above expansive vistas of what feels like the whole of Wyoming. In summer–the prime time for this trail–wildflowers are in bloom and the forests echo with the sound of birdlife. Steep climbs (and descents) take you from one awesome campsite to the next, through lush wilderness and to cold creek rivers that flow throughout the range. And at rest, you're almost guaranteed to experience at least one immaculate sunrise or sunset, lighting the tundra of the legendary Teton Range with a honey-colored glow.

THE THREE TETONS

An ever-present focal point along the TCT is a group of mountains dubbed "The Three Tetons." The name originated in the late 1800s, when French trappers nicknamed the peaks "Les Trois Tetons," or "The Three Breasts." The Indigenous Shoshone, however, know them as "Teewinot," meaning "Many Pinnacles."

Its rugged landscape will push your body and mind as you navigate steep trails

Right *A bighorn ram grazing among wildflowers near Marion Lake*
Below *The Three Tetons, rising above a lake in Grand Teton National Park*

(10)

Grand Prismatic Spring Overlook Trail

Yellowstone National Park's stunning Grand Prismatic Spring

LOCATION US **START/FINISH** Fairy Falls Trailhead/Grand Prismatic Spring Overlook **DISTANCE** 1 mile (1.5 km) **TIME** 20 minutes **DIFFICULTY** Easy **INFORMATION** www.nps.gov/yell

Take in a bird's-eye view of the wondrously colored, highly active Grand Prismatic Spring, one of the largest and most famous hot springs on earth.

The Grand Prismatic Spring is Yellowstone National Park's most photographed hydrothermal feature. And its most popular. Skip the crowded ground-level boardwalk and hike up to the overlook instead—the spectacular aerial vista gives you a much better perspective of the hot spring's enormous size and iridescent colors.

A gravel footpath leads along the desolate-looking Midway Geyser Basin, described rather accurately as "Hell's Half Acre" by English writer Rudyard Kipling when he visited in 1889, before slightly ascending into a forest of tall lodgepole pine. Your reward from the lookout up here is the whole basin—all bubbling pools, steamy craters, and water-spurting geysers—spread before you, with the astonishingly blue pool of the Grand Prismatic Spring resembling a giant open eye, lashes and all.

MARVELOUS MICROBES

The spring owes its gorgeous array of pigments to trillions of heat-loving microbes. Each band of color equates to a change in water temperature and, in turn, a unique group of microbes. Nothing survives at the center—the brilliant blue is caused by minerals scattering the sun's rays.

11

Boy Scout Trail

LOCATION US **START/FINISH** Park Boulevard (return) **DISTANCE** 16 miles (26 km) **TIME** 2 days **DIFFICULTY** Moderate **INFORMATION** www.nps.gov/joshuatree; register at the backcountry registration board before setting off

Marvel at Joshua Tree's remarkable rock formations, stark canyons, and, of course, those legendary prickly trees on this overnight backpacking quest.

Otherworldly, ethereal, vast: Joshua Tree National Park extends across California's southeastern edge, its famous prickly trees one of America's most iconic sights. Believed to have first been occupied by the Pinto some 15,000 years ago, Joshua Tree is now home to more than 100 miles (66 km) of hiking paths. And the Boy Scout Trail cuts through the very best of it.

The first few miles are flat, and then it's a slight downward incline until Indian Cove campground. It's here that you'll find the best scenery—expect mammoth boulders, towering formations, and, if you're lucky, desert wildlife like tortoises and bighorn sheep. The quiet campground is away from the hum of campers and generators found on other sites in the park, and a stone's throw from some of the west's best rock-climbing ,scrambles. And plenty of Joshua trees, of course.

Expect mammoth boulders, towering formations, and, if you're lucky, desert wildlife

Prickly Joshua trees standing in their namesake national park

12

Pacific Crest Trail

LOCATION US **START/FINISH** Campo/Monument
DISTANCE 2,650 miles (4,635 km) **TIME** 5–6 months
DIFFICULTY Challenging **INFORMATION** www.pcta.org

This epic trail forges an unbroken path from Mexico to Canada, traveling through the most sublime mountain scenery of the western United States.

The jewel in the crown of America's long-distance hiking trails, the Pacific Crest Trail (PCT) follows the pinnacles of the Cascade and Sierra Nevada ranges through some of the most spectacular landscapes in California, Oregon, and Washington.

It's a journey of superlatives and extremes. The PCT crosses barren deserts and tunnels through dense forest canopies, skirts the edge of sapphire lakes and tumbling waterfalls, and traverses the shoulders of conical volcanic peaks and glaciated granite spires. One day, you'll hike in the company of spiny barrel cacti in scorching desert heat; a few days later, you'll post-hole through thigh-high snow above 10,000 ft (3,000 m).

The majority of thru-hikers walk the PCT in a northbound direction (starting in April or May to finish by September or October), because it allows for the best weather and trail conditions at the route's widely varying elevations. Northbound hikers start in the small town of Campo near California's border with Mexico. The first 500 miles (805 km) often make or break your PCT dream: you'll face intense heat and sparse water sources in the arid Southern California desert, followed by challenging climbs and descents of some of Southern California's highest mountains. Yet they also inspire with their vast open spaces and remarkably varied terrain.

> The PCT crosses barren deserts and tunnels through dense forest canopies

Hiking along a section of the trail in Washington state, with views across to the North Cascades

TRAIL LOGISTICS

Completing the trail on a thru-hike requires starting in April/May and finishing by September/October. You'll need to cover an average of 16 to 18 miles (26 to 29 km) a day to allow for the vagaries of weather and rest days. Physical strength is critical, but so are wilderness smarts and mental toughness. You'll need strong logistics skills to figure out plans for resupply drops at remote outposts.

A rest break at the Sierra Nevada's southern tip is imperative because in the next trail stretch, there's no easy way out—not a single road crosses the Sierra crest for a daunting 185 miles (298 km). Logistical challenges aside, this range offers unparalleled scenery in the form of austere alpine landscapes and dramatically glaciated geology. The PCT ascends up and over a dozen knee-pounding passes, including six that are higher than 11,000 ft (3,350 m)—once you've made it up and over Forester Pass, though, you can rest easy in the knowledge that you've conquered the highest point along the PCT.

The PCT is nothing if not a trail of contrasts. Mellow grades around the Lake Tahoe basin precede the notoriously hot and dry Hat Creek Rim and then you're plunging into the lush green fir groves of Northern California and southern Oregon's Sky Lake Wilderness, where an ancient, massive caldera hems in the sparkling blue waters of Crater Lake. Pushing northward through Oregon, one of North America's largest volcanoes dominates the horizon. You've made it to Mount Hood (11,250 ft/3,429 m), where skiers and snowboarders ply the slopes year-round.

Just before the border with Washington comes a remarkably long descent to the Columbia River crossing at the Bridge of the Gods, the

Left *McArthur-Burney Falls Memorial State Park in California*
Below *Cinder Cone Rim, Lassen Volcanic National Park*

Monument

CANADA

WAVE GOODBYE *to Oregon as you cross over the* **Bridge of Gods** *and into Washington state*

MAKE A PIT STOP *at the charming village of* **Stehekin,** *the last settlement you'll see on the PCT*

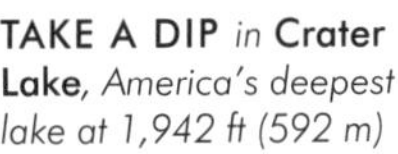

TAKE A DIP *in* **Crater Lake,** *America's deepest lake at 1,942 ft (592 m)*

Pacific Ocean

WATCH YOUR STEP *among the steaming vents and boiling pools of* **Lassen Volcanic National Park**

UNITED STATES

Campo

MEXICO

DETOUR *to* **Mount Whitney,** *at 14,505 ft (4,421 m), the highest point in the contiguous United States*

PCT's lowest elevation point. As you rise back up into the "Evergreen State," your PCT victory is creeping ever closer, and the last 512 miles (824 km) of terrain are nothing short of spectacular. There's a brief foray into temperate rainforest at Panther Creek and the rugged peaks and vast valleys of Goat Rocks Wilderness. Then, just when you think the views can't get any better, the trail leads past 14,411 ft (4,392 m) Mount Rainier, the king of the Cascades, before climbing into the Alpine Lakes Wilderness, a vast expanse of jagged peaks, and the even more impressive Glacier Peak Wilderness, an area home to giant conifers and multiple glaciers and snowfields.

For your final leg, you'll tunnel through North Cascades National Park, one of the wettest sections of the PCT. But the rain won't bother you one bit—after all, you have only 80 miles (129 km) remaining before you reach E. C. Manning Provincial Park, just over the Canadian border, and PCT glory.

another way

Named after another American environmentalist, and the cofounder of the Wilderness Society, the Benton MacKaye Trail wends its way for 300 miles (483 km) through the Southern Appalachian Mountains.

13

John Muir Trail

LOCATION US **START/FINISH** Happy Isles/Mount Whitney
DISTANCE 211 miles (340 km) **TIME** 3 weeks
DIFFICULTY Challenging; mountainous terrain
INFORMATION www.nps.gov; permit required

Traversing the finest mountain scenery in California, the John Muir Trail takes in gem-colored lakes and an arid landscape far above the Sierra Nevada tree line.

Negotiating a series of vertiginous ups and downs, the John Muir Trail is a challenging hike. Walkers must tackle the "Golden Staircase"—a steep 1,500 ft (457 m) ascent via 50 or more jaw-dropping switchbacks—and the final climb up Mount Whitney, where the moonscape summit seems to overlook the whole of California. There are few guesthouses to provide creature comforts along the way; instead, hikers must camp beside the Sierra Nevada's alpine lakes, but this is all part of the trail's charm.

Jumping into a snow-fed lake after a sweaty hike is far more energizing than a shower, and it's hard to resist the glistening depths of Lower Cathedral Lake, Thousand Island Lake, or Lake Marjorie. After drying off and setting up camp, settle down to stargaze to the soundtrack of rustling winds and screeching hawks. In the morning, the sun rises over jagged peaks, and deer and bighorn sheep clamber up the rocky slopes. With scenes like these, it's easy to see why John Muir fought so hard to protect this stretch of wilderness.

JOHN MUIR

Pioneering naturalist and author John Muir was born in Dunbar, Scotland, in 1838. He emigrated to the US with his family when he was 11 years old, and saw Yosemite Valley for the first time in 1868. He spent the rest of his life fighting for its preservation, writing the essays that helped establish Yosemite National Park in 1890.

Camping in a scenic spot by Lake Marjorie

Half Dome poking out from the far end of a misty Yosemite Valley

14

Half Dome

LOCATION US **START/FINISH** Happy Isles (loop) **DISTANCE** 16 miles (26 km) **TIME** 10–12 hours **DIFFICULTY** Challenging **INFORMATION** www.nps.gov; permit required

Yosemite National Park is full of monumental cliff faces and landmark peaks, none more so than iconic Half Dome. Summit views don't get much better than this.

A hike to the round, smooth summit of Half Dome is one of Yosemite National Park's greatest challenges, despite the route's brevity. Starting on the leafy banks of the fast-flowing Merced River, the trail steadily gets trickier. After passing the Vernal Falls, a thin ribbon of water plunging off a cliff, and the wider Nevada Falls, hikers climb through forests of fir and spruce. Giant mountains rise up all around, towering above this ocean of green trees.

Then, suddenly, it's there—Half Dome. The path runs onto the northeast ridge of this barren hulk of weathered granite. From here, the slopes of the final summit seem almost sheer, but two metal cables allow hikers to clamber the last 400 ft (122 m) to the top without rock-climbing equipment. It's an exhilaratingly steep scramble over the smooth rock surface, but the flat top of Half Dome is the perfect place to catch your breath, before heading back down to earth.

15

Kalalau Trail

LOCATION US **START/FINISH** Ha'ena State Park/Kalalau Beach **DISTANCE** 22 miles (35 km) **TIME** 2 days **DIFFICULTY** Challenging **INFORMATION** www.kalalautrail.com

Far from the bustle of sun-soaked Waikīkī Beach, Hawaii's Kalalau Trail leads walkers into a timeless Polynesian world of misty sea cliffs, turquoise bays, and primeval jungle. There are no resorts or souvenir shops—just the untrammeled Nāpali coast of Kauai. The route starts with a steady climb circling the base of fanglike Makana Mountain; tantalizing glimpses of the Pacific Ocean are granted at intervals as the trail plunges through dense scrub and spiny pandanus. Undulating switchbacks lead through an abandoned coffee plantation and over towering high cliffs, dropping down to Pu'ukulua ("Red Hill"), a ridge of crimson earth. Many choose to spend the last night camped out on untouched Kalalau Beach, under a sky full of stars, the only sound the gentle lapping of Pacific swells.

Verdant ridges reaching down to the Pacific on Kauai's spectacular coastline

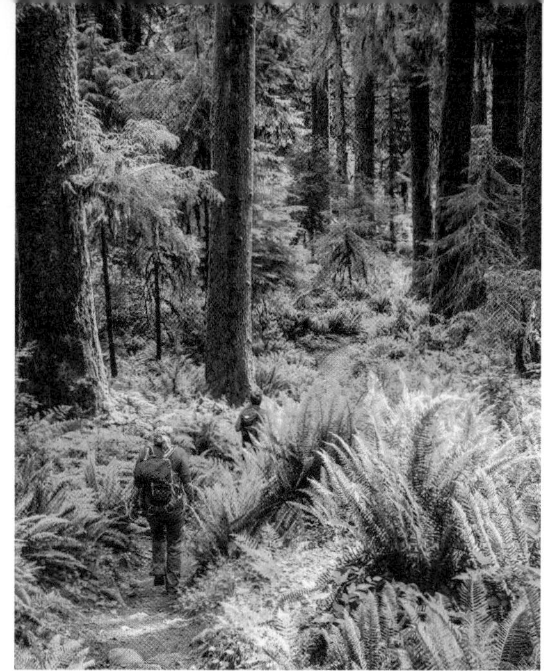

Hiking through old-growth forest on the Hoh River Trail

16

Hoh River Trail

LOCATION US **START/FINISH** Hoh River Trailhead (return) **DISTANCE** 35 miles (56 km) **TIME** 3 days return **DIFFICULTY** Easy to challenging **INFORMATION** www.nps.gov/olym

From its source on Washington state's Mount Olympus, the milky-colored Hoh River tumbles 50 miles (80 km) downstream to the Pacific Ocean. This trail tracks the waterway's journey in reverse, starting in the heart of a dripping rainforest—where mosses and ferns flourish on every surface—before meandering upstream through the subalpine meadows and old-growth forest of the glacier-carved Hoh River Valley.

The path offers an extremely gentle grade for the first 12.5 miles (20 km), followed by an abrupt 3,000 ft (914 m) ascent to Glacier Meadows. It's a leg-trembling climb—you'll have to cross a deep, sheer-sided gorge on the High Hoh Bridge and make a wet and slippery ladder ascent up a near-vertical slope. But it's worth it when you reach the top, to be greeted by an otherworldly panorama of blue-tinged crevasses cascading down Mount Olympus.

(17)

Plain of Six Glaciers Trail

LOCATION Canada **START/FINISH** Fairmont Chateau/Abbot Pass Viewpoint **DISTANCE** 9 miles (14.5 km) **TIME** 1 day **DIFFICULTY** Moderate **INFORMATION** www.banfflakelouise.com

Crack. Crack. The sound coming along the trail ahead isn't the noise of hiker boots scuffing over rocks. No, it's the sound of ever-shifting glaciers, whose crackles and snaps are carried on the wind across bright-blue Lake Louise. Hikers have long been drawn to this bewitching trail, which takes in the ice tongues, pointed peaks, and polar-blue lakes of Canada's most visited national park, Banff. The out-and-back pathway first lulls you into a false sense of security but then shifts up a gear, ascending past a log-cabin teahouse into a natural mountain amphitheater brimming with undiluted drama. The glacier views are immense, as is the panorama over a landscape of ice and rock from Abbot Pass Viewpoint, a fitting finale before descending back down to the waters of magical Lake Louise.

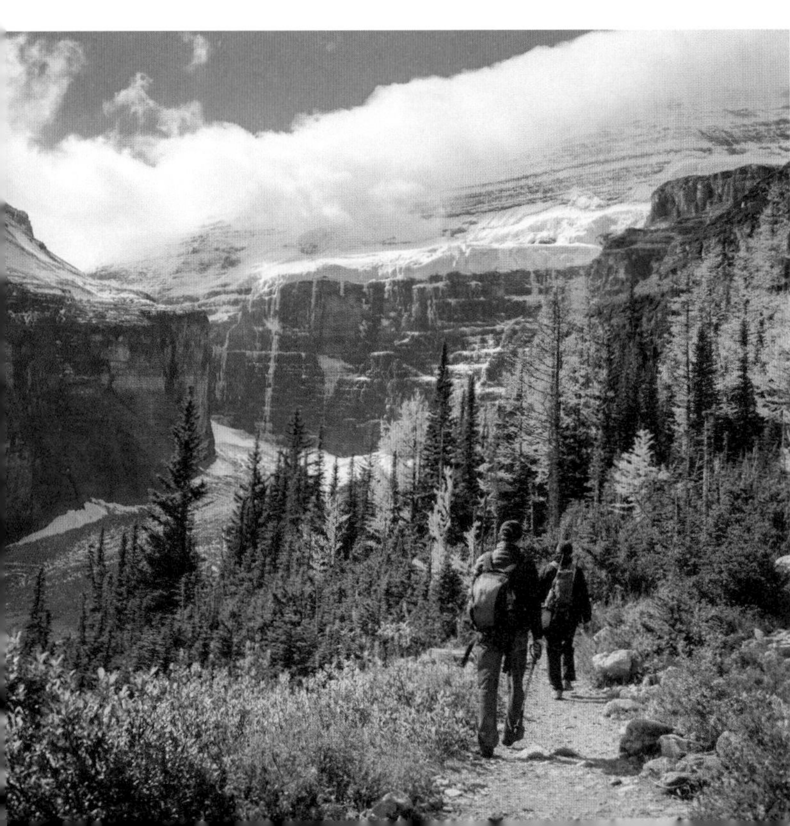

Hikers descending toward Lake Louise in Banff National Park

(18)

Grouse Grind

LOCATION Canada **START/FINISH** Grouse Mountain Base Station/Grouse Mountain Top Station **DISTANCE** 1.5 miles (2.5 km) **TIME** 1–2 hours **DIFFICULTY** Challenging, with steep sections **INFORMATION** www. grousemountain. com/grousegrind; trail open late Apr–Oct

First comes the silence—Vancouver's city buzz fades, replaced by only the scrape of rock on boot and the huff-puff of breath. Then the sky darkens as the canopy of cathedral-size pine and sitka spruce closes in, the path ahead marching steeply in a reckless zigzag before disappearing abruptly out of sight toward the summit of Grouse Mountain.

To fitness-obsessed Vancouverites, this old lumber route is Mother Nature's Stairmaster, but to the average have-a-go traveler, the Grouse Grind is an urban hiking challenge of Everest proportions. Fatigue will inevitably kick in, but don't turn back—the reward is an eye-widening view of chainsaw-cut peaks and a sea-meets-sky blast of shimmering Burrard Inlet below.

another way

Grouse Mountain is one of three gold-star mountain aeries in North Vancouver. Mount Seymour and Cypress Mountain are the two other totemic peaks, and both are home to thrilling hiking trails in summer and ski routes in winter.

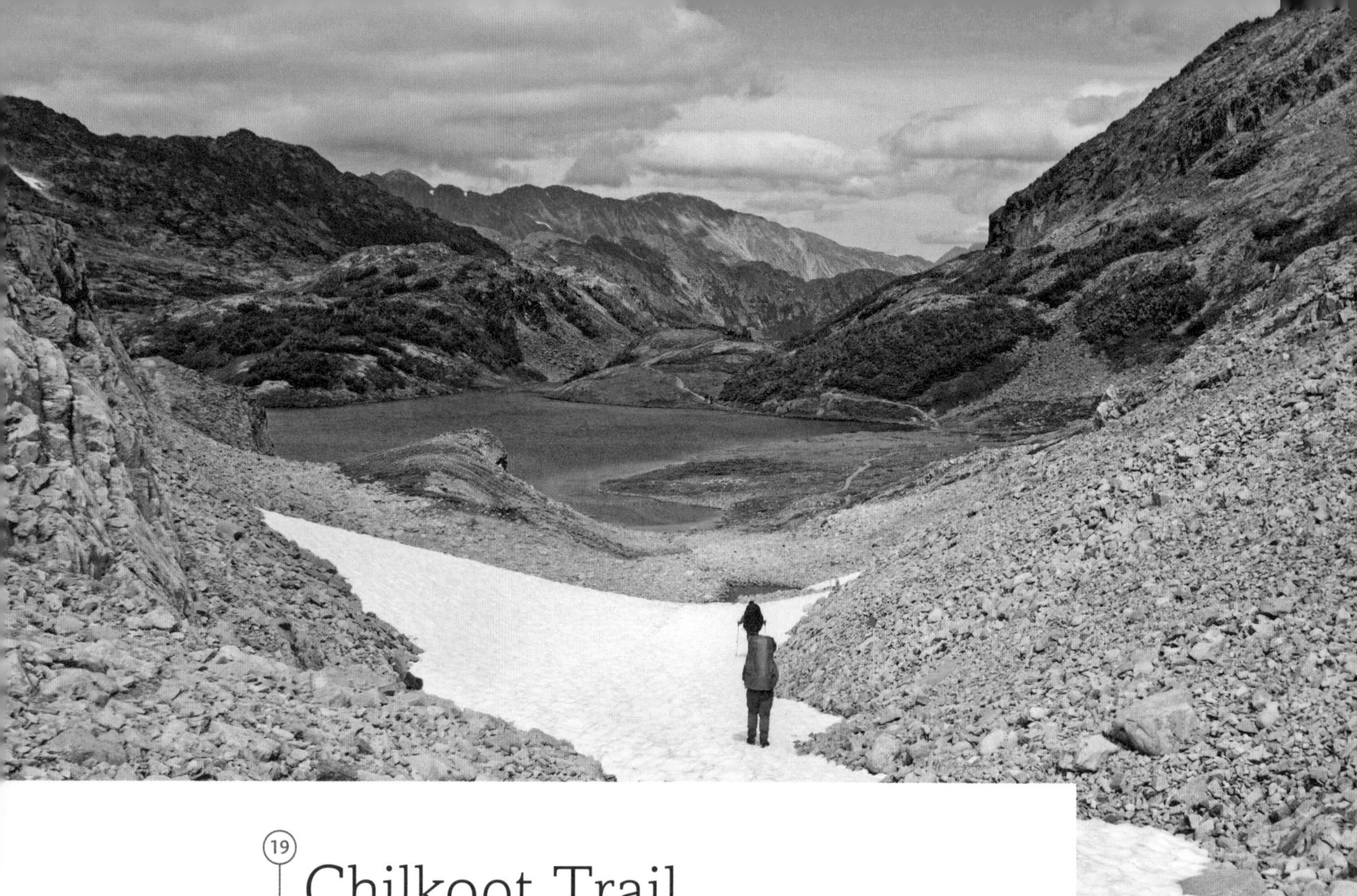

Snow lining the trail down to Morrow Lake

19

Chilkoot Trail

LOCATION US and Canada **START/FINISH** Dyea/Bennett **DISTANCE** 33 miles (53 km) **TIME** 3–5 days **DIFFICULTY** Challenging; steep climbs and changeable weather **INFORMATION** www.parks.canada.ca; permit required

Follow in the footsteps of 19th-century prospectors, who were driven to tackle this arduous but magnificent route, from the Alaskan coast to the wild Canadian interior, by a lust for gold.

When gold was discovered near the Klondike River in Canada's Yukon Territory in 1896, it sparked one of the most frantic gold rushes in history. In the two years that followed, a quiet trade route, used by First Nations peoples for centuries, was transformed into a thronging highway. Around 100,000 stampeders made the journey from Dyea, near Skagway in Alaska, to lakeside Bennett in British Columbia, all in the hope of making their fortunes.

With gold fever long gone, the old track is now tramped by intrepid hikers instead. You'll start at Dyea, where a few ruined wooden buildings are all that's left of its brief stint as a prospecting boomtown. The trail heads through coastal rainforest, crossing frothing creeks and passing a string of old miners' camps; you'll see some of the artifacts they left behind, from old boot soles to engine winches.

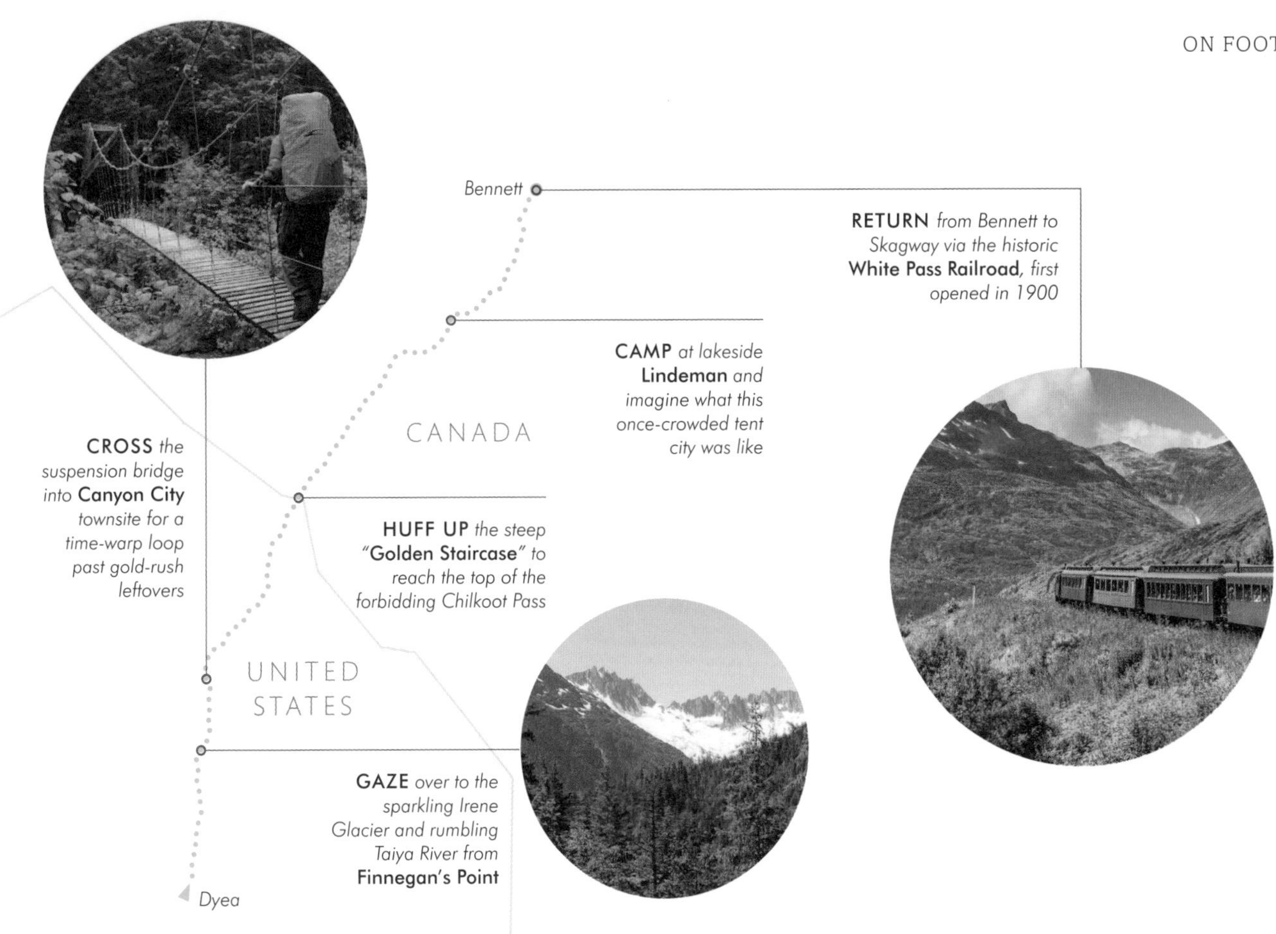

Bennett
RETURN *from Bennett to Skagway via the historic* **White Pass Railroad**, *first opened in 1900*
CAMP *at lakeside* **Lindeman** *and imagine what this once-crowded tent city was like*
CANADA
CROSS *the suspension bridge into* **Canyon City** *townsite for a time-warp loop past gold-rush leftovers*
HUFF UP *the steep* **"Golden Staircase"** *to reach the top of the forbidding Chilkoot Pass*
UNITED STATES
GAZE *over to the sparkling Irene Glacier and rumbling Taiya River from* **Finnegan's Point**
Dyea

Beyond Sheep Camp, the trail climbs into exposed highlands. The stiffest stretch is past The Scales and up the formidable 3,500 ft (1,067 m) Chilkoot Pass, which straddles the US-Canada border. The terrain here is desolate indeed. The route then descends via alpine lakes and boreal forests before finishing by Lake Bennett. This peaceful backwater was once a bustling settlement; now rusting scraps of metal and a small Presbyterian church dating from the gold-rush era are the only evidence of glories past.

THE SCALES

The Canadian government required stampeders bound for the Yukon's gold fields to carry a "grubstake," a year's worth of provisions, ranging from dried food to shovels. The Scales was the final weigh station before the push over the pass; faced with such a horrendous climb, many stampeders simply gave up here, leaving their grubstake behind.

St. Andrews Church, on the shores of Lake Bennett

20

Skyline Trail

LOCATION Canada **START/FINISH** Maligne Lake Trailhead/Signal Mountain Trailhead **DISTANCE** 27 miles (44 km) **TIME** 2–4 days **DIFFICULTY** Moderate **INFORMATION** www.parks.canada.ca/pn-np/ab/jasper; campgrounds are open Jun–Sep

You'll feel on top of the world as you explore the Skyline Trail, a sublime hike in Jasper National Park along three lone mountain passes of the Canadian Rockies.

Early morning mist rising over a lake in beautiful Jasper National Park

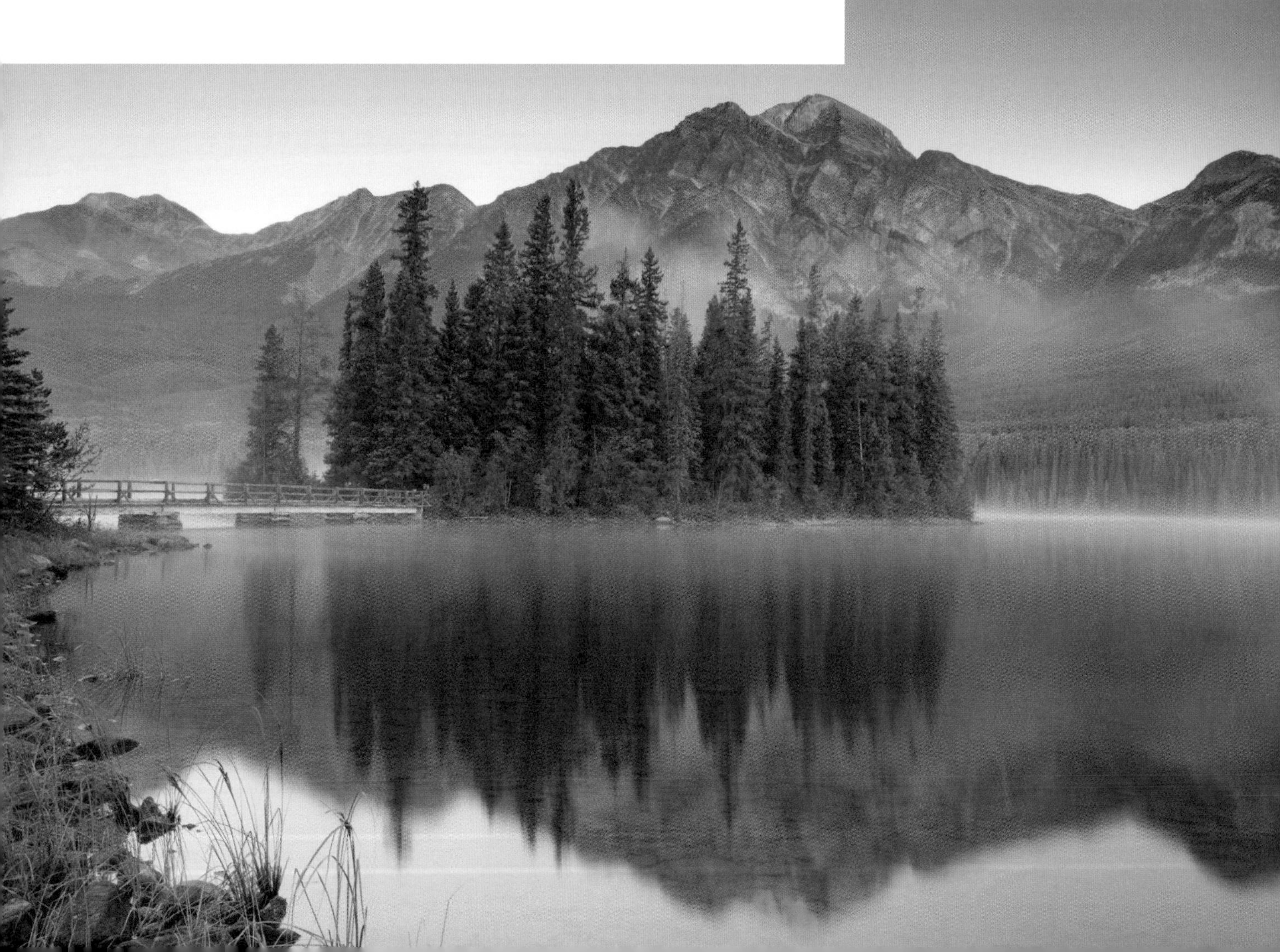

Signal Mountain Trailhead
GAZE in awe at inspiring Mount Tekarra, named after an Iroquois guide and hunter
CANADA
CANADA
Skyline Trail
FEEL the refreshing mist on your face from the cascading waterfall at Curator Campground
TAKE time out on tiny Spirit Island, at the heart of Maligne Lake
Maligne Lake Trailhead
SPOT deer as you descend from The Notch, the highest point of the trail at 8,238 ft (2,511 m)
PEEK INSIDE Shangrila, a winter-warming hut originally built in 1936 by legendary park guide Donald Philips

another way

Experienced hikers can complete the trail in two days and push on to overnight in the rustic Shovel Pass Lodge, the park's oldest backcountry lodge, where comfy linens and hot meals are provided.

Beginning on the shores of glacier-fed Maligne Lake, the Skyline Trail sets off north on a boot-worn path through some of the most monumental scenery in Jasper National Park. The initial ascent is gradual, taking you through a serene alpine forest of stunted pine and spruce, where herds of caribou often graze, and up to the first major pass. Above the treeline, the expansive mountain scenery begins to unfold: a vast terrain of grassy meadows dotted with hardy wildflowers and an endless backdrop of the lofty ridges of the Canadian Rockies.

The next morning brings another pass and an approach through a wide, verdant valley known for being prime grizzly bear country. Then you're trekking up to The Notch, the third and final pass and the highest point of the hike. It's here, on this exposed, snow-packed crest, where the Skyline Trail truly lives up to its name, placing you at eye level with the park's greatest precipices. The trail then descends into a territory of barren, rocky fields where noisy and tenacious pika have made entire networks of burrows among the piles of stones. At night, packs of timber wolves agilely patrol the forested scree slopes, following the scent of bighorn sheep.

As you continue to follow the trail down, Mount Tekarra comes into view, like a massive medieval castle carved by giants. This impressive peak stays with you, a hulking landmark at first ahead and then behind, as you make your way to Signal Mountain Trailhead and the end of this spellbinding route.

21

East Coast Trail

LOCATION Canada **START/FINISH** Topsail Beach/Cappahayden **DISTANCE** 209 miles (336 km) **TIME** 3–4 weeks **DIFFICULTY** Easy to challenging **INFORMATION** www.eastcoasttrail.com

Take in the rocky headlands, welcoming fishing villages and noisy seabird colonies of Canada's wild east on a trail that helps protect this unique natural environment.

The Avalon Peninsula, which dangles off Canada's Newfoundland and Labrador province, is where the colonial story of North America really begins. You can roam the region where the first New World explorers landed in the late 15th century and where the English founded their first overseas outposts in the early 1600s, on a superb trail that reveals Avalon's rich natural and historical heritage to hikers.

Created gradually over the years from the mid-1990s, the East Coast Trail currently traces the peninsula's easternmost shoreline from scenic Topsail Beach to the small fishing town of Cappahayden—though the intention is to extend it another 60 miles (100 km) or so to Trepassey. The trail is not a single path but rather a series of 25 separate ones, which pass through the 30-plus colorful settlements along the way. The paths range from around 2.5 miles (4 km) to 12.5 miles (20 km) and can be walked individually, each doable in a day or less, or strung together for one big adventure. There are six

Atlantic puffins on the cliffs of Witless Bay Ecological Reserve, near St. John's

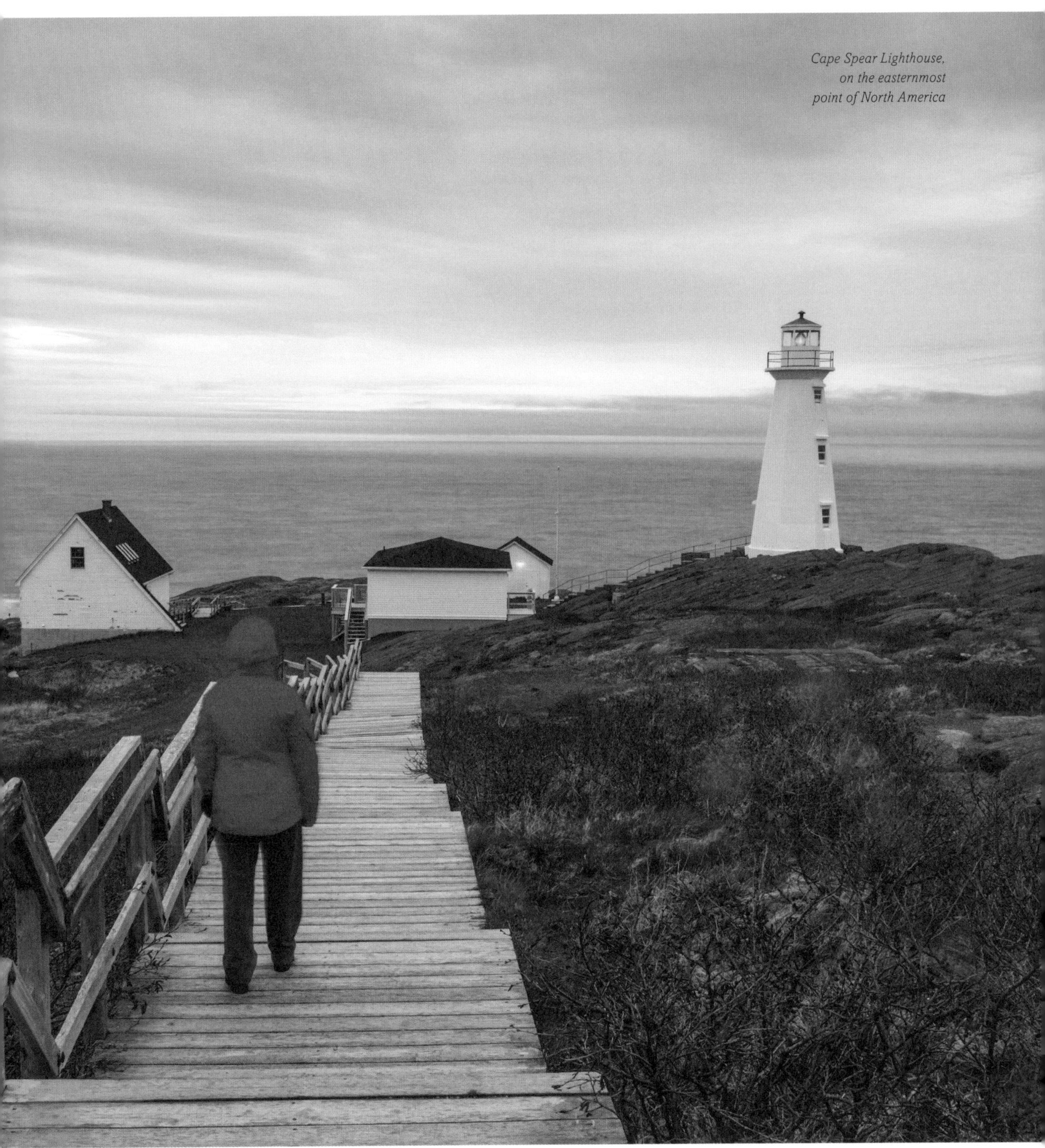

Cape Spear Lighthouse, on the easternmost point of North America

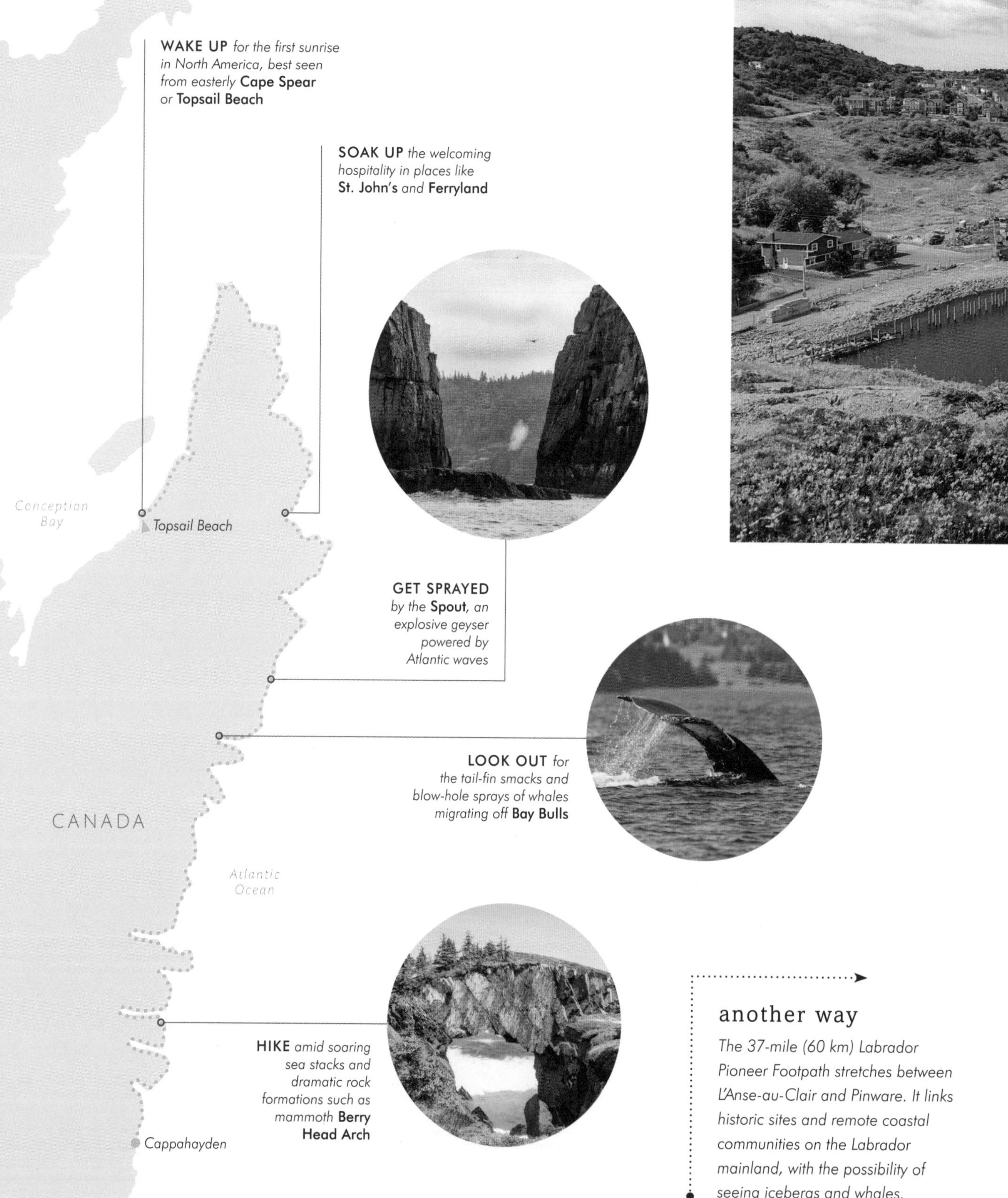

WAKE UP *for the first sunrise in North America, best seen from easterly* **Cape Spear** *or* **Topsail Beach**

SOAK UP *the welcoming hospitality in places like* **St. John's** *and* **Ferryland**

GET SPRAYED *by the* **Spout**, *an explosive geyser powered by Atlantic waves*

LOOK OUT *for the tail-fin smacks and blow-hole sprays of whales migrating off* **Bay Bulls**

HIKE *amid soaring sea stacks and dramatic rock formations such as mammoth* **Berry Head Arch**

another way

The 37-mile (60 km) Labrador Pioneer Footpath stretches between L'Anse-au-Clair and Pinware. It links historic sites and remote coastal communities on the Labrador mainland, with the possibility of seeing icebergs and whales.

Above *Hiking along the coast near St. John's*
Left *The village of Quidi Vidi*

designated campsites en route but also plenty of hotels, lodges, and B&Bs in the trailhead towns and villages.

The coastline itself is remarkable. On the trail, you'll encounter quiet coves, plunging waterfalls, and intriguing human relics, from World War II batteries to Cold War tracking stations. The crashing Atlantic Ocean is a near-constant companion, providing plenty of opportunities to see Arctic icebergs float by or the splash and spray of humpbacks, orcas, minke, and more (whale-watching is best here between June and August).

Every section of the trail is different. For a straightforward starter, try the Beaches Path, a short, low-level trail that wends for 4.5 miles (7 km) through woodland, heath, and meadows; past cobblestone beaches; and close to Witless Bay Ecological Reserve, a real hot spot for nesting seabirds and puffins.

For a slightly more challenging trek, hit the Sugarloaf Path, a moderate 5.5-mile (9 km) day-hike that begins in Quidi Vidi village, a quaint fishing community that's known for its candy-colored cottages and a microbrewery that uses iceberg water to make its refreshing beers. From here, the trail ascends quite steeply, affording sweeping views of St. John's, the capital of the province, before closely following the coast up to barren Sugarloaf Head. It finishes at Logy Bay, where bobbing boats, whales. and seals share the rough ocean waves below.

Or why not walk the whole thing? It'll take you the best part of a month, but what a month it'll be, spent on the easternmost fringes of the North American continent, with only icebergs and seabirds for company.

ICEBERG ALLEY

The waters off Newfoundland's craggy coast are known as "Iceberg Alley." Every year, chunks of ice, mostly calved off the glaciers of western Greenland, drift southward past the province. They come in all shapes and sizes, some as huge as office buildings, others small and sculptural. Good spots to see them include St. John's, Cape Spear, Bay Bulls, and Witless Bay; May and June are best times.

22

The Island Walk

LOCATION Canada **START/FINISH** Charlottetown (return) **DISTANCE** 435 miles (700 km) **TIME** 4–5 weeks **DIFFICULTY** Easy **INFORMATION** www.theislandwalk.ca

Canada's answer to Spain's Camino de Santiago embraces slow travel on an enriching loop of Prince Edward Island, with picturesque towns, quiet beaches and unmissable seafood en route.

Canada's smallest province, Prince Edward Island (PEI) lies in the Gulf of St. Lawrence, an isolated idyll of soft red soil, rolling hills and sandstone cliffs. Just the kind of place, then, to savor on a long, leisurely loop.

Created in 2021, the Island Walk is the brainchild of a local walking group, who wanted to develop a trail that meandered through the region's villages in the same way that the Camino de Santiago in Spain does. Start (and end) your sojourn around the island's perimeter in the creative capital of Charlottetown, Canada's lively birthplace of confederation. Along the way, you'll potter around PEI's more notable communities, such as Kensington, where fresh fish tacos are the order of the day, and Cavendish, whose miles of powder-soft white sand offer boardwalk shopping and soothing vistas. In North Cape, to the west, goats skitter along the beaches and you can try catching your own bluefish tuna out at sea. Around Souris and Montague, on the homeward eastern leg, look out for soaring ospreys and bald eagles—a fine way to finish your circuit of PEI.

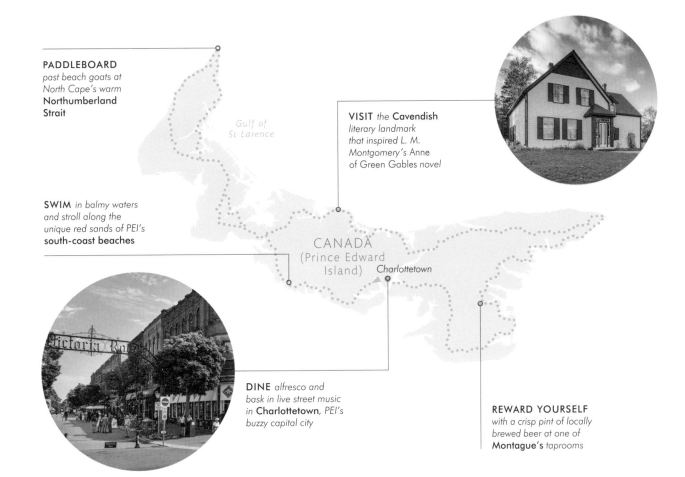

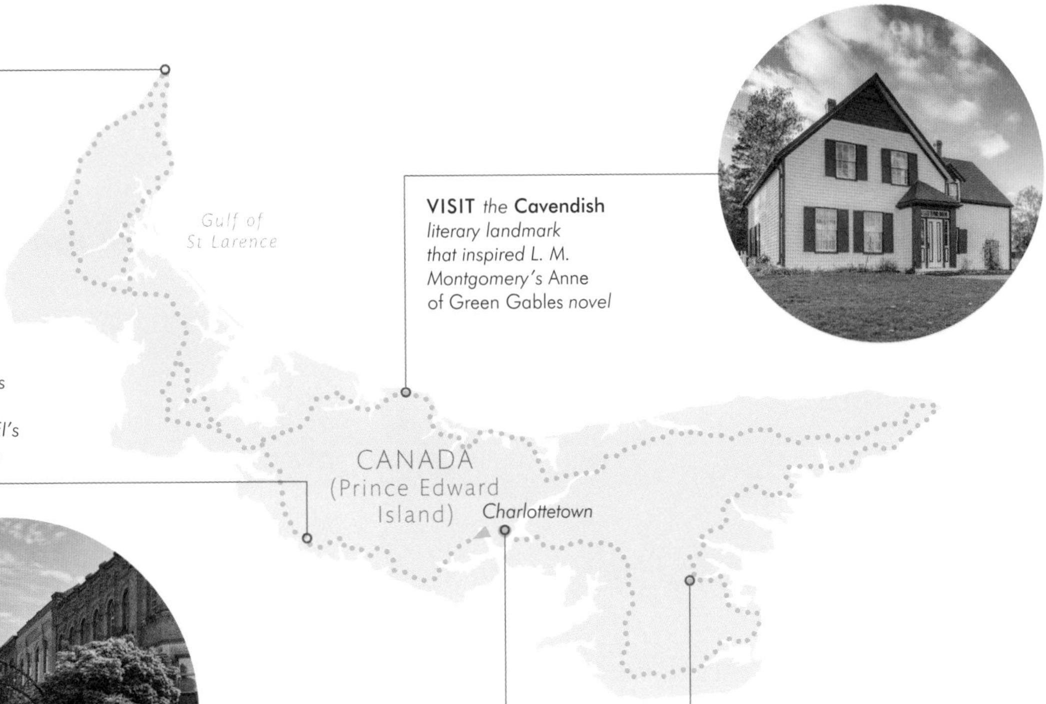

PADDLEBOARD *past beach goats at North Cape's warm* **Northumberland Strait**

Gulf of St Larence

VISIT *the* **Cavendish** *literary landmark that inspired L. M. Montgomery's Anne of Green Gables novel*

SWIM *in balmy waters and stroll along the unique red sands of PEI's* **south-coast beaches**

CANADA (Prince Edward Island)

Charlottetown

DINE *alfresco and bask in live street music in* **Charlottetown***, PEI's buzzy capital city*

REWARD YOURSELF *with a crisp pint of locally brewed beer at one of* **Montague's** *taprooms*

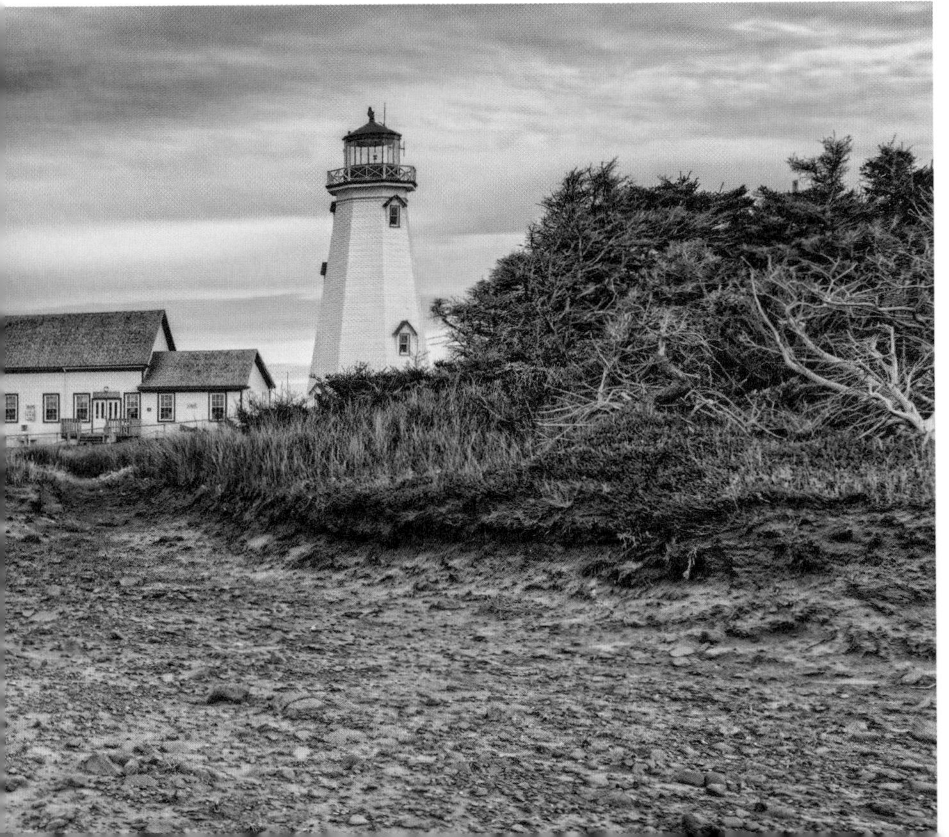

another way

For a shorter, seven-day itinerary, consider looping the heart of PEI: start at lively Charlottetown and walk clockwise via Summerside, Kensington, and Cavendish. PEI's finest stretch of beaches resides near the latter.

Pretty East Point Lighthouse, on the northeastern tip of Prince Edward Island

Left *Fall colors in Hautes-Gorges-de-la-Rivière-Malbaie* ***Above*** *Setting off into the hills on the Charlevoix Traverse*

23

Charlevoix Traverse

LOCATION Canada **START/FINISH** Saint-Urbain/Mont Grands-Fonds **DISTANCE** 57 miles (91 km) **TIME** 1 week **DIFFICULTY** Moderate **INFORMATION** www.traverseedecharlevoix.qc.ca

Hop between a network of backcountry huts, exploring pristine forests and lakes, dizzying rock walls, and impressive canyons.

The Charlevoix crater, in Quebec, was created around 450 million years ago, when an asteroid is thought to have collided with the earth. Much of the crater's 34-mile (54 km) diameter now lies beneath the St. Lawrence River, but a good portion remains on land, its loosely defined edges guiding the Charlevoix Traverse, a beautiful hiking trail that runs through the heart of the UNESCO Charlevoix Biosphere Reserve.

Tracing a route between two national parks—Grands-Jardins and Hautes-Gorges-de-la-Rivière-Malbaie—the trail takes in vast gray granite rock faces, gentle lakeland scenery, and giant canyons carved out by the Malbaie River. And you can enjoy all of this in relative comfort. With hikers overnighting in a series of cabins ready-stocked with mattresses and equipped kitchens, the traverse offers a rare chance to get deep into the backcountry with only the barest of life's essentials strapped to your grateful shoulders.

another way

Such is the lure of the Hautes-Gorges-de-la-Rivière-Malbaie that many hikers decide to stop halfway along the trail to spend a couple of days in the national park. Contact La Traversée de Charlevoix to have your car and camping gear waiting for you.

24

Coastal Hiking Trail

LOCATION Canada **START/FINISH** North Swallow River/Hattie Cove **DISTANCE** 37 miles (60 km) **TIME** 5–9 days **DIFFICULTY** Challenging **INFORMATION** www.pc.gc.ca; registration required

Tracing the shoreline of the largest freshwater lake in the world, this hike through Ontario's wilderness follows in the footsteps of the Anishinaabe peoples.

Weaving along an undeveloped shoreline of the spectacular Lake Superior in Ontario's Pukaskwa National Park, the Coastal Hiking Trail chases a faint and ancient path once used by First Nations peoples many millennia ago. Only a few cairn markers—small, human-made stone piles—lead the way as you cross over the slick lichen-covered granite slabs that are part of the massive Precambrian rock formation known as the Canadian Shield. By day, you'll pitch on and off the wave-lashed beaches that hug Lake Superior, occasionally cutting inland through thick woods and across suspension bridges that hang over raging rivers. Be prepared to share the steep, rough terrain with the timber wolves, lynx, and other reclusive creatures who roam the isolated boreal forests and boulder-strewn landscapes of this stunning part of Canada. After dark, you'll camp on deserted lakeside beaches, with just the lapping of the lake's waters to lull you to sleep. If you're after an adventure in the wilderness, this is it.

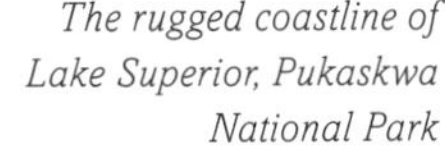

The rugged coastline of Lake Superior, Pukaskwa National Park

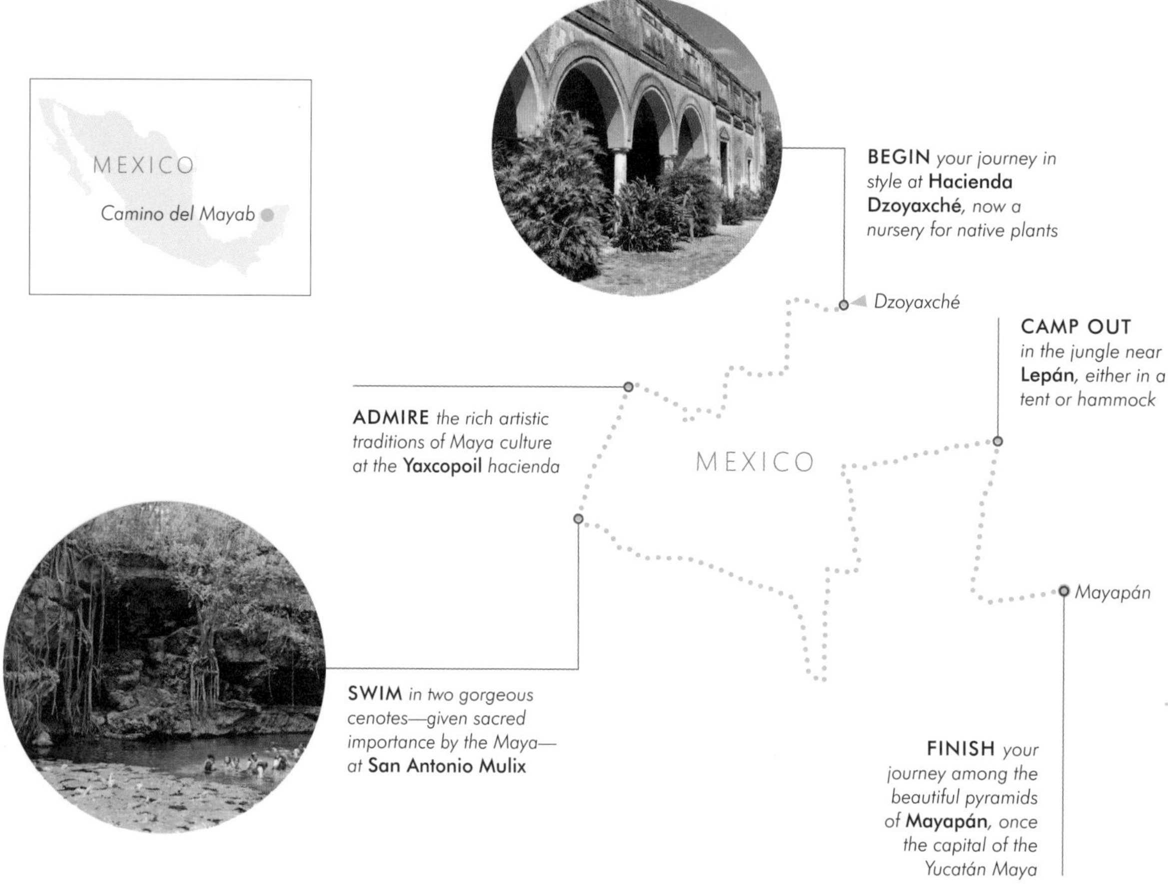
MEXICO
Camino del Mayab
BEGIN your journey in style at Hacienda Dzoyaxché, now a nursery for native plants
Dzoyaxché
CAMP OUT in the jungle near Lepán, either in a tent or hammock
ADMIRE the rich artistic traditions of Maya culture at the Yaxcopoil hacienda
MEXICO
Mayapán
SWIM in two gorgeous cenotes—given sacred importance by the Maya—at San Antonio Mulix
FINISH your journey among the beautiful pyramids of Mayapán, once the capital of the Yucatán Maya

25

Camino del Mayab

LOCATION Mexico **START/FINISH** Dzoyaxché/Mayapán **DISTANCE** 62 miles (100 km) **TIME** 5 days **DIFFICULTY** Easy to moderate **INFORMATION** www.caminodelmayab.com

Wind through the temple-strewn jungles of Mexico's Yucatán Peninsula, learning about the rich culture of the ancient Maya and staying in historic haciendas along the way.

The vibrant culture of the Maya gave Mexico some of its most defining features: magnificent Mesoamerican temples; colorfully woven *huipil* tunics; and a vivid mythological landscape, where natural sinkholes are portals to the underworld and the technicolor motmot bird is a messenger from the gods. Maya culture was decimated during the Spanish colonial conquest of the 16th and 17th centuries, leaving Mayan civilizations scattered and their temples in ruins, but the people themselves survive to this day across the Yucatán Peninsula.

Mexico's first long-distance hiking trail, the Camino del Mayab, or Maya Way, leads you through their communities, with well-maintained trails along former railroads and livestock routes. You'll cool off from the

THE ALUX

The Mayan equivalent of the sprite is the alux, a mischievous spirit. The town of Lepán is considered a hub for alux activity, with locals claiming to hear alux cries resonating out of cenotes in the middle of the night. Belief in aluxes is so widespread that in the 1990s a pyramid was built to satisfy the spirits under a bridge in Cancún, after a series of construction problems was attributed to an angry alux.

heat of the jungle in cenotes (sinkholes), enjoy classic Mayan dishes such as tamales, and explore Mayan ruins hidden in the jungle, such as the dramatic complex of temples at Mayapán, once the capital of the Yucatán Maya.

The trail offers opportunities to stop off at Maya communities living either on or near historic haciendas, colonial country estates. Some of these haciendas, including the start point Dzoyaxché, are now plant nurseries. Others have been turned into museums, such as Yaxcopoil, where Maya artifacts are exhibited along with machinery required in the processing of *henequen*, an agave used in rope making. The haciendas were once places of oppression; *henequen* was known as "green gold" for how wealthy it made the landowners, while the Maya workers earned next to nothing. This trail, however, seeks to redress this injustice, with 80 percent of proceeds going to support local Maya communities.

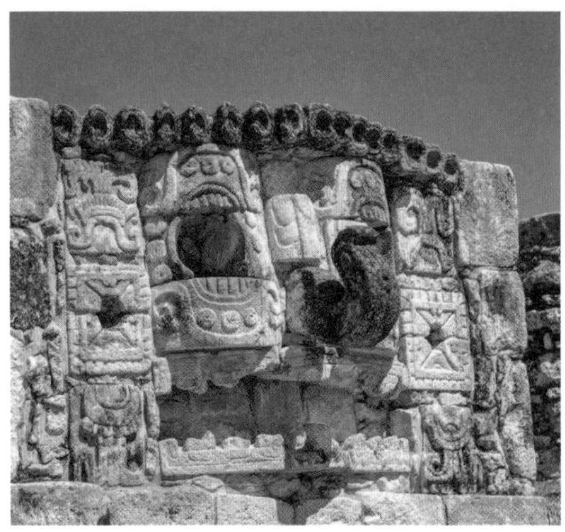

Top *The ruins at Mayapán*
Above *Stone carving of Chaac, the Mayan god of rain, at Mayapán*

The ruined church of San Juan Parangaricutiro, rising dramatically from the jungle

26

Paricutín

LOCATION Mexico **START/FINISH** Angahuan (return) **DISTANCE** 12.5 miles (20 km) **TIME** 5–7 hours **DIFFICULTY** Moderate **INFORMATION** Guide required for first leg

Amid the avocado orchards and pine forests of Michoacán rises a cinematic sight: the charred cone of Paricutín, a young volcano that emerged without warning from the middle of a cornfield in 1943. The eruption engulfed the hamlet of San Juan Parangaricutiro, leaving only the ruins of its church, which poke atmospherically through a lava field—locals still leave poignant offerings of candles and flowers on its exposed altar.

Walking to these spectral ruins from the nearby village of Angahuan is an unforgettable experience, particularly when combined with a hike to the summit of Paricutín. You can walk the path on your own, but a guide is required to lead you on the first part through the pine forest, where it's easy to get lost. Be sure to wear sturdy shoes, and be careful on the sharp volcanic rocks. It's remarkable to walk on such a new landscape, where vivid green shrubs and trees are sprouting from the black earth—a symbol, like the old church, of survival in the face of cataclysm.

27

Cerro Verde National Park

LOCATION El Salvador **START/FINISH** Cerro Verde (return) **DISTANCE** 4.5 miles (7 km) **TIME** 4–5 hours **DIFFICULTY** Moderate; steep in stretches **INFORMATION** www.elsalvador.travel

The three volcanoes in the Cerro Verde National Park couldn't be more different: extinct for 2,500 years, Cerro Verde is draped in cloud forest; Izalco is a striking cone of black ash; and Santa Ana (or Ilamatpec) has a bubbling sulfurous lagoon in its deep crater. Still, as a group, their profile is so picturesque and is said to have inspired aristocratic French aviator Antoine de Saint-Exupéry to write *The Little Prince* (1943).

You'll get a taste of all three on the trail to the summit of Santa Ana, the highest point in El Salvador at 7,812 ft (2,381 m). Starting on Cerro Verde, where vendors sell cheese-filled *pupusas*, the country's signature snack, you head down past Izalco and up a zigzag path to sublime views of Santa Ana's crater. The turquoise shimmer of Lago Coatepeque in the crater below is a temptation—ease tired calves with a refreshing dip in its cool waters.

The turquoise shimmer of Lago Coatepeque in the crater below is a temptation

28

Cerro Negro

LOCATION Nicaragua **START/FINISH** Leon (return) **DISTANCE** 2 miles (3.5 km) **TIME** 4–5 hours **DIFFICULTY** Moderate; steep in stretches **INFORMATION** www.visitnicaragua.us

The youngest volcano in Nicaragua, Cerro Negro exploded into life in 1850 and has erupted over 230 times since, leaving a wide skirt of blackened ash around its base. The shadeless trail to the top rises only 1,312 ft (400 m) but can take up to an hour as you trudge through scree and battle blustery winds to reach the smoking fumaroles and vents at the summit. In places, the ground beneath you is so warm you can feel the heat through your shoes.

Panoramic views of the Maribios chain of mountains are spectacular, but for adrenaline seekers, the thrills and spills of sandboarding down the western slope are the main attraction. For safety, volcano surfers don a *Breaking Bad*-style coveralls, gloves, and goggles before whizzing down the gritty gravel on a rudimentary wooden board at speeds up to 60 mph (95 km/h). Start early for the chance of a second wild ride.

Whizzing down the dusty slopes of Cerro Negro

29

Somoto Canyon

LOCATION Nicaragua **START/FINISH** Somoto (return) **DISTANCE** 4.5 miles (7.5 km) **TIME** 6 hours **DIFFICULTY** Moderate; steep in parts **INFORMATION** www.visitnicaragua.us

The remarkable Somoto Canyon was virtually unknown to the outside world until 2004, when two Czech geologists stumbled across the gorge. It now appears on the Nicaraguan 50 cordoba note and is the highlight of the Rio Coco Geopark, Central America's first.

This trail starts in dry forest, leading to a vantage point overlooking the spot where the Comali and Tapacali rivers join to form the mighty Rio Coco. It then cuts deep through ancient rocks, the sheer walls of the canyon rising 492 ft (150 m) in places, and separated by only a few yards in the narrowest sections. From here, the journey gets wet and wild: scramble over rocks and plunge into deep pools that lie 66 ft (20 m) below, before floating dreamily downstream toward journey's end.

another way

Instead of hiking through Somoto Canyon, hop in a boat; friendly locals can row you upriver, where you can slowly glide beneath the canyon's clifftops in sedate leisure.

30

El Mirador Trail

LOCATION Guatemala **START/FINISH** Carmelita (loop)
DISTANCE 60 miles (96 km) **TIME** 6 days **DIFFICULTY** Moderate
INFORMATION www.turismocooperativacarmelita.com

Go on an intrepid adventure to a series of ancient Mayan ruins that lie hidden deep in the wild jungles of northeastern Guatemala.

Built half a millennia before Guatemala's Mayan city of Tikal, the archaeological wonder of El Mirador is thought to have flourished from around the 6th century BCE to the 1st century CE. It can be reached only via a sweaty six-day hike along a crude, lowland jungle track, which, for most visitors, is half the fun.

From the village of Carmelita, your guide from the community-run cooperative will lead you deep into the jungle along relatively flat dirt paths laced with tree roots. With camping supplies typically carried by mules, you can focus on spotting bright-billed toucans and howler monkeys, perhaps even a jaguar's paw print.

The loop trek also takes in the El Mirador "suburbs" of El Tintal, Nakbé, Wakna, and La Florida. But these partly excavated Mayan ruins pale in size and splendor to the main event. The impressive stone structures at El Mirador—including La Danta, one of the largest pyramids in the world—loom out of the trees, rising up from a jungle that seems determined to engulf them once more.

LA DANTA

The pyramid of La Danta is a staggering 236 ft (72 m) tall, making it one of the largest ancient buildings ever constructed; the base tier alone covers nearly 45 acres (18 hectares). Each block within the pyramid weighs just over 1,000 lb (450 kg) and required 12 people to carry it. Archaeologists estimate it took the equivalent of 15 million days of labor to build.

Below *The pyramid of La Danta poking through the treetops* ***Right*** *Climbing up steps toward La Danta on the El Mirador Trail*

Descending through mountain mist atop Cerro Chirripó

(31)

Cerro Chirripó

LOCATION Costa Rica **START/FINISH** San Gerardo de Rivas (return) **DISTANCE** 22.5 miles (36 km) **TIME** 2 days **DIFFICULTY** Challenging **INFORMATION** Organize permits at www.sinac.go.cr

Climb Costa Rica's highest summit, through fabulously contrasting topographical zones, to experience a vista that sweeps from the Caribbean coast to the Pacific.

Cloud forest is one of the natural wonders of Costa Rica. But at San Gerardo de Rivas, you'll simply be climbing through it, bound for the loftiest land in the nation: 12,536 ft (3,821 m) high Cerro Chirripó. Plenty of hikers come to scale the mountain's summit, but the national park surrounding it remains substantially less busy than other protected areas in Costa Rica. Exploring here will make you feel quite the trailblazing adventurer.

You can tackle the 11 miles (18 km) from trailhead to top in one day, ascending 9,843 ft (3,000 m) as you go, and hike out the way you came the day after. In a single ascent, you'll pass through more topographical zones than many countries can claim in their entirety. You'll begin in pastureland before hitting the stupendously biodiverse belt of cloud forest and then open scrub known as *páramo* (tundra). You'll emerge, finally, onto rocky mountaintop, which offers one of the few chances in the world to gaze at the Caribbean and the Pacific in one wondrous panorama.

Exploring here will make you feel quite the trailblazing adventurer

32

Pipeline Road

LOCATION Panama **START/FINISH** Gamboa (return) **DISTANCE** Up to 11 miles (17.5 km) **TIME** Up to 1 day **DIFFICULTY** Easy **INFORMATION** www.tourismpanama.com

They say to never judge a book by its cover. The inauspicious-sounding Camino del Oleoducto, the Pipeline Road, actually leads into a protected tropical-forest paradise, brimming with birdlife—all just 40 minutes' drive from the skyscrapers of Panama City. Set out early morning, when the sun leaks through the canopy and birds begin to flit and call. With more than 500 recorded species along the trail, it's an avian paradise. Even the uninitiated are likely to spot something exciting: the rainbow-colored bill of a swooping toucan, perhaps, or the dazzling head of a crimson-crested woodpecker hammering away at the bark of a tree. Chances are you won't break the world record, though; in 1985, a staggering 385 bird species were identified during one feather-filled 24-hour period.

WHAT'S IN A NAME?

The Pipeline Road gets its name from the oil pipeline it was built to service, which was made by the US Navy in World War II. Its construction was precautionary, should the war ever reach Central America and the Panama Canal be shut down. At the time, the canal, along with 5 miles (8 km) of land on either side, was US territory.

33

Comandancia de la Plata

LOCATION Cuba **START/FINISH** Alto del Naranjo (return) **DISTANCE** 5 miles (8 km) **TIME** 4 hours **DIFFICULTY** Moderate **INFORMATION** Obligatory guides are available to hire in nearby Santo Domingo

A sinuous road rises into the cloud forest-coated Sierra Maestra mountain range, its verges a picture of Cuban rural life that belies the region's past. In 1958, Fidel Castro and his fellow rebels established their headquarters here, deep in the mountainous foliage; a year later, they mustered the men and munitions to topple then-dictator Fulgencio Batista, changing Cuba irrevocably.

Their well-preserved rebel camp—which Batista never discovered—provides a poignant focus to this jungle tramp, its wooden buildings offering harrowing insights into guerrilla life; the hospital is located far from the other structures, so the screams of the wounded would not alert soldiers to remaining rebels. At Comandancia de la Plata, it feels as if the revolution is not yet over, that you're still in the remote, rugged middle of it.

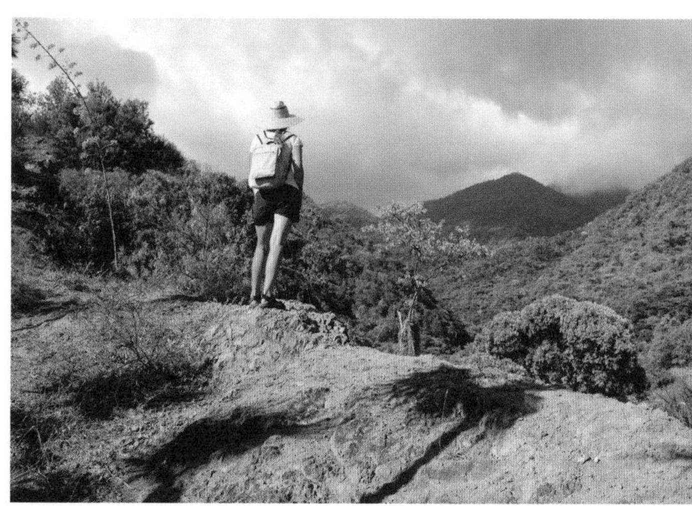

The cloud forest-coated Sierra Maestra mountain range

Quadirikiri Cave, Arikok National Park

34

Arikok National Park

LOCATION Aruba **START/FINISH** Arikok National Park Visitor Center (loop) **DISTANCE** 8.5 miles (13.5 km) **TIME** 4 hours **DIFFICULTY** Moderate to challenging **INFORMATION** www.arubanationalpark.org

Prising yourself away from some of the Caribbean's loveliest beaches might be a struggle on Aruba, an island that, along with Bonaire, Curaçao and Sint Maarten, forms the lion's share of the Netherlands' overseas territories. But you'll thank yourself once you're deep within Arikok National Park, a surreal desertscape of lumpy lava and a spectacularly chiseled coastline.

The park's best trail runs east from the visitor center, via island high-point Sero Jamanota. It takes in Fontein Cave, with its Arawak cave art, and Dos Playa, a dazzling double act rated by many as Aruba's best beaches—look for the turtles that nest there. It's less the boulder-bestrewn terrain and more the shadeless conditions that makes these trails tough, so load up with water and start early—there's a white-sand beach waiting once you're done.

another way

You could also explore the park's north, ascending Sero Arikok, the island's best viewpoint, before forging on to cool off in the azure natural pool of Conchi, where incoming tides crash over the ramparts of volcanic rock.

35

La Ciudad Perdida

LOCATION Colombia **START/FINISH** El Mamey/Santa Marta **DISTANCE** 31 miles (50 km) **TIME** 4–6 days **DIFFICULTY** Challenging **INFORMATION** www.colombia.travel

In 1972, a couple of Colombian looters hunting for tropical bird feathers in the forests of the Sierra Nevada de Santa Marta mountains pulled back some tangled roots and found the ruins of a forgotten city. They had discovered Teyuna, a township once home to 2,000 Tairona people dating from 650 CE—some 650 years older than Machu Picchu in Peru.

Today, travelers brave the hothouse humidity of the tropical jungle to reach the remains of La Ciudad Perdida, the Lost City. A Wiwa guide—a direct descendant of the Tairona—leads the way to the sacred site, along sandy paths that weave through Wiwa villages and zigzag back and forth across the tannin-colored Buritaca River. On the final ascent, more than a thousand ancient stone steps climb ever upward until, at last, you see it: ahead, the great tiers of Teyuna's oval terraces floating over the tree canopy like a castle in the clouds.

36

Blue Mountain Peak

LOCATION Jamaica **START/FINISH** Penlyne Castle (return)
DISTANCE 11 miles (17 km) **TIME** 1 day **DIFFICULTY** Challenging
INFORMATION www.blueandjohncrowmountains.org

Roam across the roof of Jamaica on a vigorous hike in the heart of the nation's lush Blue and John Crow Mountains National Park, where some of the finest coffee in the Caribbean is grown.

If you'd climb a mountain for a great coffee, then this challenging rainforest trail has your name on it. The classic hike to Blue Mountain Peak, Jamaica's highest point at 7,402 ft (2,256 m), begins in the misty mountain village of Penlyne Castle. It's surrounded by coffee plantations like Whitfield Hall, which is also a rustic hiking lodge where you can sample Jamaica's famed Blue Mountain coffee from the source.

You'll certainly need the caffeine hit for this hike. Most walkers set off shortly after midnight, to reach the summit in time to watch the sun rise—on a clear day you can see Kingston to the south, and maybe even the hazy form of Cuba to the north. If you huffed and puffed up the steep trail in the dark, you can take your time to admire the national park's incredible biodiversity on the descent. Look out for the endangered yellow-and-black Homerus swallowtail, the largest butterfly in the Americas, on your way back to Penlyne Castle for a celebratory cup of Joe.

> If you'd climb a mountain for a great coffee, then this rainforest trail has your name on it

Verdant coffee fields covering the slopes of Blue Mountain Peak

Left Sunlight illuminating a path in El Yunque National Forest
Below One of the 13 species of coqui frog that are found in El Yunque's rainforest

37

El Yunque

LOCATION Puerto Rico **START/FINISH** Palo Colorado Information Center (return) **DISTANCE** 4.8 miles (7.7 km) **TIME** 4–5 hours **DIFFICULTY** Moderate; some steep sections **INFORMATION** www.fs.usda.gov/elyunque

A hike up the mist-draped slopes of El Yunque takes in several levels of tropical rainforest, the trail overhung by giant ferns and wild hibiscus, with all of eastern Puerto Rico laid out below.

Rustling trees. The chirping of coqui frogs. The distant gurgling of running water. There's little other sound on the well-marked trail to the summit of El Yunque (3,540 ft / 1,080 m), a mostly gentle climb through jungle-smothered mountains and bubbling cascades on the eastern side of Puerto Rico.

Beginning in the heart of El Yunque National Forest, the path (one of many) snakes through lush sierra palm forest for 1.9 miles (3 km) before reaching a short spur to the jagged peaks known as Los Picachos. Lizards scurry through a dripping undergrowth of white ginger flowers and wild papaya, and you may glimpse flashes of green as Puerto Rican todies flit among the branches above. Beyond Los Picachos, the final section of the trail slices through a cloud forest of shorter twisted trees draped with mosses and vines. Finally, there's the summit, a cluster of communication masts and a stubby stone observation tower. When the clouds clear, you can see as far as San Juan and the Caribbean, glimmering in the distance.

THE SPIRITS OF EL YUNQUE

The Taíno—the Indigenous people of Puerto Rico—regarded El Yunque as a sacred mountain. This was the home of Yukiyú (or Yúcahu), their chief deity, creator of all life on earth. The Taíno believed that Yukiyú would protect them from the malevolent deity Guabancex (or "Juracán"), and it remains true today that El Yunque acts like a protective wall, taking the blow of hurricanes and storms as they hit the island from the east.

38

Waitukubuli National Trail

LOCATION Dominica **START/FINISH** Scotts Head/Fort Shirley **DISTANCE** 96 miles (155 km) **TIME** 2 weeks **DIFFICULTY** Easy to moderate; individual sections range from easy to very difficult **INFORMATION** www.waitukubulitrail.dm

Trek from one end of Dominica to the other on this rainforest trail through the island's mountainous interior of bubbling hot springs and bird-filled jungle.

There can't be too many hikes that span the length and breadth of an entire country. But Dominica's Waitukubuli Trail, the longest in the Caribbean, does exactly that. And between its 14 sections, the route takes in virgin rainforest and wave-washed beaches, botanical gardens and coffee estates, and the magnificent Morne Trois Pitons National Park, home to volcanic attractions like Boiling Lake and the Valley of Desolation.

A dozen or so mountains rear up across the island—"Waitukubuli" is the Indigenous name for the island itself and means, suitably enough, "tall is her body"—giving Dominica a much more rugged and wild feeling than most of its Caribbean counterparts. The trail, therefore, can be tough going, but for an insight into the island, Waitukubuli is difficult to beat. The trail immerses you in the island's rich wealth of flora and fauna—including vibrant orchids and heliconias, bushy candlewood trees and Sisserou parrots. Dominica isn't known as "The Nature Island" for nothing.

another way

Many of Waitukubuli's segments are individual trails in their own right. Punchy Segment 1, from Scotts Head to the Soufriere Estate, involves open climbing in parts, and ends with a well-earned dip in the bathlike waters of Soufriere's sulfur springs.

Steaming hot springs in Morne Trois Pitons National Park, a dramatic sight on the Waitukubuli Trail

The shadowy peak of Gros Piton, providing an impressive backdrop to an idyllic beach

39

Three Peaks Challenge

LOCATION St. Lucia **START/FINISH** The 758 Adventurers drop-off at each of the three mountain trailheads **DISTANCE** 8 miles (12.5 km) **TIME** 1–3 days **DIFFICULTY** Challenging **INFORMATION** The Three Peaks Challenge is run by The 758 Adventurers

Tackle the tropical version of the UK's Three Peaks Challenge, clambering, scrambling, and rope-climbing your way up to each of St. Lucia's three key summits.

Vacationers are no longer visiting the Eastern Caribbean island of St. Lucia just to relax in its blissful beach resorts. Adventure tourism has taken off in this precipitous, rainforest-draped country, and nothing fires the adrenaline like the Three Peaks Challenge. Created in 2023 by local operator The 758 Adventurers, this guided ascent sees you summiting the island's most talismanic peaks: Gros Piton, Petit Piton, and Mount Gimie, St. Lucia's highest peak at 3,117 ft (950 m).

Whether you choose to climb the mountains on separate days or tackle the trio in one gut-busting stretch, you'll need fitness in spades. Here, you'll stomp through sticky jungle and over slippery roots and rocks and, on occasion, haul yourself up by ropes to reach the summits. Gradients are abrupt, but the rewards are some of the Caribbean's loveliest vistas and the knowledge that you've taken on the island's trickiest topography—and come out on top.

THE PICTURE-BOOK PITONS

The volcanic plugs of Gros Piton and Petit Piton are St. Lucia's most defining landmarks. Together they form a UNESCO World Heritage Site, soaring in spires straight from the sea on the island's western flanks. Although covering a relatively small geographic area, their wildlife is diverse, their thick dwarf forest harboring five endemic bird species and mammals such as opossums.

40

Caminho dos Diamantes

LOCATION Brazil **START/FINISH** Diamantina/Ouro Preto **DISTANCE** 247 miles (395 km) **TIME** 27 days **DIFFICULTY** Challenging **INFORMATION** www.institutoestradareal.com.br/en/caminhos/caminhos-dos-diamantes

Built by the Portuguese—or, more accurately, the laborers they conscripted—this old diamond-trading route makes for an eye-opening, long-distance walk through eastern Brazil.

This is a hike with history. The Caminho dos Diamantes is part of the Estrada Real, or Royal Road, which snakes for more than 620 miles (1,000 km) through southeastern Brazil, linking together a string of time-burnished towns and villages. It is not, however, a single route—or a new one. The beginnings of the Estrada Real stretch back to the late 17th century, during the colonial era in South America, when the Portuguese were still establishing a hold on the country. This extended not just to Brazil's people, but to its minerals, too. By the 1690s,

The trail provides an insight into the region's remarkable artistic heritage

Left The Baroque town of Ouro Preto, marking the end of the trail **Below** A rugged escarpment greets a hiker near the city of Itambé do Mato Dentro

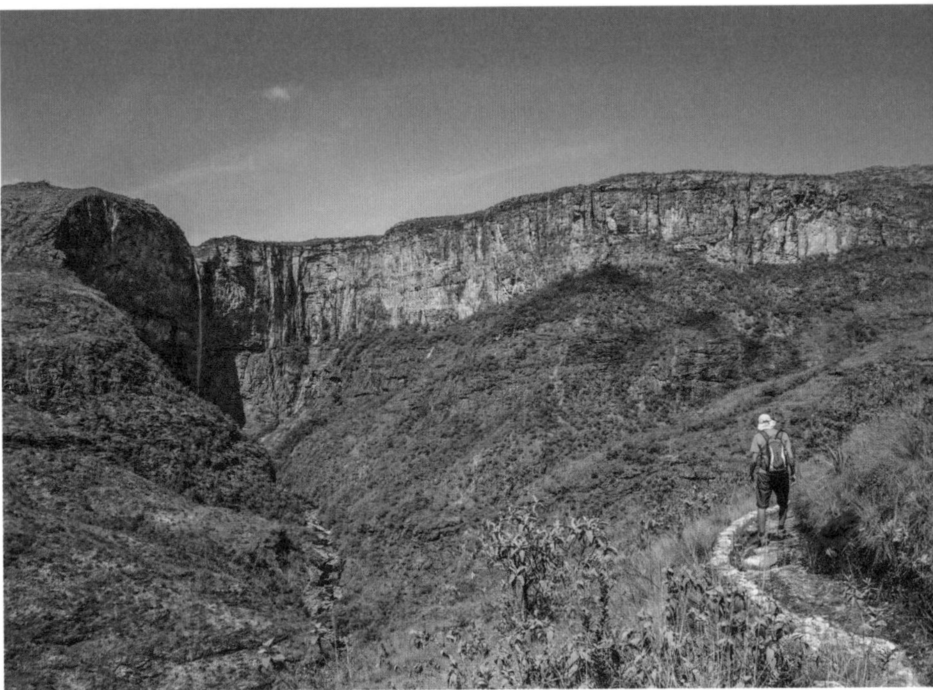

construction was underway on the first in a network of four trading roads, to allow Portuguese mule trains to carry gold and diamonds from the mines to the sea. These routes, which interlink at different points, are now collectively known as the Estrada Real. As the products of slave labor, the roads have an inescapable dark side, but they also provide an insight into the region's remarkable artistic heritage. This is particularly true of the 247-mile (395 km) section of the Estrada Real known as the Caminho dos Diamantes, or Diamond Way.

As its name suggests, the road's main aim was to help transport diamonds across the Brazilian countryside, in this case from the northern slopes of the Minas Gerais district to the colonial hub of Ouro Preto. Diamonds were discovered in the aforementioned hills in the 1720s, leading to the rapid nearby growth of what is now the town of Diamantina. As such, today's trail—which can generally be walked in around four weeks if you're taking the time to absorb the

another way

The oldest of the routes making up the Estrada Real is the Caminho Velho, or Old Path, which leads between Ouro Preto and the port of Paraty. It can be driven in around eight days.

places you pass through along the way—begins north in Diamantina and finishes south in Ouro Preto. It's possible to complete the trail on bike and on horseback, even in a vehicle, but tackling it on foot is the best way of tracing its historic legacy.

Both Diamantina and Ouro Preto are now listed as UNESCO World Heritage Sites, thanks largely to the stately Baroque architecture that still dominates their skylines. The two towns give you a flavor of what to expect on the trail that runs between them—a history of wealth and power that still feels within touch, and a route that's dotted with historic urban landmarks. The path

Diamantina

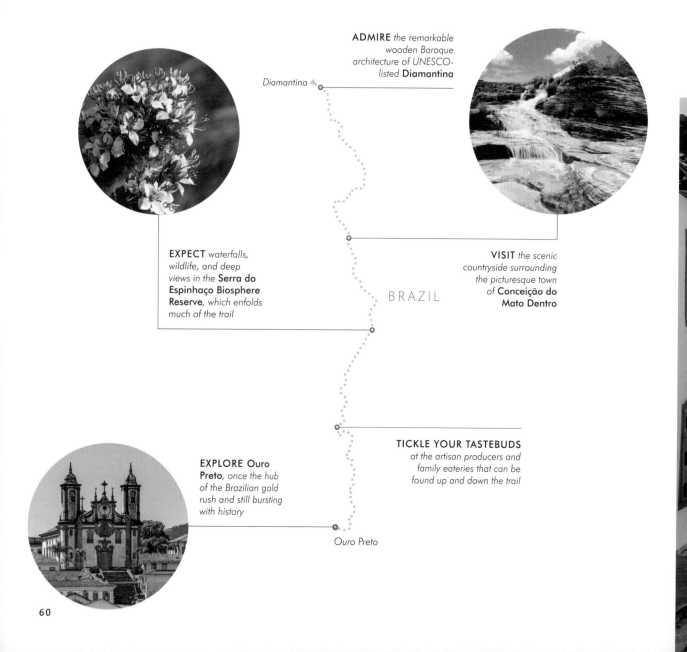

ADMIRE *the remarkable wooden Baroque architecture of UNESCO-listed* **Diamantina**

EXPECT *waterfalls, wildlife, and deep views in the* **Serra do Espinhaço Biosphere Reserve,** *which enfolds much of the trail*

VISIT *the scenic countryside surrounding the picturesque town of* **Conceição do Mato Dentro**

BRAZIL

TICKLE YOUR TASTEBUDS *at the artisan producers and family eateries that can be found up and down the trail*

EXPLORE Ouro Preto, *once the hub of the Brazilian gold rush and still bursting with history*

Ouro Preto

leads through eight other notable towns and cities in the region, all of which have their own ties to the colonial period. As well as granting accommodations, restaurants, and other welcome amenities for weary hikers, these settlements also hold genuine riches for travelers interested in the often complex legacy of Portuguese rule in the country.

The natural beauty of the route is a big part of the appeal, too, with the path passing through large swathes of the wildlife-rich Serra do Espinhaço Biosphere Reserve and meandering among the Minas Gerais countryside—think rumpled, green, wooded hills, with plenty of ascent and descent to manage as you move down the map. By combining a fascinating history and a landscape of real beauty with the vibrancy of modern Brazil, the Caminho dos Diamantes is a trek that will wow you in more ways than one.

INCONFIDÊNCIA MINEIRA

Ouro Preto is a fascinating place, not just for its integral role in the gold-rush era but as the symbolic home of the famed Inconfidência Mineira, a Brazilian independence movement set up in the 1780s after being inspired by the American Revolutionary War. The separatist group was ultimately unsuccessful, but succeeded in bringing together poets, priests, and philosophers, before the leaking of their plans led to the ringleaders being arrested.

Above *A waterfall on the Cipó River, near Diamantina* ***Left*** *Gloria's House Institute, once the residence of Diamantina's diamond supervisors*

PINCH YOURSELF *at* **Machu Picchu**, *one of the world's most iconic ancient sites*

Machu Picchu

PERU

SCAN THE SKIES *for Andean birdlife, which ranges from hummingbirds to condors*

HAUL UP *the* **Abra Mariano Pass**, *the highest point of the trek, at some 15,000 ft (4,600 m) above sea level*

CROSS *the* **Rio Blanco**, *a glacial tributary of the Amazon*

PERU

Choquequirao

MARVEL *at* **Choquequirao**, *which was reputedly used as a refuge by Inca ruler Manco II in the 1530s*

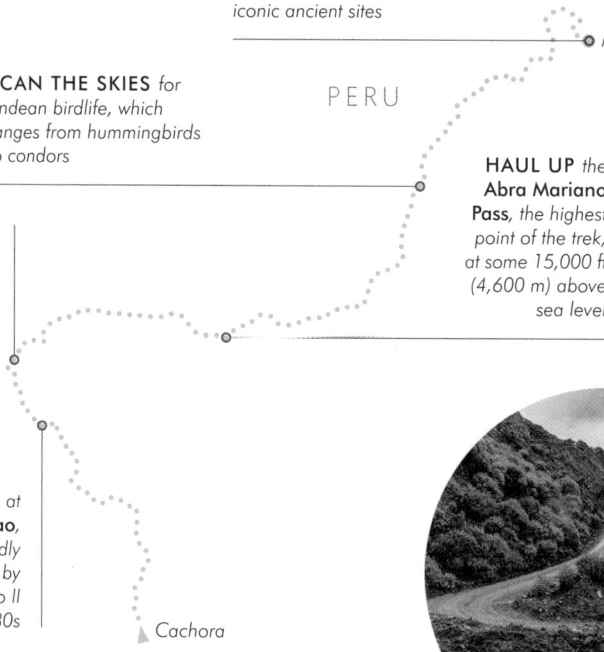

Cachora

41

Choquequirao

LOCATION Peru **START/FINISH** Cachora/Machu Picchu
DISTANCE 83 miles (133 km) **TIME** 9 days **DIFFICULTY** Challenging
INFORMATION www.perutravel.com; Mar–Oct is best for hiking

Various treks fall under the category of "alternative Inca Trails," but this nine-day epic through the Central Andes is one of the best, taking in the far-flung mountain ruins of Choquequirao.

If Machu Picchu is the star of a million-and-one photographs, the Inca citadel of Choquequirao is its remote, media-shy cousin, a cluster of crumbling temples and ancient terraces, two days' walk from the nearest settlement. This long-distance route actually takes in both sites, making it not just a wonderful mountain trek but a fascinating journey into Peru's pre-Columbian past.

One of the main joys of the hike is that, unlike the classic three-night Inca Trail, groups of other walkers are decidedly thin on the ground. The path begins in the secluded rural village of Cachora, a few hours west of Cusco, then ventures into the hulking, cactus-dotted hills. Two days in, you'll reach Choquequirao, after which this trail is named, the 15th-century remains of ceremonial shrines and coca plantations. Some of the mountainside site is yet to be excavated, but what's visible is mightily impressive. Moving on, you'll be ringed by the giant peaks of the Willkapampa Range for almost a full week, with testing ascents to negotiate as you wind over ridges and down into plunging river valleys.

Rejoining the throng as you approach journey's end comes as a shock, but the trail culminates at Machu Picchu itself, which makes for an unforgettable end to any hike.

Above *Hiking the rock trail that runs between Choquequirao and Machu Picchu*
Right *The Incan ruins at Choquequirao*

THE TRAIL LESS TRAVELED

The four-day Inca Trail that leads to Machu Picchu is one of the most legendary treks in the world. But the trail and its sites are becoming increasingly crowded. The Choquequirao Trail is the best of several other centuries-old Inca trails in the region that offer a similarly rewarding experience, but with far fewer fellow hikers.

Left The crater of Rano Kau
Below Moai statues keeping watch over Easter Island

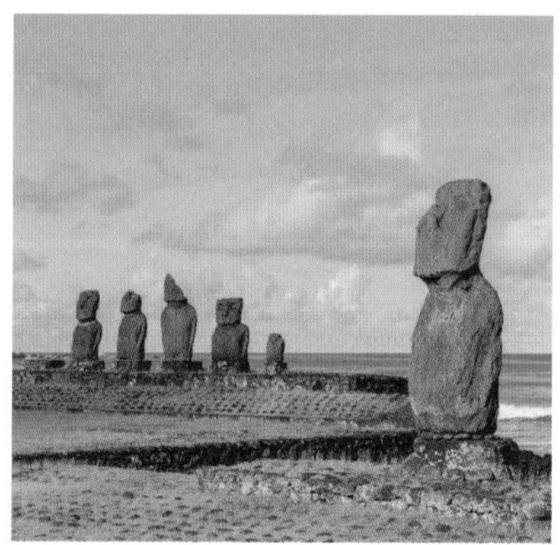

42

Birdman Trail

LOCATION Rapa Nui (Easter Island) **START/FINISH** Hanga Roa (return) **DISTANCE** 9 km (6 miles) **TIME** 1 day **DIFFICULTY** Easy **INFORMATION** www.easterislandtourism.com

Follow in the footsteps of the men who took part in an epic annual contest of courage, daring, and endurance on the remotest inhabited island on earth.

Rapa Nui—known to many as Easter Island—is renowned for its *moai*, inscrutable monolithic statues sculpted from volcanic rock. But they are only one aspect of the island's rich cultural heritage. This easy-to-follow trail retraces a route once used during the Birdman contest, an annual competition that ran for more than 150 years in the 18th and 19th centuries. The winner's patron would be named "Tangata Manu" (Birdman) at a ceremony at the village of Orongo and gain authority over the island for the next 12 months.

The route starts in the town of Hanga Roa, climbs up to the crater rim of the Rano Kau volcano, and finishes in Orongo, whose ruins sit on a clifftop above the Pacific. At this point, Birdman contestants would climb down the 984 ft (300 m) cliffs, swim through shark-infested waters, scale the nearby islet of Motu Nui, and compete to claim the first egg laid by a sooty tern that season. Fortunately, your only responsibility once you're finished is to kick back and enjoy the views.

THE LUCK BIRD

Birds play an important role in the myths and legends of Rapa Nui, understandably so in a remote place devoid of most animal life. The sooty tern is known as the manutara, the "luck bird." According to Rapa Nui tradition, the creator-god Make Make brought the birds here from Motu Motiro Hiva, Chile's modern-day Isla Salas y Gómez.

43

Climbing Aconcagua

LOCATION Argentina **START/FINISH** Puente del Inca (return) **DISTANCE** 44 miles (70 km) one-way **TIME** 3 weeks **DIFFICULTY** Challenging **INFORMATION** Permit required

The climb up Mount Aconcagua, the highest summit outside the Himalayas, is a breathtaking challenge for hardy trekkers, with few technical skills required.

The biggest mountain in the Americas, Aconcagua (22,840 ft / 6,962 m) is one of the famed "Seven Summits"—the highest peaks on every continent. While it may be high, it's fairly accessible: crampons may be required for the final push, but on the whole it's a grueling hike, with the lung-busting altitude the biggest enemy.

Thought to derive its name from the Quechua *ancho cahuac* or "white sentinel," Aconcagua was first conquered in 1897, when Swiss climber Matthias Zurbriggen found a way up via the Horcones Valley. This is the trail most trekkers ascend today, with the help of well-placed camps and an army of muleteers. The route begins at the park gate, near Puente del Inca, and climbs the mountain's northwest flank via dry valleys, snow-spikes, scree slopes, and brutal icy winds. It's vital to acclimatize well: around two-thirds of hikers don't make the summit. Those that do get the ultimate view, across peaks and glaciers to the Pacific beyond.

another way

Most hikers opt for the Normal Route but a nontechnical alternative is the Polish Traverse, which is slightly longer and begins on Aconcagua's opposite side, climbing via the Vacas Valley.

Trekkers climbing the snowy slopes of Aconcagua, en route to the mountain summit

Mount Fitz Roy, Parque Nacional Los Glaciares

(44)

Huemul Circuit

LOCATION Argentina **START/FINISH** El Chaltén (return) **DISTANCE** 41.5 miles (66.5 km) **TIME** 5 days **DIFFICULTY** Challenging **INFORMATION** www.elchalten.com

On this trek—rightfully billed as Patagonia's toughest trek—you'll battle howling winds, raging rivers, and monstrous mountains for views of the Southern Patagonian Ice Field.

Traveling as far south as Patagonia, you'll be forgiven for thinking you'll have its gnarly mountains, calving glaciers, and ice fields all to your intrepid self. Not so. Chile's Parque Nacional Torres del Paine's boom in popularity has had a snowball effect, forcing serious hikers to stray ever off-piste for a real adventure. And that's where the Huemul Circuit comes in, a savage beast of a trek that drops you into the icy depths of Argentina's nearby Parque Nacional Los Glaciares.

The deal: four days of dawn-to-dusk trekking, bare-bones wild camping, and challenging terrain, including crossing raging rivers with full gear on a "Tyrolean traverse," a steel-cable setup that requires specialist equipment. The Huemul Circuit will take every ounce of your strength, nerve, and stamina. But it will be worth every minute.

Why? Just look around you. The beauty beggars belief, be it morning sunlight dancing on turquoise Lago Viedma; or the soul-soaring moment you reach the Passo del Viento to see the Southern Patagonian Ice Field unfurl at your feet, like a frozen highway to another world. Experienced hikers only need apply.

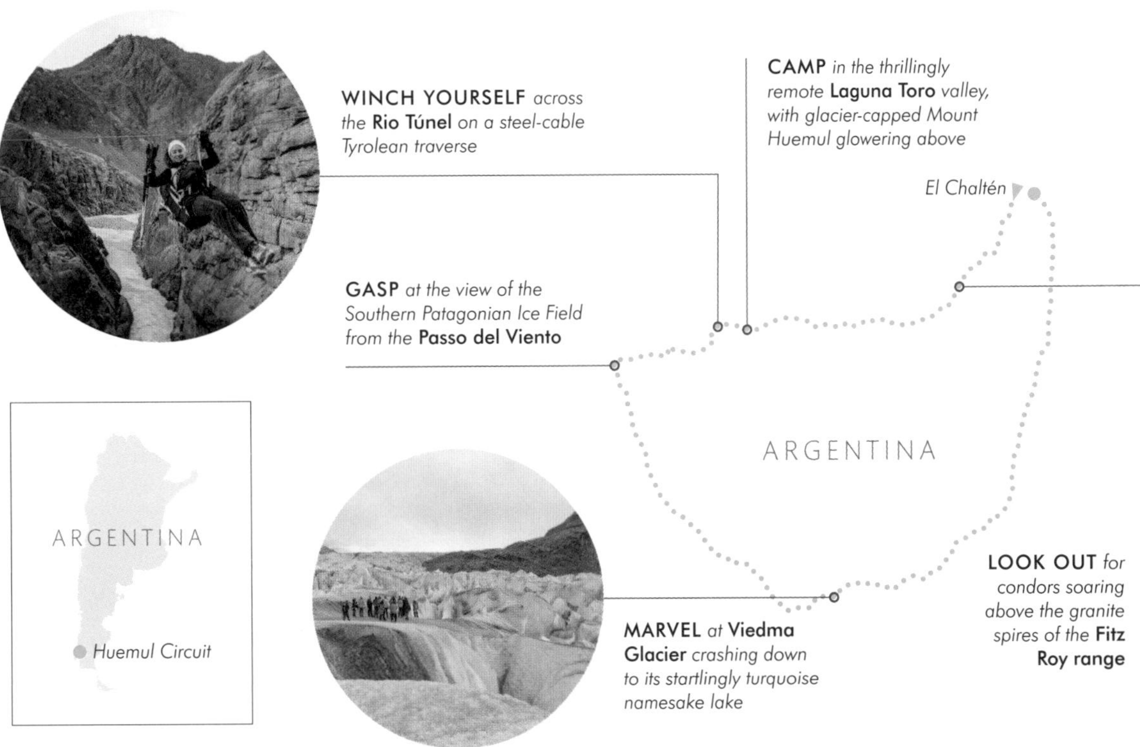

WINCH YOURSELF *across the* **Rio Túnel** *on a steel-cable Tyrolean traverse*
CAMP *in the thrillingly remote* **Laguna Toro** *valley, with glacier-capped Mount Huemul glowering above*
El Chaltén
GASP *at the view of the Southern Patagonian Ice Field from the* **Passo del Viento**
ARGENTINA
LOOK OUT *for condors soaring above the granite spires of the* **Fitz Roy range**
MARVEL *at* **Viedma Glacier** *crashing down to its startlingly turquoise namesake lake*
ARGENTINA
Huemul Circuit

45

The O Circuit

LOCATION Chile **START/FINISH** Torre Central campground (loop) **DISTANCE** 73 miles (118 km) **TIME** 9 days **DIFFICULTY** Challenging **INFORMATION** www.parquetorresdelpaine.cl; trekking without a guide is permitted only Oct–Apr

The O Circuit takes in all the highlights of Patagonia: lumbering glaciers, rugged granite peaks, and wind-blasted forests.

Tracing a wide loop around the Paine Massif range that dominates Torres del Paine National Park, the O Circuit is a breathtaking introduction to Patagonia. Each day, the scenery changes. Ochre steppes fold into groves of wind-contorted beech trees. Teal-colored lakes grow into soaring granite peaks. The forceful Paine River becomes the motionless Lago Dickson, with its amphitheater of hanging glaciers.

A steep, lung-emptying climb brings you to John Gardner's Pass, one of the region's finest vantage points. Down below, the Southern Patagonian Ice Field stretches onward, stained in ribbons of mineral black and cobalt blue. Closer still, Glacier Grey sits silently at your feet, with bergs the size of apartment buildings crumbling into the greedy, milky waters of Lago Grey.

It's from this pass that the circuit joins the truncated W section of the route. On the final day, a steep scramble up into the eastern spur of the mountains reveals the park's ultimate gift: the three *torres*, or towers, after which it's named, casting their orange-hued reflection into the gleaming waters of Lago Torres below.

Chunks of ice in the waters of Lago Grey

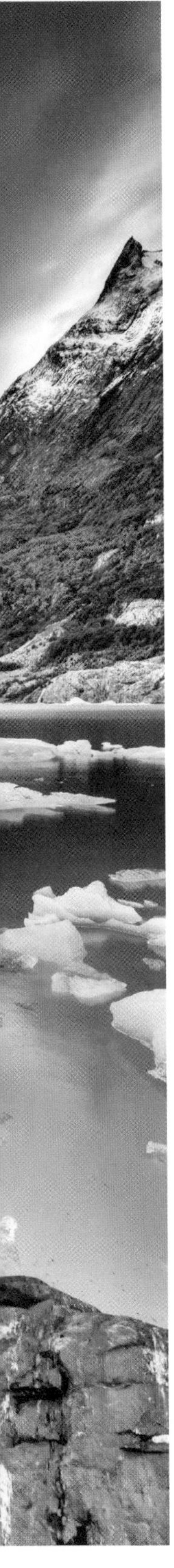

46

Shackleton Crossing

LOCATION South Georgia **START/FINISH** King Haakon Bay/ Stromness Bay **DISTANCE** 32 miles (51 km) **TIME** 3 days **DIFFICULTY** Challenging **INFORMATION** www.gov.gs

This route recreates the life-or-death crossing by Ernest Shackleton, the great 20th-century polar explorer, of a stunningly remote South Atlantic island.

South Georgia forms a sub-Antarctic sliver of ice and snow, its nearest inhabited neighbor, the Falkland Islands, 864 miles (1,390 km) away. But when Ernest Shackleton landed here in May 1916 after an epic 16-day open-boat journey across the roughest waters on earth, this inhospitable island promised salvation.

His ship *Endurance* was sunk by an Antarctic ice pack, and with the rest of the crew stranded on Elephant Island, Shackleton and five colleagues struck out to South Georgia to seek help from whalers. Shackleton, Frank Worsley and Tom Crean then trekked 32 miles (51 km) from King Haakon Bay across the uncharted interior to Stromness whaling station, where they plotted the rescue of their comrades. More than a century on, few have retraced this route. The trek is brutal, marked by blizzards and mountainous ascents. But unlike Shackleton, you'll have the benefit of thermal clothing, tents, and skis, not to mention an experienced guide following a properly mapped route through some of the most dramatic scenery in the world.

SIR ERNEST SHACKLETON

Sir Ernest Shackleton (1874–1922) first ventured to Antarctica on Robert Scott's 1901 *Discovery* expedition. He returned in 1908 on the *Nimrod* but was forced to turn back before reaching the South Pole. After the *Endurance* expedition, Shackleton returned to Antarctica for a fourth time but died en route in 1922. He is buried at Grytviken on South Georgia island.

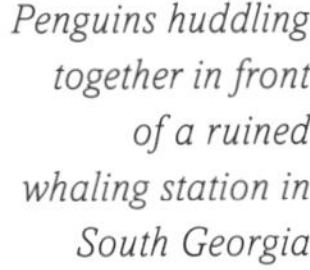

Penguins huddling together in front of a ruined whaling station in South Georgia

BY ROAD

"Nothing behind me, everything ahead of me, as is ever so on the road." Jack Kerouac's words in On the Road *capture the endless possibilities of getting behind the wheel. This is the land of the road trip. Go coast to coast in a camper or RV, hit Alaska's remote Dalton Highway, or head further south to ride Guatemala's chicken buses or cross Cuba in a Cadillac.*

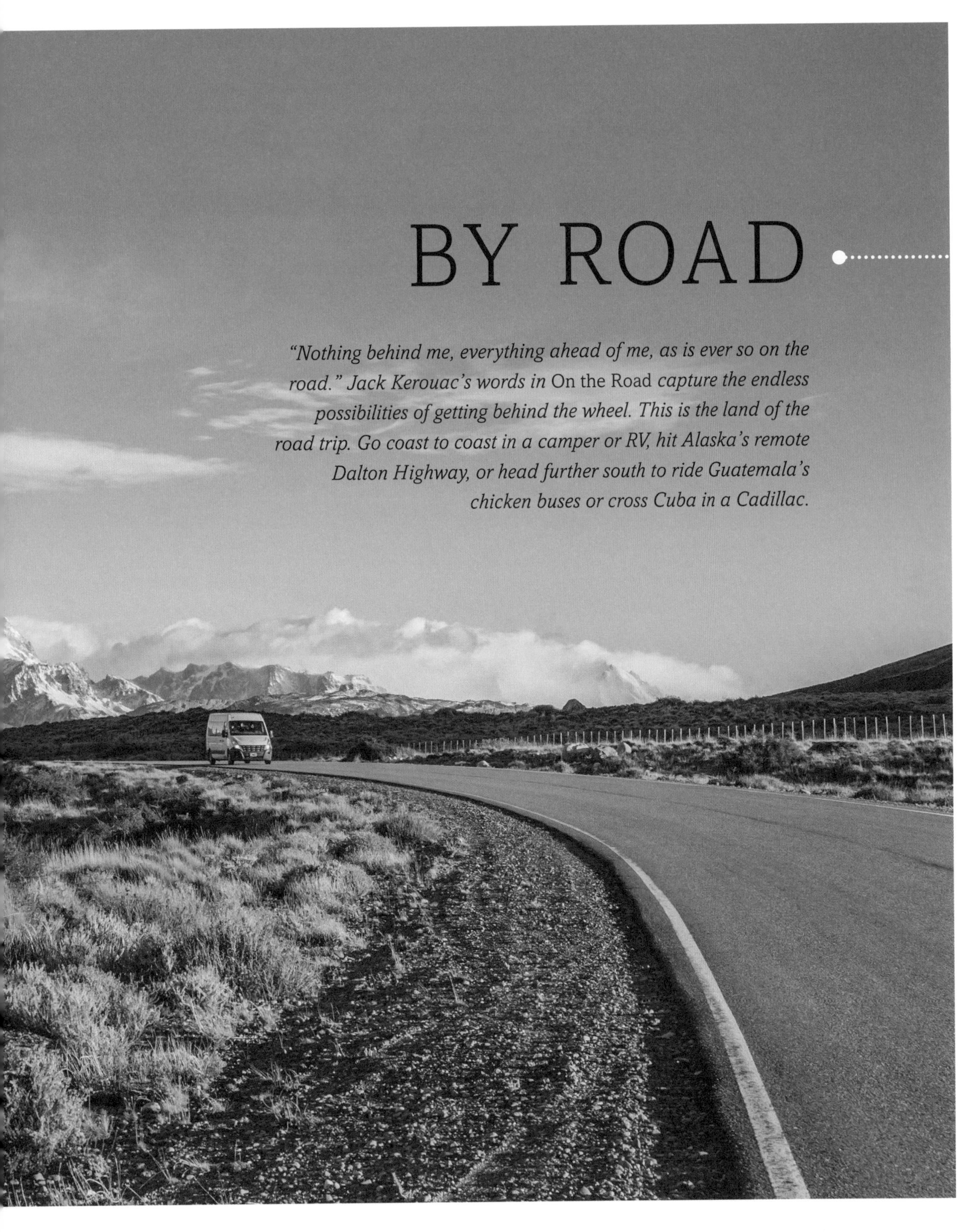

KEY TO MAP

.... Long route

• End point

***Previous page** Driving along Argentina's Ruta 40*

AT A GLANCE

BY ROAD

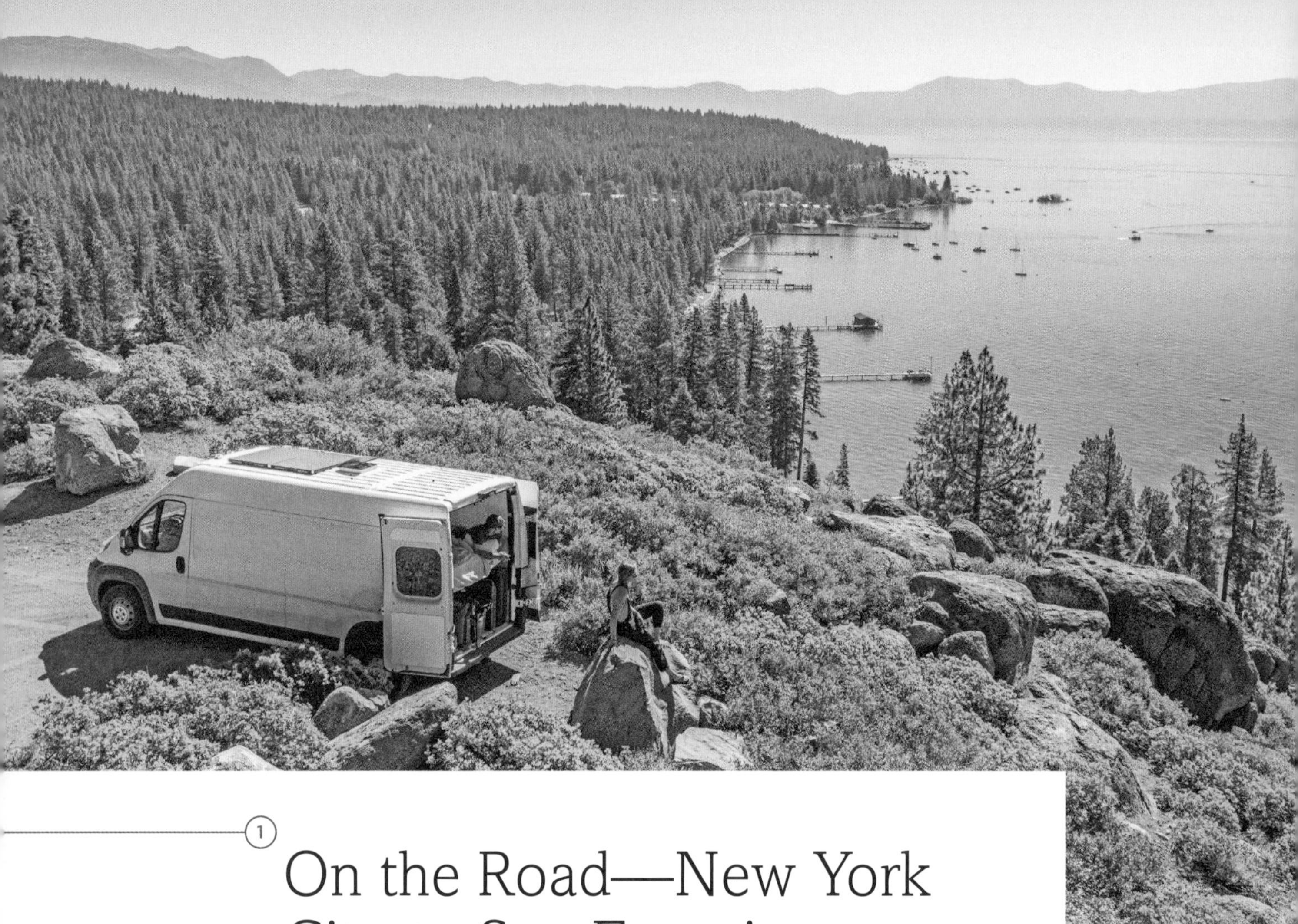

1

On the Road—New York City to San Francisco

Taking a break from the road by the shores of Lake Tahoe, California

LOCATION US **START/FINISH** New York/San Francisco **DISTANCE** 2,900 miles (4,667 km) **TIME** 2–3 weeks **ROAD CONDITIONS** Good **INFORMATION** This trip primarily follows Interstate-80 (I-80), which traces some of the routes taken by Jack Kerouac in his book *On the Road* (1957)

Follow the route of road-tripping novelist and poet Jack Kerouac, taking in the small towns, snowy peaks, and wide-open plains that symbolized the freedom of the Beat Generation.

Jack Kerouac's *On the Road* is considered the defining work of the Beat Generation, a group of writers who railed against the constrictions of postwar mainstream America. Hitting the road was the ultimate escape, and *On the Road* captured this quest for freedom, tracing the lives of Sal Paradise (based on Kerouac himself) and Dean Moriarty as they crisscrossed the country.

Like Kerouac's protagonists, you're starting in New York City and heading way out west—although one transcontinental traverse should be enough. Leave the built-up East Coast behind and follow I-80 through the deep green forests of the Allegheny Mountains and on to Chicago, a popular stop with the freeform-loving Beats for its legendary jazz clubs. Cross the mighty Mississippi at Davenport,

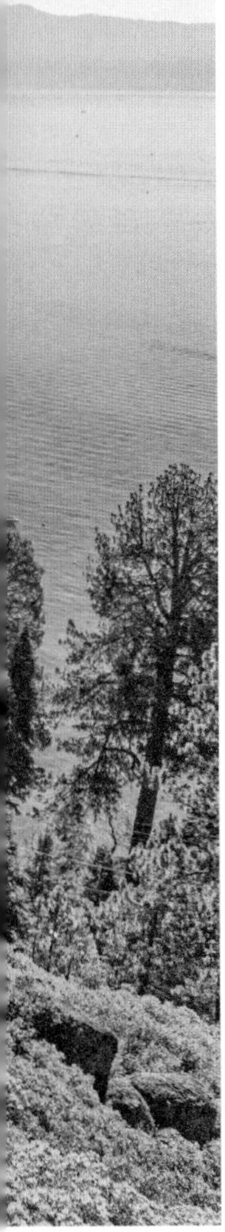

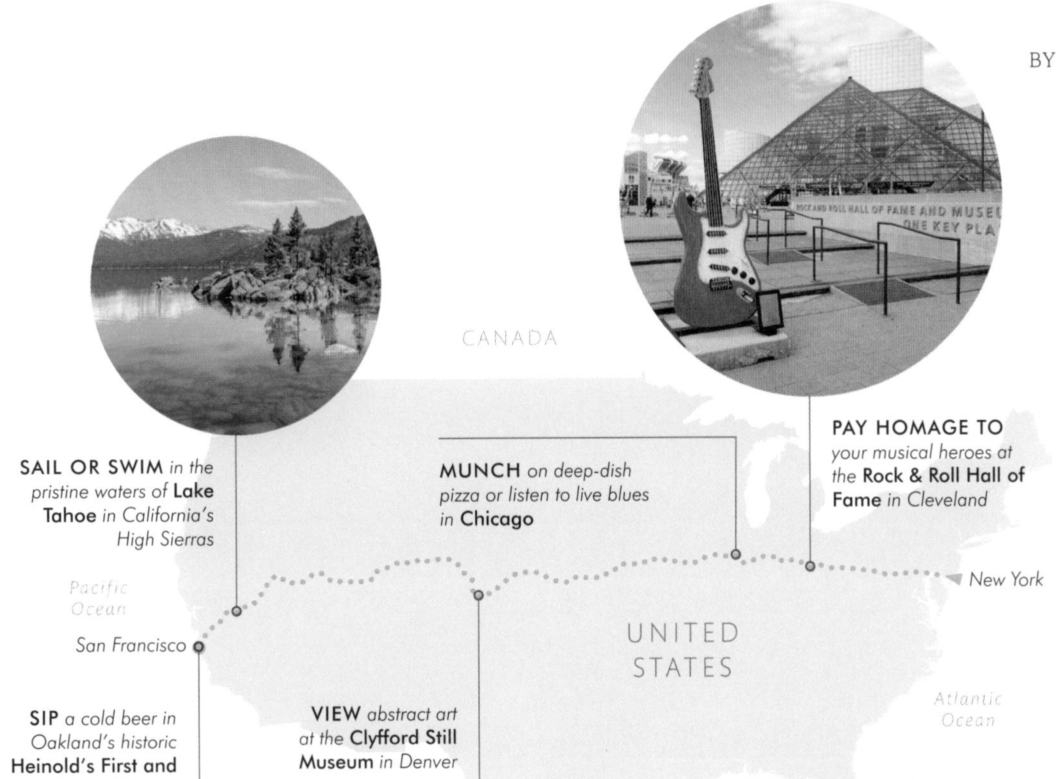

CANADA

SAIL OR SWIM *in the pristine waters of* **Lake Tahoe** *in California's High Sierras*

MUNCH *on deep-dish pizza or listen to live blues in* **Chicago**

PAY HOMAGE TO *your musical heroes at the* **Rock & Roll Hall of Fame** *in Cleveland*

Pacific Ocean

San Francisco

New York

UNITED STATES

Atlantic Ocean

SIP *a cold beer in Oakland's historic* **Heinold's First and Last Chance Saloon**

VIEW *abstract art at the* **Clyfford Still Museum** *in Denver*

Gulf of Mexico

MEXICO

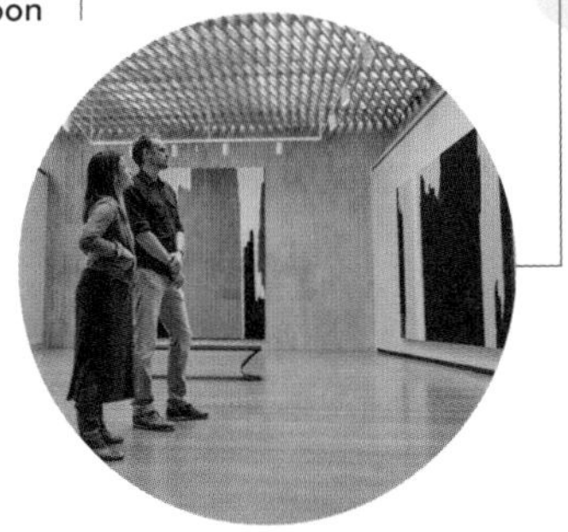

another way

To follow the route as closely as possible by train, take the Pennsylvanian from New York to Pittsburgh, then the Capitol Limited for Chicago. The California Zephyr (p174) goes from Chicago to Emeryville for San Francisco.

Iowa, just as Kerouac's characters did, and then follow their journey through Nebraska, where the Midwest transitions to the Wild West, the "verdant farmfields of the Platte" giving way to "long flat wastelands of sand and sagebrush." Detour down to Denver, Colorado, home of Kerouac's infamous travel companion Neal Cassady (Dean Moriarty in *On the Road*), before crossing Utah's deserts and salt lakes, where you'll still witness the lights of Salt Lake City "glimmering almost a hundred miles across the mirage of the flats." For Sal and Dean, the end of the road was San Francisco—as it is for you, too, I-80 gliding across the beautiful blue bay and into the city.

Oakland Bat Bridge, San Francisco

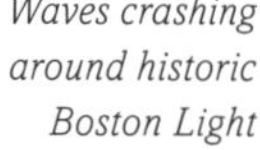

Waves crashing around historic Boston Light

2

New England Lighthouse Trail

LOCATION US **START/FINISH** Newburyport Rear Range Light/Stonington Lighthouse Museum **DISTANCE** 352 miles (566 km) **TIME** 9 days **ROAD CONDITIONS** Well-maintained paved roads **INFORMATION** www.newenglandlighthouses.net; many lighthouses open only May–Oct

Follow New England's lighthouse trail for a road trip that shines a beam on dramatic coastal landscapes, a rich maritime culture and almost 200 storied towers.

Danger or salvation? Hope or banishment? We project all sorts of meaning onto those mysterious soaring lighthouses. But in New England, especially, the brilliant beams also symbolize new beginnings, having helped establish the early trade routes that built the nation.

New England is home to nearly 200 lighthouses, dotted along the coastal edges and seaside towns of Maine, New Hampshire, Vermont, Massachusetts, Connecticut, and Rhode Island. A good jumping-off point for this maritime driving tour is Newburyport Rear Range Light, the only place in the world where you can dine at the top of a lofty light. Having navigated the spiral staircase, diners squeeze elbow-to-elbow at the table in the lantern room, which seats just four. The guestbook reads like a love letter to the stoical brick tower, evidence of the various marriage proposals and anniversaries that this lighthouse has witnessed since it was built in 1873.

New England is home to nearly 200 lighthouses, dotted along coastal edges

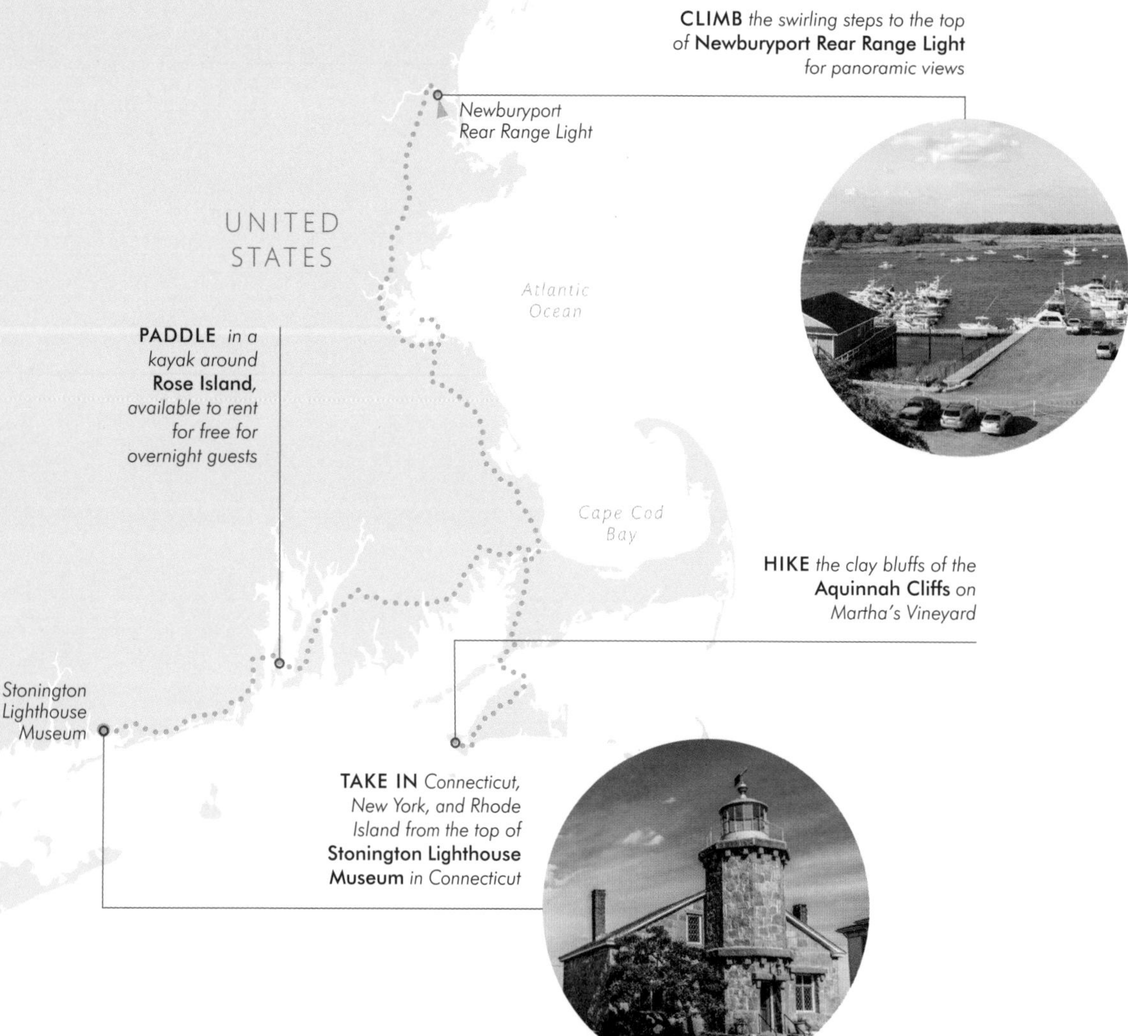
CLIMB *the swirling steps to the top of* **Newburyport Rear Range Light** *for panoramic views*
Newburyport Rear Range Light
UNITED STATES
Atlantic Ocean
PADDLE *in a kayak around* **Rose Island,** *available to rent for free for overnight guests*
Cape Cod Bay
HIKE *the clay bluffs of the* **Aquinnah Cliffs** *on Martha's Vineyard*
Stonington Lighthouse Museum
TAKE IN *Connecticut, New York, and Rhode Island from the top of* **Stonington Lighthouse Museum** *in Connecticut*

SOME LIGHT READING

For essential reading while on the road, pick up a copy of Virginia Woolf's 1927 novel *To the Lighthouse*, which uses the lighthouse's symbolism to explore human themes such as desire and control. Alternatively, pack a copy of children's book *Moominpappa at Sea*, for a charming tale of finding one's true nature with the help of a steadfast light, written by the Finnish author Tove Jansson.

A short drive south brings you to Boston Light, the first established lighthouse in the US. Built off the stormy Massachusetts coast in 1716, Boston Light is tended to in the high season by Sally Snowman, the only female lighthouse keeper in the country. Catching a boat out of Boston, and with gulls squawking overhead, you'll glide past the pioneering lighthouse, set on the small but mighty Little Brewster Island.

Heading further south, along roads lined with wooden fish shacks and sprawling salt marshes, brings you to Cape Cod, where a ferry chugs cars and pedestrians over to Martha's Vineyard. It's a favorite with playwrights, presidents, and pop stars alike, who come for the storybook fishing villages, white sandy beaches, and five stunning lighthouses that ring the treasured island. Gay Head Light

__Above__ Waves washing the shoreline by the Aquinnah Cliffs on Martha's Vineyard __Right__ A seagull flying by Rose Island Lighthouse

is worth driving to the westernmost point for; it's located in the region of Aquinnah, and the nearby shops and cafés are operated by the Wampanoag people. Stop off at the charming Martha's Vineyard Museum to admire its game-changing Fresnel lighthouse lens, plus cabinets crammed with seafaring curiosities, including whale's teeth painstakingly engraved with intricate pictures by idle sailors.

As you drive farther along the coast to Newport, Connecticut, the shoreline jostles with working fishing boats and high-rolling yachts. Here, visitors can play at being lighthouse keeper with an overnight stay on Rose Island. Following a stint as a military torpedo station, local preservationists spruced up the white clapperboard lighthouse keeper's lodge, filling the apartment with antique furnishings and erecting a flag mast that chimes in the wind. Blissfully, there's very little to do for overnight guests beyond embracing the deep sense of calm brought on by watching boats sail gracefully past the lighthouse windows. It's a view that can be matched only at your last stop, Stonington Lighthouse Museum, where a climb to the top reveals a sea-swept panorama that takes in Connecticut, New York, and Rhode Island.

another way

From Boston, keep heading north to the coast of Maine, home to 65 magnificent lighthouses. Try to time your visit for early September, when Maine Open Lighthouse Day sees 20 usually off-bounds lights open to visitors for one day only.

3

North Maine Woods

LOCATION US **START/FINISH** Greenville/Moosehead Lake **DISTANCE** 44 miles (70 km) **TIME** 2–3 days **ROAD CONDITIONS** Unpaved roads; 4WD essential **INFORMATION** www.destinationmooseheadlake.com

A bucket-list moose safari on backcountry roads is the ultimate way to experience this rarely visited wonderland in the far northeastern corner of Maine.

With trees so tall they shield the sun and moose that weigh up to 1,400 lb (635 kg), the North Maine Woods exists as a wilderness of epic proportions and a place where nature has long had the upper hand. American naturalist Henry David Thoreau recounted his traverse of the heavily forested area more than 150 years ago in his travelogue *The Maine Woods*, and it still remains just as wild. In summer, the Acadian forest fills with hibernation-starved black bears and the largest number of moose in the contiguous United States. What you won't find here are many people. Set your GPS for Moosehead Lake, the largest in Maine, for a band of seemingly impenetrable woodlands and a region with a matrix of ungraded forest roads to explore. Stop to paddle on golden ponds, surrounded by hemlock and jack pine, and discover the area's oversize wildlife—the forests enveloping the lake's hub town of Greenville are inhabited by some 25,000 moose.

Moose in the North Maine Woods

A lonely cannon on the battlefield at Gettysburg

4

Civil War Battlefields Trail

LOCATION US **START/FINISH** Gettysburg/Appomattox **DISTANCE** 323 miles (520 km) **TIME** 1 week **ROAD CONDITIONS** Good **INFORMATION** www.battlefields.org

Take in some of the most poignant memorials to the American Civil War, scattered amid country lanes and farming towns in Maryland, Pennsylvania, and Virginia.

Driving south through the pastures and cornfields of Pennsylvania, it's hard to imagine the desperate fighting that took place at Gettysburg in 1863, the deadliest battle in US history. It's a quiet tourist town today, ringed by hundreds of statues, marble columns, and grand monuments, part of the Gettysburg National Military Park. Begin your tour here, spending time at the park museum, then drive on to the moving State of Pennsylvania Monument, where Union forces beat back "Pickett's Charge" on the third and final day of fighting. The route continues to beautifully restored Harpers Ferry, where you can learn about John Brown's failed rebellion to end slavery, before crossing into Virginia to trace the paths of the Confederate and Union armies from the battlefields of Bull Run to Richmond, the Confederate capital. The final stretch runs deep into rural Virginia, ending where the war did: at the simple Appomattox Court House where General Grant accepted the surrender of the main Confederate army in 1865.

JOHN BROWN'S BODY

Harpers Ferry is indelibly linked to John Brown, a fiery abolitionist who battled proslavery forces in "Bleeding Kansas" in the 1850s. His failed attempt to start a rebellion among the South's enslaved population, by seizing the armory at Harpers Ferry in 1859, helped spark the Civil War. He was viewed as a martyr in the North, and "John Brown's Body" was a popular song that emerged soon after his execution.

5

The Crooked Road

LOCATION US **START/FINISH** Bristol/Galax **DISTANCE** 330 miles (531 km) **TIME** 1 week **ROAD CONDITIONS** Well-maintained roads **INFORMATION** www.thecrookedroadva.com

Crowd participation is encouraged along this route, a musical-heritage trail taking in front-porch pickers, old-time museums, and boot-stomping barn dances.

Country music's Big Bang moment occurred in 1927, when a talent scout from Victor Records traveled along winding rural roads to set up a makeshift studio in Bristol, a sleepy two-state town straddling the border between Tennessee and Virginia. The Bristol Sessions featured the first recordings of country music's pioneers, including Jimmie Rodgers and the Carter Family, unleashing a quintessentially American sound from the hills and hollows of Appalachia.

Nowadays, Bristol is the headline act on the Crooked Road, a heritage music trail that weaves through southwest Virginia, amplifying the sounds of country, Americana, roots, and bluegrass

LISTEN IN *at the* **Grundy Music Jam,** *which attracts the finest pickers from the local coal country community*

VISIT County Sales *in Floyd, home to the world's largest selection of traditional country music—and a Friday Night Jamboree*

HOTFOOT IT *to the* **Country Cabin II** *in Norton for a clogging dance class*

UNITED STATES

Galax

Bristol

HEAR *world-class musicians playing at August's* **Old Fiddlers Convention** *in Galax*

UNITED STATES

The Crooked Road

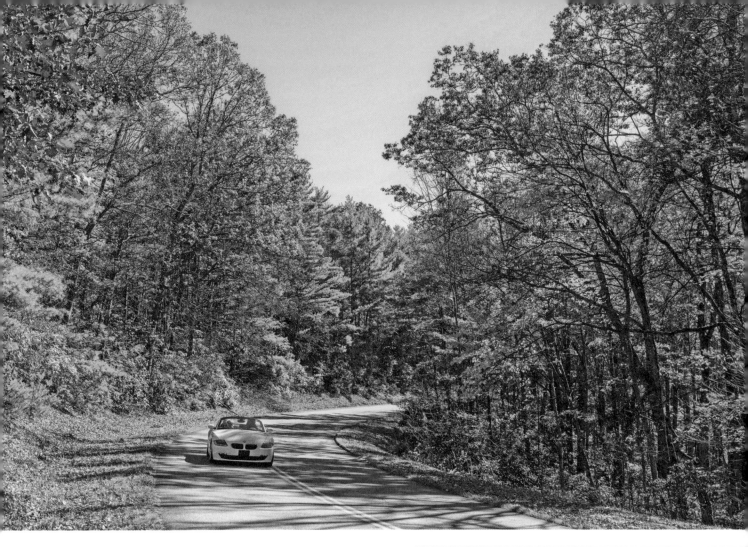

music along the way. A suitable start to your trip is at the Birthplace of Country Music Museum in Bristol, the best place—arguably in the whole of the US—to tune in to the early recording sessions and brush up on the subsequent commercialization of country music.

It's then up to the Carter Family Fold in Hiltons, where, on a Saturday night, you can witness a hoedown in full swing. Here, the rustic 800-seat barn vibrates to the sound of furious fiddles and fast-picking banjos, as the wooden jamboree dance floor becomes a joyful swirl of flat-foot and square dancers.

Follow the road to Blacksburg, where on Wednesday evenings throughout the summer the downtown market square transforms into an open-air rehearsal space of old-time folk tunes. There's no need for stage fright: music enthusiasts of all levels are encouraged to pull up a chair and join the ditty. Or you can finish your trip with a live bluegrass show at the Rex Theater in Galax, held on Friday evenings. Either way, you'll be leaving Virginia on a high note.

Top *Driving along the Crooked Road*
Above *Listening to a performance at the Blue Ridge Music Center in Galax*

Chesapeake Bay, the focus of the Virginia Oyster Trail

6 Virginia Oyster Trail

LOCATION US **START/FINISH** Virginia Beach/ Alexandria **DISTANCE** 204 miles (328 km) **TIME** 5–7 days **ROAD CONDITIONS** Good **INFORMATION** www.virginiaoystertrail.com

A road trip along the Virginia coastline is a seamless essay on the region's history, imbued as it is with the rise, fall, and rise again of the proud fishing traditions of the Chesapeake Bay oystermen. At the center of the state's centuries-old oyster industry is the Virginia Oyster Trail, a loosely themed experiential route focusing on shellfish restaurants, coastal farms, and oyster companies. It's possible to plan your own weeklong driving adventure, connecting the dots from Virginia Beach in the south all the way north to Alexandria. The common denominator, of course, is the quality of the oysters—which is all the invitation you need to drive, eat, slurp, and repeat.

THE WORLD'S THEIR OYSTER

Oysters were once overlooked in the US, in favor of Atlantic lobster and Gulf Coast shrimp. But times change and they are now in such demand that the oystermen of Chesapeake Bay pull in up to 25,000 oysters a day per boat.

7 Kentucky Bourbon Trail

LOCATION US **START/FINISH** Louisville/ Lexington **DISTANCE** 150 miles (241 km) **TIME** 4 days **ROAD CONDITIONS** Good **INFORMATION** www.kybourbontrail.com

Dense forests of oak and hickory, the rich aromas of smoky wood and corn mash, and tempting no-frills barbecue shacks—welcome to Kentucky bourbon country. This taster of the state's finest distilleries (assuming there's a designated driver on hand) begins in Louisville, home of the iconic Jim Beam, before continuing on to historic Bardstown, the "Bourbon Capital of the World." Here lie the red-brick Barton 1792 Distillery, homely Heaven Hill, and elegantly contemporary Lux Row. Further south, Maker's Mark Distillery provides a rustic contrast to the Spanish Mission-style Four Roses distillery, which sits in nearby Lawrenceburg. The final stretch of the tour passes through prime horse country, with a stop at Woodford Reserve Distillery before arriving at Lexington, America's horse-racing capital. Your journey ends here, with a final taste of bourbon at "brew-distillery" Town Branch.

8

Dolly Parton's Tennessee

LOCATION US **START/FINISH** Knoxville/ Nashville **DISTANCE** 180 miles (290 km) **TIME** 3 hours **ROAD CONDITIONS** Well maintained and paved **INFORMATION** www.dollywood.com; www.tnvacation.com

Combine a great American singer with the equally great Greyhound bus service, and you have a (short) journey to remember. Country legend Dolly Parton was born in Knoxville, in the foothills of the Great Smoky Mountains, which is where you'll board a bus to Nashville—after visiting the nearby Dollywood theme park, and snapping an obligatory photo with Knoxville's supersize Dolly mural, of course—just as Dolly did, at age 18. Armed with a plastic bag of clothes and a cup of ambition, she rode toward the bright lights of Tennessee's state capital, just as you will. It's a journey of only a few sweet hours, offering just enough time to gaze at the passing white clapboard churches and reflect on the anticipation the singer must have felt before stepping into the honky-tonk-lined unknown. As music history tells, it all worked out just fine for Dolly, who celebrated 50 years at the Grand Ole Opry, the home of country and western, in 2019.

9

Civil Rights Trail

LOCATION US **START/FINISH** Selma/ Montgomery **DISTANCE** 54 miles (87 km) **TIME** 2 days **ROAD CONDITIONS** Good **INFORMATION** www.civilrightstrail.com

The US Civil Rights Trail stretches across 14 states and includes poignant landmarks such as the Central High School National Historic Site in Little Rock, Arkansas, where a group of Black American students helped pave the way for desegregation. One of the most historic events to take in on a drive lies to the east, in Alabama, where the brutal treatment of peaceful protesters in 1965 helped lead to the Voting Rights Act later that year. The Selma to Montgomery National Historic Trail takes in the Brown Chapel AME Church, where the marches began, as well as the Edmund Pettus Bridge, where the marchers met a wall of state troopers armed with batons and tear gas. End your tour at the Dexter Avenue King Memorial Baptist Church in Montgomery, where Dr. Martin Luther King Jr. once served as pastor.

another way

You can link together other Civil Rights sites in Alabama on a drive that starts in Anniston, a stop on the original anti-segregation Freedom Ride from Atlanta, and ends in Tuscaloosa, the scene of former state governor George C. Wallace's failed "stand" for segregation in 1963.

Dolly Parton performing at the Grand Ole Opry

10

Blues Highway

LOCATION US **START/FINISH** Memphis/Vicksburg **DISTANCE** 224 miles (360 km) **TIME** 3 days **ROAD CONDITIONS** Good **INFORMATION** www.visitmississippi.org; www.tnvacation.com

Few road trips sound better than the legendary Blues Highway, which wiggles from Tennessee to Mississippi and rings with blues, soul, gospel, and R&B music.

In the vast plains that sweep out alongside the Mississippi River, the stomping, soul-stirring Delta blues was born, rooted in the field hollers and chants of enslaved African Americans. A who's who of music greats later traversed beat-ridden Highway 61, from Bessie Smith to Muddy Waters, and music still carries drivers from Memphis to Vicksburg, a section of road now known as the Blues Highway. Major stops include the Stax Museum of American Soul Music in Memphis and Tunica's Gateway to the Blues Visitors Center & Museum, but this is as much about the region's ramshackle juke joints that shake with the sound of the harmonica and slide guitar, and its pint-size churches thrumming with gospel music. The ghost of the King of Rock and Roll is never far away—you'll find Elvis in Memphis, where his iconic voice was first laid down on acetate at Sun Studios, and where his home, Graceland, still serves as a pilgrimage site for fans. Catch the sounds of today at Clarksdale's Ground Zero Blues Club, a place that is just as legendary.

DEVIL AND THE DELTA BLUES

Born in Hazlehurst, Mississippi, Robert Johnson was a star of the Delta blues, but his musical gift apparently came at a high price. After an early performance was poorly received, he vanished, only to reappear several years later having mastered his art. Legend has it he sold his soul to the devil at the crossroads of Highway 61 and 49 in Clarksdale; in return, the devil bestowed on him great musical talent.

The famous Sun Studios in Memphis

Middle Falls, Gooseberry Falls State Park

11

North Shore Scenic Drive

LOCATION US **START/FINISH** Duluth/Grand Portage **DISTANCE** 154 miles (248 km) **TIME** 3 days **ROAD CONDITIONS** Good **INFORMATION** www.northshorevisitor.com

Scooting along the edge of Lake Superior, this waterside driving route knits together fishing towns, cascade-filled state parks, and stellar beaches.

The glory of mammoth Lake Superior is on full display on this route from Duluth to Grand Portage in Minnesota. While drivers now come for the views, the region's inhabitants have long milked its natural bounty. Its North Shore was first settled some 10,000 years ago, by Indigenous peoples who fished for trout and salmon. Then came the fur trappers, loggers, and miners, who turned the area into a hive of industry.

The drive is studded with sights recounting this layered human history, from the North Shore Commercial Fishing Museum in quaint Tofte to the Grand Portage National Monument, which preserves an old fur-trading depot and explores Anishinaabe heritage. In between, the route sews together a patchwork of pinch-yourself views, from Split Rock Lighthouse, perched on a craggy, tree-tufted bluff, to the tumbling curtains of water that make up the Gooseberry Falls State Park. Topping them all? Lake Superior itself, of course.

another way

The mammoth Superior Hiking Trail hugs the North Shore, spooling out for 310 miles (499 km). You'll skirt plunging river gorges, beat along forest tracks, gaze up at rushing waterfalls, and stop at viewpoints offering rippling lake vistas.

An arrow-straight stretch of Route 66 in Southern California

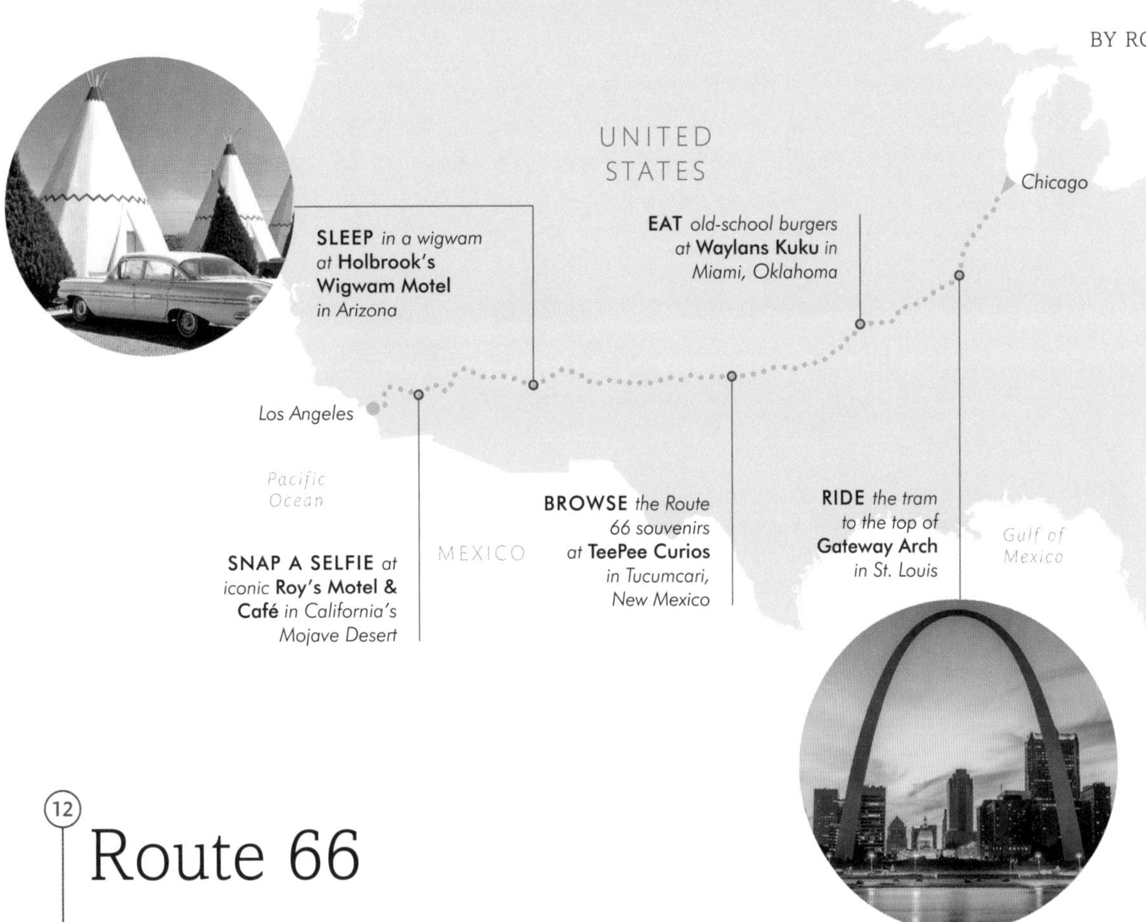
UNITED STATES
Chicago
SLEEP in a wigwam at Holbrook's Wigwam Motel in Arizona
EAT old-school burgers at Waylans Kuku in Miami, Oklahoma
Los Angeles
Pacific Ocean
MEXICO
BROWSE the Route 66 souvenirs at TeePee Curios in Tucumcari, New Mexico
RIDE the tram to the top of Gateway Arch in St. Louis
Gulf of Mexico
SNAP A SELFIE at iconic Roy's Motel & Café in California's Mojave Desert

12

Route 66

LOCATION US **START/FINISH** Chicago/Los Angeles
DISTANCE 2,448 miles (3,940 km) **TIME** 1–2 weeks
ROAD CONDITIONS Good **INFORMATION** www.national66.org

Few journeys are as iconic as crossing America on Route 66, the original transcontinental highway, taking in everything from small towns on the prairies to the Mojave Desert.

Steeped in legend, the "Mother Road" is an enduring symbol of the classic American West. Although Route 66 was decommissioned in 1985, its path can still be traced via a blend of county roads, interstate highways, and scenic byways.

The route begins in Illinois, slicing southwest through rich farmland. It then crosses the swirling waters of the Mississippi at St. Louis, before skirting the densely wooded Ozarks in Missouri. Heading into Oklahoma, Route 66 offers a dose of 1950s nostalgia, lined with diners, quirky Americana, and whimsical museums—eat apple pie at Clanton's Café, stop for selfies at the Blue Whale of Catoosa, and admire the Arcadia Round Barn. Vast fields of corn and wheat dominate the Texas Panhandle, while New Mexico brings wilder, more mountainous terrain. This arid land has been inhabited by Indigenous peoples for thousands of years—view ancient rock drawings at the Petroglyph National Monument or learn about Indigenous history at the Sky City Cultural Center in the Acoma Pueblo. In Arizona, you'll hurdle the mountains at Sitgreaves Pass—dark ridges fill the horizon, the winding road the only sign of civilization.

Entering the final leg of the journey, the road runs across the burning sands of California's Mojave Desert, peppered with retro-architectural icons of old Route 66 that give way, finally, to the Los Angeles basin and the stirring sight of the glimmering Pacific beyond.

Fort Atkinson State Historical Park, Nebraska

13

Lewis and Clark Scenic Byway

LOCATION US **START/FINISH** South Sioux City/Fort Calhoun **DISTANCE** 131 miles (211 km) **TIME** 5 hours **ROAD CONDITIONS** Well-maintained roads **INFORMATION** www.visitnebraska.com/lewis-clark-scenic-byway

Drivers can reach some of the finest sights in Nebraska on this history-rich road trip, which traces a portion of the 19th-century Lewis and Clark Expedition.

In 1804, Captain Meriwether Lewis and Lieutenant William Clark struck out from Illinois under the orders of President Thomas Jefferson. Their mission: to survey the swathe of land acquired by the 1803 Louisiana Purchase and to explore the wild Pacific Northwest, which was then largely uncharted by white settlers.

The journey would be a grueling one, lasting more than two years and spanning some 8,000 miles (12,875 km). Their mammoth odyssey crossed into the northeastern corner of what is modern-day Nebraska—a leg of their arduous trip that can now be driven in comfort along the bucolic Lewis and Clark Scenic Byway.

The route trails the wriggling Missouri River, crop-filled valleys opening out on the side of the road, as it weaves between centuries-old forts and history-steeped towns. Highlights include Fort Atkinson State Historical Park, the first US Army post west of the Missouri River, and the bird-filled Boyer Chute National Wildlife Refuge. Following in the footsteps of pioneers has never felt quite so easy.

> It weaves between centuries-old forts and history-steeped towns

14

Chasing Storms in Tornado Alley

LOCATION US **START/FINISH** Oklahoma City (return) **DISTANCE** 310 miles (500 km) per day **TIME** 6–11 days **ROAD CONDITIONS** Good **INFORMATION** www.stormchasing.com

The wide open spaces of the Great Plains are the theater for some of earth's most dramatic storms—and the heavy-duty cars that chase them.

The Great Plains is defined by open space. The land is low, an endless expanse of prairie and wheat fields, and the sky is high, unblemished by topography taller than a cornstalk. In summer, the air between the two comes alive, morphing into supercells: giant, fearsome thunderstorms that press down on the land like anvils. Sometimes, the right conditions combine and these storms form tornadoes, viciously rotating columns of air that chew up the earth.

Witnessing a supercell or tornado is an awe-inspiring experience, and the Great Plains has a devoted coterie of storm chasers who hunt them down and get you close, but not too close—tornadoes can reach wind speeds of up to 310 mph (500 km/h). Most tours spend about a week tracking them across a region known as Tornado Alley and have meteorologists who provide weather briefings and forecasting lessons.

Tornadoes are dangerous and destructive. But chasing them is irresistible—an adrenaline rush like no other.

another way

Many tours also operate out of Denver, Colorado; Wichita, Kansas; Tulsa, Oklahoma; and Rapid City, South Dakota. It should go without saying, but under no circumstances should you attempt this type of adventure independently.

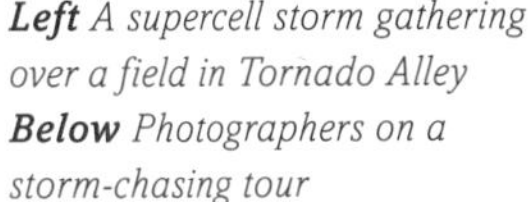

Left *A supercell storm gathering over a field in Tornado Alley*
Below *Photographers on a storm-chasing tour*

15

Fredericksberg Wine Road

LOCATION US **START/FINISH** Fredericksburg/ Austin **DISTANCE** 78 miles (126 km) **TIME** 3 days **ROAD CONDITIONS** Good **INFORMATION** www.wineroad290.com

Flecked with bluebonnets and awash with wine, Highway 290 wiggles through Texas's bucolic Hill Country. This is not the Lone Star State as you might imagine. You'll enter a world of lush vine-striped banks and quaint little towns that could be plucked straight out of Europe—this is one of Texas's premier wine-growing regions, its granite-based soils producing fat, juicy grapes.

The wine road is anchored by Fredericksburg, a charming town founded by immigrants from Germany in the mid-1800s. As you push east, wineries pop up along the route: tasting rooms are tucked into old farmhouses, and glasses of Mourvedre are sipped on stone patios. Before breaking south for Austin, you'll come to Johnson City, jumping-off point for Pedernales Falls State Park; pack a picnic and raise a toast to your grape escape.

Bluebonnets, Texas Hill Country

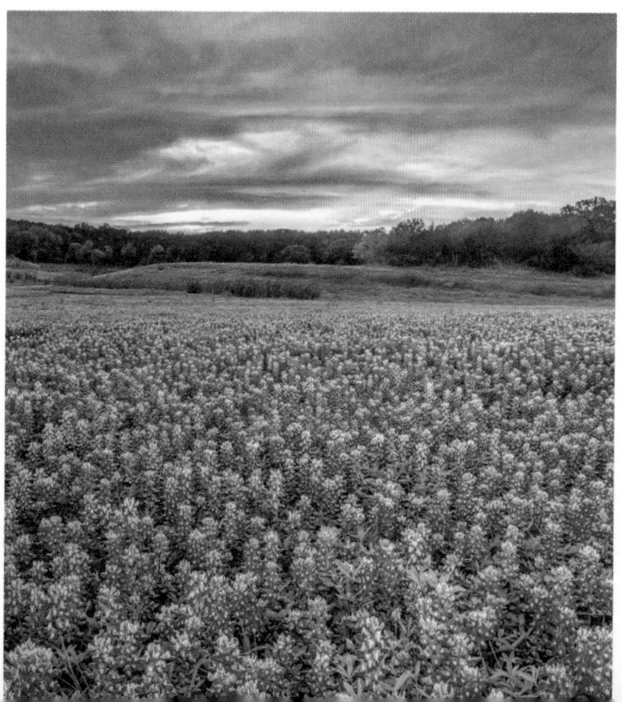

Santa Fe, New Mexico

16

High Road to Taos

LOCATION US **START/FINISH** Santa Fe/Taos **DISTANCE** 76 miles (122 km) **TIME** 1 day **ROAD CONDITIONS** Paved roads, in good condition **INFORMATION** www.newmexico.org

History is writ large in this rugged route that winds from Santa Fe to Taos. It is laced with vestiges of Colonial Spain, from stuck-in-time villages to centuries-old mission churches: the 1816-built Santuario de Chimayó remains an important pilgrimage site, and devotees come to rub the chapel's healing holy dirt on their bodies. The 18th-century San Jose de Gracia de las Trampas is another wonderfully preserved relic from the era. Beyond the bones of time, Mother Nature is the High Road's star: the route beats a path through the craggy Sangre de Cristo Mountains, fringed by rugged juniper-scattered plains. Artists are drawn by the wildly scenic landscapes, too, and towns such as Chimayo, Cordova, and Truchas are stuffed with shops and galleries showcasing traditional crafts practiced here for centuries, from weaving and woodcarving to pottery.

17

Going-to-the-Sun Road

LOCATION US **START/FINISH** West Glacier/ St. Mary **DISTANCE** 50 miles (80 km) **TIME** 3–4 hours **ROAD CONDITIONS** Paved road **INFORMATION** Sections closed winter and spring

Twisting through Glacier National Park, the dramatic Going-to-the-Sun Road climbs over the Continental Divide—expect gasp-worthy views of glacier-carved landscapes that get bigger and better the higher you go. From West Glacier, the route spins along the flat shore of Lake McDonald before lazily ascending a valley corridor squeezed by soaring peaks. The route tops out at Logan Pass, a wildflower meadow with mountain goats and bighorn sheep, before exiting East Side Tunnel to a view that explodes in size from a scooped green valley to scads of peaks. As you descend to the end-point of turquoise St. Mary Lake, be ready for the road to offer up a final treat: grizzly bears, regular visitors to the plains at Two Dog Flats on Going-to-the-Sun Mountain's eastern side.

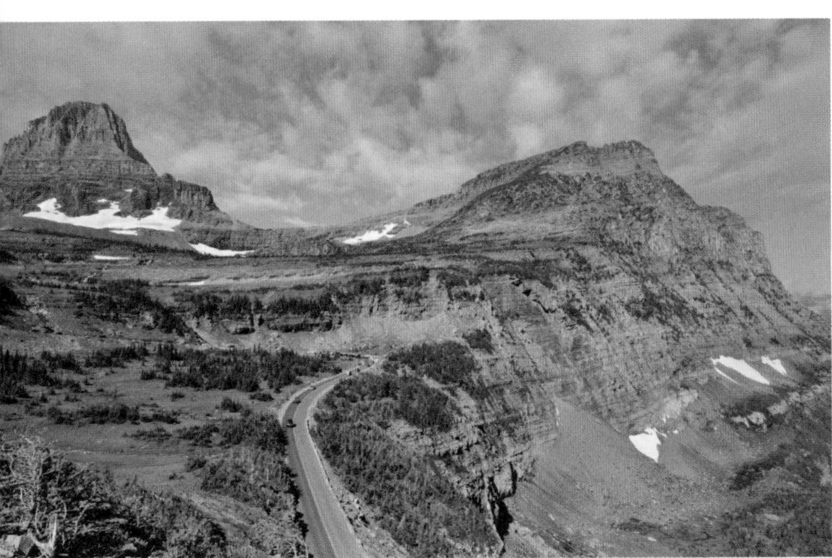

Crossing the Continental Divide at Logan Pass

18

Hāna Highway

LOCATION US **START/FINISH** Kahului/Hāna **DISTANCE** 52 miles (84 km) **TIME** 2–8 hours **ROAD CONDITIONS** Multiple blind bends **INFORMATION** www.roadtohana.com

If Heaven has a highway, then surely it looks like the Road to Hāna, 52 Edenic miles (84 km) along the northeast coast of Maui. You can drive the route in two hours, but the highway deserves an entire day to discover its beaches, hiking trails, and waterfalls. Explore lush arboretums, spelunk the Hāna Lava Tube, and dig your toes into the black-sand beach at Wai'ānapanapa State Park. Along the way, roadside stalls sell shave ice and Maui's famed banana bread. If you're here in winter, break at Ho'okipa Beach to watch surfers ride some of Hawaii's biggest waves.

The best advice? Get someone else to do the driving, so you can gawk. If you do take the wheel, proceed with caution—the road has more than 600 curves and 50 one-lane bridges before it delivers you to the isolated community of Hāna.

HĀNA LEGENDS

Legend has it that the ocean goddess, Namakaokaha'i, defeated her younger sister, the fire goddess Pele, in battle on a hill near Hāna's Kōkī Beach. Later, when a visiting Moloka'i chief doubted the spot's sacredness, Pele turned him into a giant eel. As he slithered into the sea, he left an enormous scar in the lava rock that you can still see at Liho'ula Beach.

Driving through Big Sur across the picturesque Bixby Bridge

19

Pacific Coast Highway

LOCATION US **START/FINISH** Los Angeles/San Francisco **DISTANCE** 455 miles (732 km) **TIME** 2–6 days **ROAD CONDITIONS** Good **INFORMATION** www.visitcalifornia.com/road-trips

Stretching between LA and San Francisco, the Pacific Coast Highway has some of the most spectacular oceanside scenery in the world.

A drive along California's Pacific Coast Highway is the stuff of road-trip dreams: cruising alongside the glittering ocean, soaking up the warmth of the sun, and feeling the kiss of salty sea air on your face. So what are you waiting for? Hop in a convertible, wind the rooftop down, and hit the road.

Heading north for San Francisco, the coast opens up almost as soon as you leave Los Angeles, with the arid hills and canyons of Malibu seeming to crumple into the vastness of the ocean. Soon, the mountains begin to fall away, signaling your arrival at pretty Santa Barbara, an affluent seaside city of Spanish colonial-style buildings with red-tiled roofs and white-washed stucco walls. The highway hugs the city's palm-lined beaches along a gently curving bay, continuing past more tempting stretches of sand to Gaviota, where you can bathe in soothing hot springs.

From Gaviota, the road cuts inland through a landscape of rolling hills, where detours to the Danish town of Solvang and Santa Ynez wine country offer an escape from the endless blue of the Pacific. The coast reappears at Pismo Beach, "clam capital of the world," crammed with American diners cooking up the delicious mollusks in chowders and stews, or deep-fried.

> Hop in a convertible, wind the rooftop down, and hit the road

Above *Monarch butterflies, found in Pacific Grove*
Right *Vineyards in Santa Ynez*

MISSION STATEMENT

The Pacific Coast Highway passes some of California's most famous Catholic Missions. Starting in 1769, early Spanish colonizers built a chain of 21 missions from San Diego north to Sonoma, all 30 miles (48 km) or so apart—around a day's ride on horseback. Nine of them were established by padre (and now saint) Junípero Serra, including the Mission San Diego de Alcalá and Mission San Carlos Borromeo del Rio Carmelo, in Carmel, where Serra is buried.

To the north is turreted Hearst Castle, once the opulent home of newspaper tycoon William Randolph Hearst and a worthy stop on your trip. Wander around his colonnaded swimming pools, fringed with statues of Roman gods and goddesses, before driving on to nearby Piedras Blancas, where the less-regal figures of huge, blubbery elephant seals loll on the sand, their deep bellows echoing across the beach.

If you thought the scenery was good so far, just wait for the next stretch of road through Big Sur. Here, the coastal mountain ranges run right down to the ocean, the highway wriggling far above jagged-edged cliffs and through dense redwood forests. The road winds its way through a patchwork of state parks, laced with appealing hiking trails and pretty cascades, and pristine beaches where whales and otters frolic off the coast. Big Sur ends with a bang at Point Lobos State Natural Reserve, graced with trails rich in birdlife and craggy granite pinnacles that reach down into rugged blue coves.

North of Point Lobos, the highway cuts through the rocky promontory and gnarled cypress trees of the Monterey Peninsula. This area is peppered with charming seaside towns, including Carmel, with its ornate 18th-century Spanish mission, and quiet

CATCH the huge waves—or watch the local pros do it—at Half Moon Bay
San Francisco
EXPLORE the forested gullies and remote beaches of beautifully rugged Big Sur
UNITED STATES
SEE elephant seals frolicking in the sand at Piedras Blancas
Pacific Ocean
Los Angeles
MAKE a pilgrimage to the Santa Ynez wine region, inspiration for the movie Sideways
VISIT the so-called Queen of the Missions, Old Mission Santa Barbara, with its lovely gardens

another way

Head south of LA instead, on the shorter hop along the I-5, which hugs the coast to San Diego; or north of San Francisco, where Hwy-1 threads through the giant redwoods of Northern California.

Pacific Grove, known for its winter flocks of orange-and-black monarch butterflies. Monterey itself is steeped in history, from Spanish adobe homes to Steinbeck's Cannery Row, a restored area of weathered tuna factories now housing a worthwhile aquarium.

The final stretch of highway passes cooler, storm-wracked beaches, artsy Santa Cruz, and surfing hot spot Half Moon Bay, eventually hitting San Francisco on its quieter western side. The road here snakes through a final bank of hills before suddenly dropping down to the Golden Gate and its famous russet-red bridge, often shrouded in fog. The tarmac goes on and on, but it's time to roll up the rooftop, as this is where the road-trip dream officially ends.

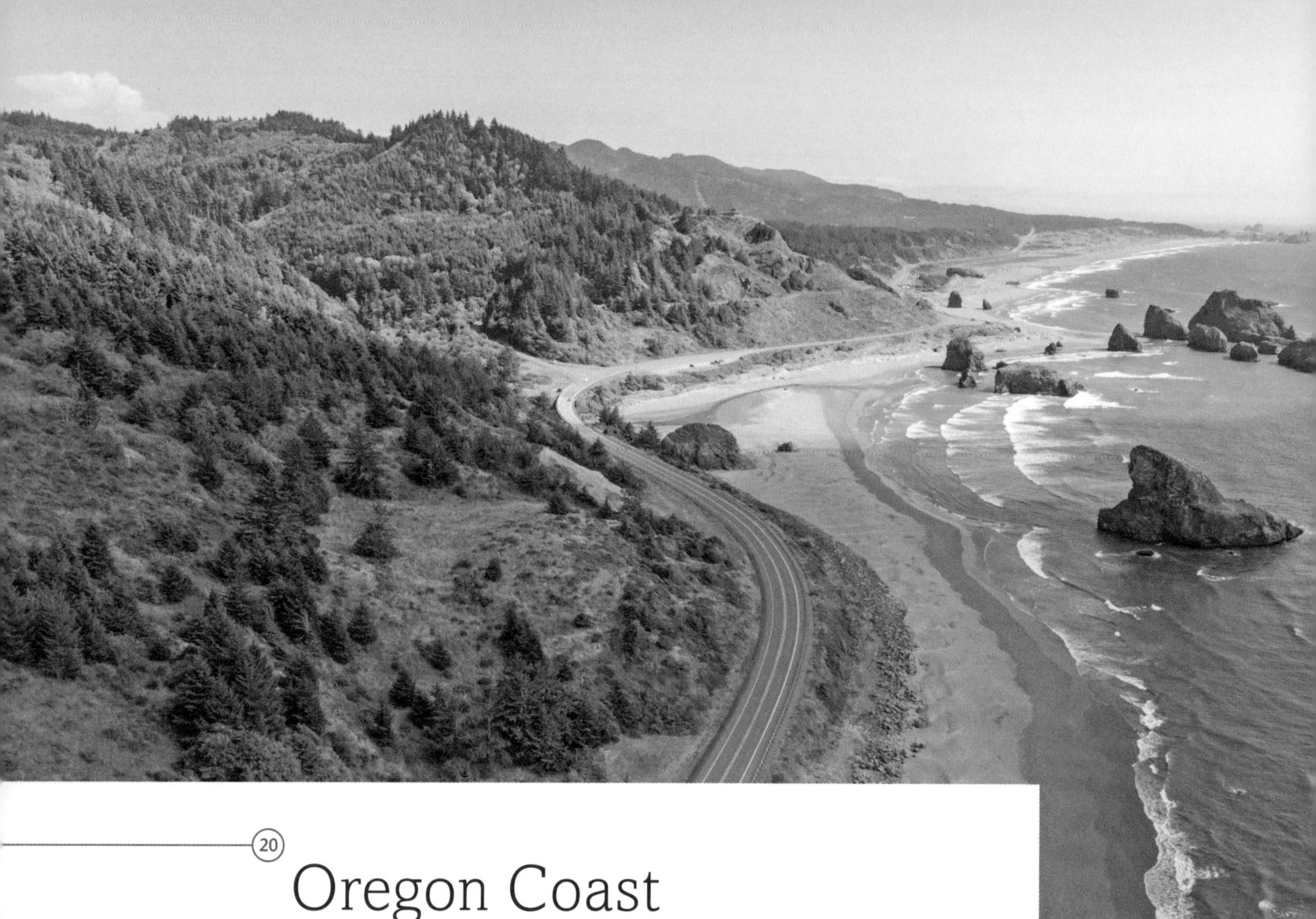

The Oregon Coast Highway 101 hugging the shoreline

20

Oregon Coast Highway 101

LOCATION US **START/FINISH** Astoria/Brookings **DISTANCE** 338 miles (544 km) **TIME** 4 days **ROAD CONDITIONS** Well-maintained paved roads **INFORMATION** www.traveloregon.com; www.stateparks.oregon.gov

Unfurling like a ribbon down Oregon's Pacific seaboard, this windswept coastal road reveals a dizzying hit-list of craggy headlands, peeping lighthouses, and quaint fishing towns.

Built in the 1920s, the Oregon Coast Highway 101 is a remarkable feat of engineering, slipping through tunnels and vaulting over bridges. It twirls high along the coastal mountains, edged by misty maritime forest and sheer drops that fall away to the frothing ocean. For a road trip to remember, begin as far north as Astoria, where the Columbia River marks out the border with Washington state (and the highway officially begins), and then cruise toward northern California, home to groves of redwoods spiking toward the sky. Trailheads

It twirls high along the coastal mountains, edged by misty forest and sheer drops

along the way provide ideal stopping points, squiggling down toward driftwood-strewn beaches with sea stacks breaching like whales in the waters of the Pacific Ocean. There are real whales here, too—most notably the Pacific gray, which pass along the coast in huge numbers during winter and spring—plus Steller sea lions basking on rocky rookeries and seabirds circling in the skies.

One of the star attractions is Oregon Dunes National Recreation Area, a sea of sandy mounds laced with hiking trails and filled with campgrounds and picnic spots. The southern Samuel H. Boardman State Scenic Corridor is another particularly stunning stretch. If time is tight, you could just drive this section of twisted rock formations, little-trodden beaches, and breathtaking panoramas. But once you've got a taste for 101, you won't want to stop.

A walkway running along Cape Arago on the central Oregon coast

HIKE *in* **Ecola State Park**, *an oasis of sitka spruce forest and sea-stack-studded shores*

SAMPLE *ice cream and Cheddar cheese at the long-running* **Tillamook Creamery**

Astoria

OVERNIGHT *at the charming bed-and-breakfast in the keeper's home at clifftop* **Heceta Head Lighthouse**

Pacific Ocean

UNITED STATES

VENTURE *to* **Sea Lion Caves** *to see hordes of Steller sea lions frolicking on wave-lashed rocks*

GET YOUR THRILLS *with a sandboarding lesson at* **Oregon Dunes National Recreation Area**

Brookings

another way

One for serious hikers, the Oregon Coast Trail runs for 362 miles (583 km), routing through thick fir forests, across Pacific-lapped beaches, and along rocky capes. You can complete one of the 10 sections, or backpack the entire route.

21

Reinig Road: the Twin Peaks route

LOCATION US **START/FINISH** Seattle/Snoqualmie Pass **DISTANCE** 54 miles (87 km) **TIME** 1–2 days **ROAD CONDITIONS** Well-maintained highways **INFORMATION** www.snoqualmiewa.gov; www.discovernorthbend.com

For Twin Peaks *fans, this trip is the stuff of dreams: a relentlessly beautiful mountain valley and a succession of towns that stitch together memories from the original cult TV show.*

It's impossible not to think of *Twin Peaks* when looking at Snoqualmie Falls. David Lynch's landmark TV series was shot extensively in the cafés, hotels, and forests of Snoqualmie, one hour east of Seattle, and today *Twin Peaks* fandom means the city is ground zero for lovers of cherry pie and damn fine cups of coffee (both references to the series, for the uninitiated).

From I-90, Reinig Road veers north onto the Snoqualmie Parkway, first directing road-trippers to the Snoqualmie Falls and Salish Lodge & Spa, which was featured heavily (as the Great Northern Hotel) in the opening credits and throughout the series. Next, it's onto a succession of production locations that, mostly, still look the same as when they were first filmed in the early 1990s. Detour to the Roadhouse Bar in Fall City to see the fictional town's biker bar, then it's onward for a stop at the Double R Diner in North Bend—to go the full Agent Cooper, take a black coffee on one of the retro red bar stools.

The city is ground zero for lovers of cherry pie and damn fine cups of coffee

Fit for an opening scene, the tumbling cascades of Snoqualmie Falls

Left *The Dalton Highway, running alongside the region's oil pipeline* ***Above*** *Musk oxen at the side of the highway*

(22)

Dalton Highway

LOCATION US **START/FINISH** Livengood/Deadhorse **DISTANCE** 414 miles (666 km) **TIME** 2–4 days **ROAD CONDITIONS** 4WD essential **INFORMATION** www.dot.alaska.gov/highways/dalton

You begin in a town called Livengood and end in one called Deadhorse. This will not be a joyride. But for the intrepid, Dalton presents the ultimate road-trip challenge.

Built to service oil fields on Alaska's North Slope and terminating on the forbidding coast of the Beaufort Sea, the Dalton Highway is one of the northernmost roads in the world. It's only occasionally paved, services are nonexistent for long stretches, and even in the narrow summer window, driving conditions are difficult. The wilderness extends for hundreds of miles on either side of you. Civilization here is two lanes wide.

On the highway, you're utterly enveloped in Alaska's maximum nature: conifer-spiked and bog-speckled boreal forests; the frigid majesty of the Brooks Range; and the flat, frozen North Slope tundra, where you'll have only your thoughts for company—traffic is mostly semitrailers delivering fuel and supplies to the oil fields. Once you embark, you'll have only two opportunities for lodging and fuel: Yukon Crossing, near which you can explore Alaskan fishing camps; and Coldfoot, a former gold-mining settlement near the drive's halfway point. Beyond that, it's just caribou and musk oxen roaming the land—it's no wonder the Dalton has been described as the loneliest road on the planet.

another way

If you'd rather not hazard the highway on your own, you can join a tour that takes you up the Dalton from Fairbanks to Deadhorse by van and then flies you back (or vice versa).

23

Icefields Parkway

LOCATION Canada **START/FINISH** Lake Louise/Jasper **DISTANCE** 144 miles (232 km) **TIME** 2 days **ROAD CONDITIONS** Winter tires required Nov–Apr **INFORMATION** www.icefieldsparkway.com

Every curve of this route unveils astonishing scenery: jewel-colored lakes, sweeping valleys, and ancient glaciers. Fuel up, put on several layers, and head out on an icy adventure.

Following the double-lane Highway 93 North, the Icefields Parkway winds through two national parks—Banff and Jasper—in the Canadian Rocky Mountains, where peaks easily reach a staggering 12,467 ft (3,800 m). Accessible for most of the year, this superb stretch of road has plenty of turnouts to take in jaw-dropping views, or to reach hiking trails to thundering waterfalls and picturesque picnic spots.

The alpine environment here harbors cougar and regal elk, and mountain goats casually trotting along absurdly dangerous cliffs. Besides the wildlife and the splendid grandeur of the Rockies, the route's star attraction is the Columbia Icefield, one of the largest masses of glacial ice on earth, resembling a frozen river slowly inching down for over 15.5 miles (25 km) between walls of sky-high mountains. It's a monumental landscape that's befitting for a monumental part of the world.

A monumental landscape befitting for a monumental part of the world

The Icefields Parkway running through some of Alberta's most breathtaking scenery

Admiring the stunning views at Revelstoke Mountain Resort

24

Powder Highway

LOCATION Canada **START/FINISH** Fairmont Hot Springs (loop) **DISTANCE** 293 miles (472 km) **TIME** 7–10 days **ROAD CONDITIONS** Good paved roads **INFORMATION** www.powderhighway.com

A self-styled Route 66 for skiers and snowboarders, this circuit through British Columbia is ideal for those in search of heavenly powder.

On a winter odyssey into the British Columbia interior, a number of things strike you from behind the wheel. The Rocky ranges constantly fill the windshield and peer imperviously from the horizon. The views of vermillion-colored lakes and star-studded skies seem endless. And the road has a tendency to end abruptly at the foot of mountains—where the only way is up.

Such snowscapes are the stock in trade of the Powder Highway, a snazzy cluster of connected winter resorts and Nordic ski areas in the Kootenay Rockies. Along the way, the highway carves its way through glacial valleys and up-and-over improbable passes between serene backcountry towns such as Rossland, Golden, and Nelson, a former mining town now home to trendy cafés and craft breweries. Hit the uncrowded trails of Fernie and soak in the views at Panorama, and make sure you earmark stops at Revelstoke, for the greatest skiing vertical in North America, and Kicking Horse Resort, home to Canada's highest restaurant. Winter is coming.

another way

Over the provincial border, Alberta has an equal number of dazzling winter resorts. Take your pick from Mount Norquay, Sunshine Village, Lake Louise, and Nakiska. Journey's end has to be Banff, so perfect it looks like a screensaver.

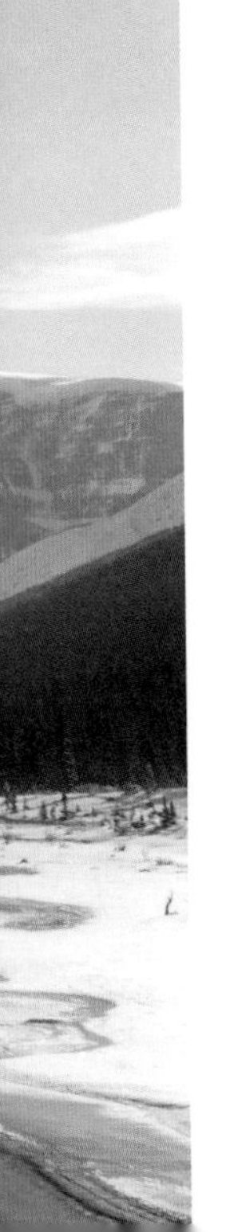

The remains of Viking houses, L'Anse aux Meadows National Historic Site

25

Cowboy Trail

LOCATION Canada **START/FINISH** Calgary/ Longview **DISTANCE** 63 miles (101 km) **TIME** 2–3 days **ROAD CONDITIONS** Well maintained **INFORMATION** www.thecowboytrail.com; www.calgarystampede.com

Think of Calgary and images of city slickers and a 1980s Texan-style oil boom might spring to mind. And yet, more traditional High Noon adventures are on tap when road-tripping south through the high ranching pasture, harnessed between the vast Canadian prairie and the Rocky Mountains.

Along Highway 22, from Cochrane to Longview, you can witness a First Nations powwow, harness your inner cowboy at a working farm, or tumble back in time at Bar U Ranch, a National Historic Site and once one of North America's largest ranches. This whole area absorbed Old West settlers in the 1880s when immigrants transformed the buffalo-grazed grasslands into bumper-to-bumper cattle farms. Visit in July and bookend a trip with the Calgary Stampede, the world's largest rodeo—the perfect time to don a stetson and sample a prairie oyster (also known as a deep-fried bull testicle).

26

Viking Trail

LOCATION Canada **START/FINISH** Deer Park/ St. Anthony **DISTANCE** 327 miles (526 km) **TIME** 4–6 days **ROAD CONDITIONS** Good **INFORMATION** www.vikingtrail.org

Offering the chance to hike across mesalike formations and explore ancient fishing villages, the island province of Newfoundland isn't exactly your typical Canada, even if the scenery is just as incredible.

Viking tales are legion in the coastal mountains and Atlantic-facing communities here, and Route 430—the so-called Viking Trail—has all the drama of an epic Norse saga. At the end-of-the-world tablelands of Gros Morne National Park, geologists helped prove the theory of continental drift. At L'Anse aux Meadows National Historic Site, you can poke around Viking house remains, sod longhouses, and a turf-topped chieftain's hall. It was here, 1,000 years or so ago, that Viking explorer Leif Erickson marshaled Icelandic and Greenlandic sailors to Canada's eastern shores, founding the first European settlement on this side of the Atlantic.

27

Cabot Trail

LOCATION Canada **START/FINISH** Baddeck (return) **DISTANCE** 186 miles (298 km) **TIME** 2–7 days **ROAD CONDITIONS** Good **INFORMATION** www.cbisland.com

The Cabot Trail, which twirls around Nova Scotia's wild Cape Breton Island, is one of the world's most scenic drives. The views from the asphalt are jaw-dropping—pull over at lookouts like Cape Smokey, dramatic Cap Rouge, and MacKenzie Mountain, where you might see whales blowing offshore. But it's also a lifeline to the communities scattered around the island's valleys and shores. By making the drive, you'll get a glimpse into the First Nations, Acadian, and Gaelic cultures that make this place so unique.

You could make the trip in a day, but it's worth taking your time and stopping often. Linger in lakeside Baddeck, home to the Alexander Graham Bell National Historic Site. Stop at St. Ann's Gaelic College, which hosts regular céilidhs. Go lobster fishing from lovely Ingonish. Learn about Acadian folk art at the little harbor of Chéticamp. And enjoy the unfurling of craggy coast and tree-cloaked hills at every bend.

28

Sugar Shack Country

LOCATION Canada **START/FINISH** Montreal/Quebec City **DISTANCE** 168 miles (271 km) **TIME** 4–5 days **ROAD CONDITIONS** Good **INFORMATION** www.bonjourquebec.com; usually open mid-Mar to mid-Apr

Quebec makes a compelling case for the sweetest place on earth. Every winter, 3 million gallons of maple syrup is harvested, stoking an industry for *pouding chômeur* (baked sugar and cream) and *Grandpère* dumplings.

Such rewards await road trippers in dozens of historic sugar shacks on backcountry roads between Montreal and Quebec City. Often out of sight, these postcard timber cabins and modern banquet-style halls come with sample rooms and tables for a traditionally syrup-heavy Quebec supper. For a belly-hugging tour along the St. Lawrence River, map a route between many of the finest, including Sucrerie de la Montagne, Chez Dany, L'Erabliere du Cap, and L'En Tailleur. Just don't tell your dentist.

another way

A far less calorific journey (also beginning in Montreal) is the Route Verte, a colossal cycle route through Quebec that's crisscrossed by the longest network of bike trails in North America.

Kidston Island Lighthouse in Baddeck

The colorful streets of Campeche, on the west coast of the Yucatán Peninsula

Across the Yucatán

LOCATION Mexico **START/FINISH** Campeche/Tulum **DISTANCE** 373 miles (600 km) **TIME** 1 week **ROAD CONDITIONS** Well-maintained paved roads **INFORMATION** www.yucatan.travel/en

Nowhere paints a picture of Mexico more vividly than the Yucatán Peninsula, home to fine Maya ruins, stately colonial cities, and a sugar-white Caribbean coastline.

Mexico's precolonial history echoes throughout the Yucatán Peninsula, in the mesmerizing form of Mayan ruins and cenotes—sinkholes that had a ritual significance for the Maya people. This interplay between cultural history and natural beauty is what characterizes the Yucatán and makes it such a magnificent setting for a self-drive road trip.

The vibrant city of Campeche sets the tone for this vivid corner of Mexico. Known as the Rainbow City for its spectrum of pastel-hued houses, it couldn't be more different from mega-resorts like Cancún. Vintage cars sit elegantly on the pavements, kids play rowdy games of *fútbol* in the streets, and stalls sizzle with the sound (and smell) of *pan de cazón*—shredded dogfish, squeezed between stacked tortillas and slathered in spicy tomato sauce.

Vintage cars sit elegantly on the pavements and kids play rowdy games of *fútbol*

Yucatán cuisine is likely to be a highlight of your adventure as you cross the peninsula from west to east. In Mérida, your next stop after Campeche, be sure to try the street-food favorite *cochinita pibil*: a mouthwatering suckling-pig dish with Mayan origins and a European influence in the addition of Seville oranges—a fusion that is pure Yucatán. By the time you get to the Caribbean coast, the food takes on a tropical flavor; rice and beans with fried plantain is a common fixture on beach-shack menus, as is ocean-fresh ceviche.

TICA
DJC-69-81

CENOTES AND THE MAYA

The Maya imbued Yucatán's many cenotes with sacred importance, seeing them as portals to the underworld. In a practical sense, they used these sinkholes as a source of drinking water, but in the religious realm, they were the site of ritual sacrifices. Ancient finds have confirmed that people were thrown in, along with gold and jade jewelry, to appease the rain god Chaac.

Even more memorable than the food, but displaying the same fusion of Old and New World influences, is the architecture. Mérida, the Yucatán capital, is justly applauded for its gorgeous Spanish colonnades and its Catholic cathedral, built by the Spanish on the site of Mayan ruins. To the east, the magnificence of the Maya stands proud at Chichen Itza, one of the world's most famous archaeological sites, built a thousand years ago yet looking, in places, brand new. Its centerpiece is majestic El Castillo, a perfectly preserved step pyramid whose alignment highlights the ingenuity of Maya architects: each equinox, the sun strikes the

MARVEL *at the genius of Mayan architects at* **Chichen Itza,** *the greatest surviving Mesoamerican complex*

DELVE *into Mayan culture at the* **Gran Museo del Mundo Maya** *in Yucatán's princely capital, Mérida*

Gulf of Mexico

SWIM *in the atmospheric* **Cenote Samula,** *as beams of sunlight break through a hole in the cave roof*

STROLL *amid the colorful mansions and colonial fortresses of* **Campeche,** *a UNESCO World Heritage Site*

MEXICO

Tulum

BASK *on the soft sand of* **Playa Ruinas,** *in the shadow of clifftop Maya temples*

Campeche

Above *Playa Ruinas beach, in the shadow of the El Castillo Mayan ruins*
Right *Sea fan coral, the Great Maya Reef*

steps to cast the shadow of a descending serpent, in honor of the feathered snake deity Kukulcán to whom the temple was built.

For all the jaw-dropping human culture along the way, you'll be awestruck by Yucatán's natural beauty, too, which inspired the Maya to imbue the landscape with such a rich tapestry of myth. The Anillo de Cenotes, near Valladolid, is a vast ring of natural sinkholes caused by the same meteorite that wiped out the dinosaurs, and which the Maya used for ritual sacrifices; today, they're a place to swim, snorkel, and cool off from the Mexican sun. On the coast, you'll find some of the most gorgeous beaches in Mexico, while the Great Maya Reef is home to some of the world's finest reef diving off Isla Cozumel.

The Yucatán is most charming, though, when the human and the wild combine. As you hit the east coast and run out of road at Tulum's Playa Ruinas, Mayan ruins perched above the beach make for an unforgettable end to your journey.

another way

If you can't resist a purely coastal drive, stick to the lesser-visited west coast of the peninsula, heading north from Campeche to explore the flamingo-rich mangroves of Ria Celestún and finishing in Mérida.

Brightly adorned chicken buses

30

Chicken Buses

LOCATION Guatemala **START/FINISH** Antigua/Chichicastenango **DISTANCE** 66 miles (106 km) **TIME** 2.5 hours **ROAD CONDITIONS** Hairpin bends **INFORMATION** www.visitguatemala.com

The cheapest transport in Guatemala, and the most exhilarating, is the so-called chicken bus: retired school buses from the US that have been stripped out, sprayed like a street mural, and fitted with a horn so loud you'd think a train was coming. Infamous for having no maximum limit on passengers, they careen around corners with a hair-raising desperate-to-dash attitude.

Despite the name, it's rare to share a seat with livestock except on market days, but you will get to see (and taste) the real Guatemala, with passengers decked out in an amazing array of traditional textiles, and stops for hawkers to push street food to everyone on board. Many visitors get their chicken-bus experience on the ride from Antigua to Guatemala City, but for scenery and an immersion into K'iche Maya culture, the trip to Chichicastenango can't be beat.

31

Ruta de las Flores

LOCATION El Salvador **START/FINISH** Nahuizalco/Ataco **DISTANCE** 20 miles (32 km) **TIME** 3 days **ROAD CONDITIONS** Good **INFORMATION** www.elsalvador.travel/en

Named after the coffee flowers that burst into bloom from November to February, the Ruta de las Flores is one of the most scenic circuits in El Salvador, taking in five pretty pueblos with whitewashed churches, colorful murals, and cobbled streets. Start at the market in Nahuizalco, where stalls spill over with exotic fruits, before heading to Salcoatitán, famous for its crafts. Spend a night in Juayúa, whose weekend food fair is dedicated to local dishes, and trek out to the stepped waterfalls of Chorros de la Calera. Next stop, Apaneca, is dedicated to adventure: try the zipline "sky bikes," tubing track and eco-friendly maze. Spend a final night exploring the craft stores and quirky corners of colonial Concepción de Ataco before ending with a morning bean-to-cup tour of El Carmen Estate. Dating back to the 1930s, this is the place to revel in the gourmet-bean glories of pacamara and geisha, a suitably floral ending to your trip.

another way

Explore the Ruta de las Flores in one day, starting with breakfast and a coffee tour at El Carmen Estate in Ataco, lunch and various activities in Apaneca, and a final stop in Nahuizalco.

Vintage American cars cruising along the Malecón in Havana

Waves crashing over St. Lucy's North Point

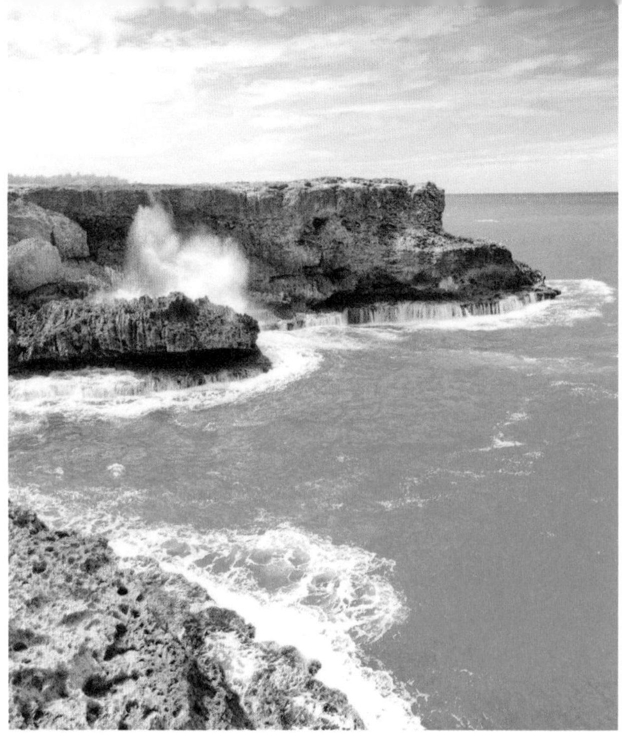

(32)

Cuba in a Cadillac

LOCATION Cuba **START/FINISH** Havana/ Santiago de Cuba **DISTANCE** 499 miles (804 km) **TIME** 7–10 days **ROAD CONDITIONS** Some potholes **INFORMATION** www.infotur.cu

You can hardly come to Cuba and not hit the road in a vintage convertible. Pick one up in candy-colored Havana, then join the rainbow parade of *yanqui* motors as they zip east past glittering seas and powder-soft sands. Most journeys then plunge inland toward the lush Península de Zapata, rich in wildlife and revolutionary history, before tracing the coastline to Punta Perdiz, where it's easy to succumb to the lure of the beach. Back in the driver's seat, follow the road past dusty villages, up through the town of Santa Clara, and down the spine of the island. As the tarmac chips away, Sierra Maestra's peaks rear up on the horizon, and the highway wriggles through a series of sharp bends before revealing the jaw-dropping sight of pristine beach after pristine beach, all the way to Santiago.

(33)

St. Lucy Loop

LOCATION Barbados **START/FINISH** Speightstown (loop) **DISTANCE** 25 miles (40 km) **TIME** 3–4 hours **ROAD CONDITIONS** Mostly tarred; the dirt road to Cove Bay is inaccessible after heavy rain **INFORMATION** Signposting is sketchy

The rugged, windswept contours of St. Lucy, Barbados's most northerly parish, are a million miles from the island's sun-soaked-beach image—but just as beautiful. A 10-minute drive northeast from the starting point of Speightstown takes you to a world of crinkly coastlines peppered with dramatic views and hidden coves, each with its own character. The cliff-enclosed sands of Archer's Bay are accessed via steep steps, while at fairly flat Little Bay, the seething surf foams over limestone formations, spouting through blowholes and curling into rock pools. At the grassy promontory overlooking nearby Cove Bay, you'll have serried ranks of palms (and possibly a few cows) for company as you watch the relentless swell heave and retreat. Time your arrival at North Point for lunchtime, where the clifftop restaurant provides the perfect vantage point to experience the ocean's thunderous waves crashing against the rocks, sending clouds of spray high into the air.

(34)

Zona Cafetera

LOCATION Colombia **START/FINISH** Manizales/Ibagué **DISTANCE** 119 miles (191 km) **TIME** 5–7 days **ROAD CONDITIONS** Good **INFORMATION** www.colombia.travel

Journey through the Colombian coffee region during peak harvest time, meeting coffee growers and relaxing in the area's laid-back mountain towns.

Cruising through Colombia's coffee country in a vintage Jeep, visiting working *fincas* to sample the region's rich arabica, is an energizing experience. The vibrant cities and towns of the Zona Cafetera include Manizales, where glorious views can be had of the Andean foothills, covered with fertile plantations, and Pereira, where coffee helps to fuel a buzzing nightlife scene. In the charming town of Salento, further south, the Finca el Ocaso provides tours through their coffee fields and the chance to learn how a planted seed becomes a piping-hot cup of joe.

The countryside of the Zona Cafetera is Colombia at its most enchanting. Driving southeast of Salento leads to the verdant mountainsides of the Cocora Valley, studded with spindly palm trees, their tops often wreathed in mist, a striking collision of the alpine and the tropical. The volcanic hot springs of nearby Machín are perfect for winding down at the end of your trip—and before a night in the folk bars of Ibagué, Colombia's vibrant musical capital.

YIPAOS

The favored mode of transportation in coffee country is the Yipao, the local name for the Willys Jeep. Known as "mechanical mules," these robust machines are often overflowing with coffee, bananas, and other fruits of the fields. There is even a Yipao Parade, held each June and July, in the city of Armenia.

The Cocora Valley, in Colombia's Zona Cafetera

The sun setting over the pretty cobblestone streets of Paraty

35

Costa Verde

LOCATION Brazil **START/FINISH** Santos/Itaguai **DISTANCE** 303 miles (485 km) **TIME** 2 days **DIFFICULTY** Well-paved road; check for landslides and floods in Dec **INFORMATION** www.visitbrasil.com

Often called Brazil's most beautiful coastal route, the winding road that shadows the Costa Verde seems a world away from the country's traffic-clogged cities.

If you put your foot down, you could motor along the BR101 highway, which shadows the Costa Verde, in about eight hours. But who would want to do that, when the aptly named "Green Coast" is so packed with scenic wonders? Start in the port city of Santos and head north to the outskirts of Rio, or vice versa, and take your time— Brazilian-style—soaking up the scenery slowly over a couple of days.

Looming high above the winding highway, the lush Atlantic Forest spills over granite peaks; ceiba trees are draped with bromeliads and flowers embroider the overgrown banks. Hundreds of offshore islands sprinkle the coastline, while the route winds past whitewashed colonial churches standing guard over quiet villages and roadside stalls selling sizzling grilled fish. The unmissable highlight, however, is the historic port of Paraty, situated midway along this stretch of coast. The town's cobblestoned lanes are lined with cafés and boutique *pousadas* (guesthouses), making it an idyllic spot to rest before hitting the road again, and returning to the hubbub of a city once more.

Beautifully sited Huancavelica, lying between mountains

(36)

Into the Andes: Lima to Cusco

LOCATION Peru **START/FINISH** Lima/Cusco **DISTANCE** 764 miles (1,230 km) **TIME** 7–9 days **ROAD CONDITIONS** Some good roads, many rough tracks; hairpin bends and sheer drops throughout **INFORMATION** Driving yourself is not advised; most motorists will find conditions difficult, and ample public transportation serves the route

Hop on a bus for this spellbinding high-altitude pootle and enjoy a trundle that gets you far closer to Peru's rugged, tradition-rich soul than any well-trodden tourist route ever could.

To debunk a popular misconception, the cities of Lima—Peru's classy, culinary capital—and Cusco—the captivating center of the ancient Inca world—are not the country's highlights. The real pinnacle of Peru is the bit in the middle: the Andes, and the culture and scenery stashed within the range's serrated 13,125 ft (4,000 m) peaks. Think clamoring produce markets and impromptu fiestas; unsigned dirt-track highways in cinematically stark terrain; prehistoric sites and companionable moments with locals debating the state of the roads and of life. A brimful of

The real pinnacle of Peru is the bit in the middle

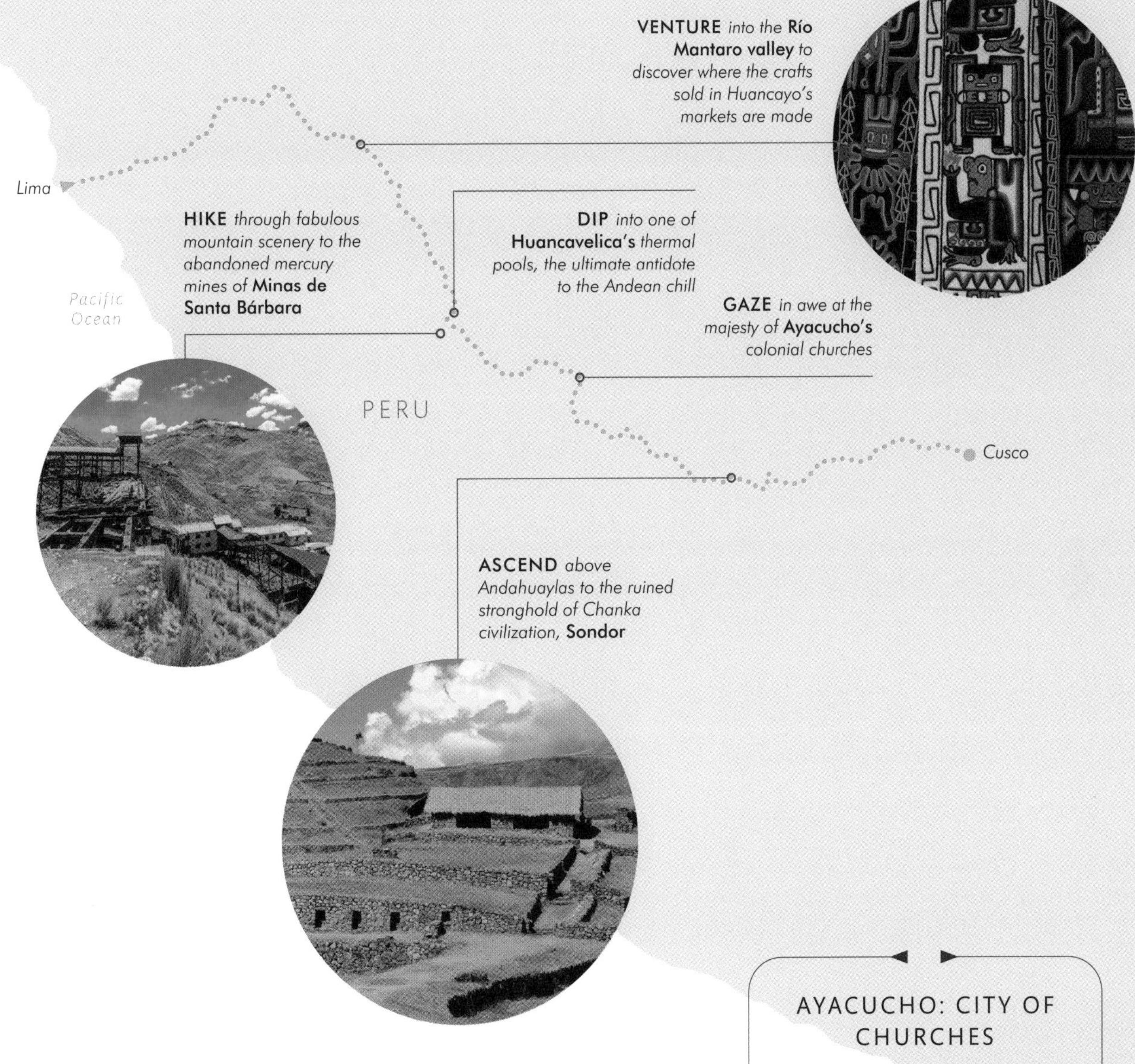

VENTURE *into the* **Río Mantaro valley** *to discover where the crafts sold in Huancayo's markets are made*
Lima
HIKE *through fabulous mountain scenery to the abandoned mercury mines of* **Minas de Santa Bárbara**
DIP *into one of* **Huancavelica's** *thermal pools, the ultimate antidote to the Andean chill*
Pacific Ocean
GAZE *in awe at the majesty of* **Ayacucho's** *colonial churches*
PERU
Cusco
ASCEND *above Andahuaylas to the ruined stronghold of Chanka civilization,* **Sondor**

undiluted Peru, harder to encounter on its coast (being more developed) or in its jungle (where taking tours is necessary), is what you get served on this sensational motor from seaboard to sierra.

Embark on this overland odyssey and you'll be signing up for the succulent taste of clay-baked lake trout in Jauja, the unheralded workmanship of the crafts fashioned in the Río Mantaro valley outside Huancayo, and the moment of magic when you step into an Ayacucho church—there are dozens to choose from—and behold the intricate interior for yourself. The way is long and winding, more mud than tarmac. But this is a journey that's about belligerent donkeys and back-of-beyond lunch breaks, not check-it-off-the-bucket-list sights, the kind of trip that will be full of wonderful, one-of-a-kind stories to tell back home.

AYACUCHO: CITY OF CHURCHES

The city of Ayacucho is famous for its 33 colonial churches, each one representing a year of Jesus's life. Pick of the bunch for visitors are the Monasterio de Carmelitas Descalzas; the Capellania Santo Domingo, its huge altar adorned with gold leaf; and the Catedral Basílica de Nuestra Señora de las Nieves (Our Lady of the Snows), which contains Stations of the Cross paintings from Rome.

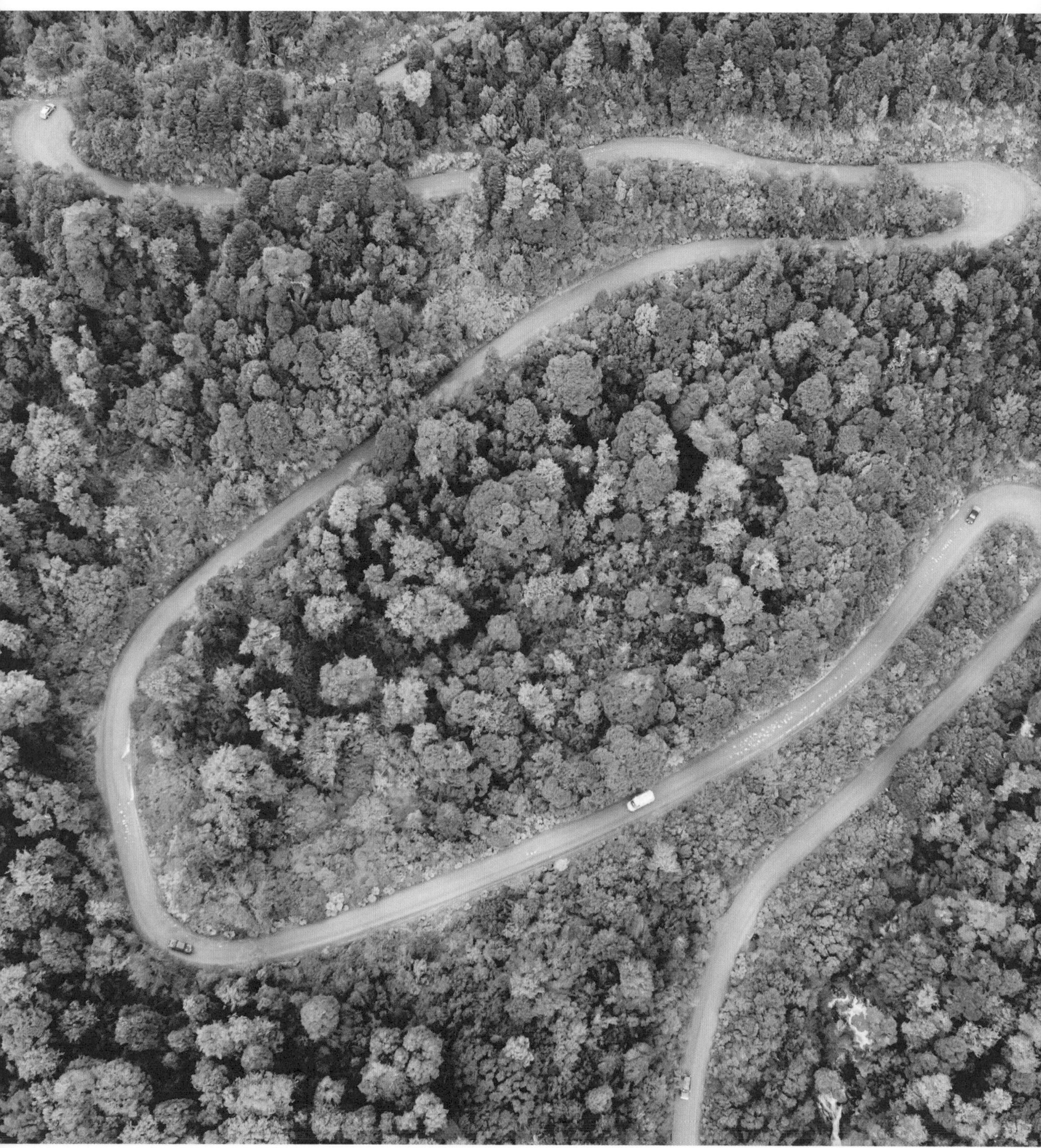

The Carretera Austral snaking through forest between Puyuhuapi and Cisnesg

37

Carretera Austral

LOCATION Chile **START/FINISH** Puerto Montt/Villa O'Higgins **DISTANCE** 750 miles (1,208 km) **TIME** 2 weeks **ROAD CONDITIONS** Mixture of paved, gravel, and dirt **INFORMATION** www.chile.travel/en

Tracing the route of the Andes, the "Southern Highway" takes drivers through the dramatic and sparsely populated landscapes of Chilean Patagonia.

Built to connect remote frontier communities in Chilean Patagonia, the Carretera Austral (Southern Highway) is a journey into the heart of one of the world's last remaining wildernesses. Long sections of the road remain unpaved and are dotted with deep potholes, but bold drivers are well compensated with views of smoldering volcanoes and iceberg-filled fjords, swathes of rainforest, and open steppe sprinkled with grazing guanacos.

Best driven from north to south, the Carretera Austral (also known as Ruta 7) starts in the port city of Puerto Montt and finishes in tiny Villa O'Higgins, close to the Argentinian border. As you drive south, initially hugging the shimmering coastline, Chile slowly breaks up into a tangle of islands, peninsulas, and channels. Stretch your legs at Pumalín, one of the country's newest national parks and home to snow-covered mountains and thundering waterfalls; trails here lead through moss-scented forests of towering alerce trees, some more than 3,000 years old.

Chile slowly breaks up into a tangle of islands, peninsulas, and channels

Beyond Pumalín, the highway weaves between mountains of emerald green forest as it traces the route of two serpentine rivers—first the Frio, then the Palena—tinged with hues of electric blue and turquoise. Take a detour and head east to the picturesque town of Futaleufú, where you can swap your car for a raft and tackle the world-class whitewater rapids on its namesake river.

Back on the main road heading south, you'll soon reach Puyuhuapi, a mist-shrouded village on the shoreline of a gorgeous fjord. Take time out here to visit one of the hot springs and call into the nearby Parque Nacional Queulat, home to a famous "hanging glacier" seemingly suspended from a cliff face high above a beautiful lake.

South of Puyuhuapi, the road deteriorates as the scenery grows grander. Between the city of Coyhaique and the hamlet of Villa Cerro Castillo, you'll reach the highest point on the drive, a 3,537 ft (1,078 m) pass with views to match. From there, the highway loops through largely uninhabited wilderness until you reach the vast Lago General Carrera, the second-largest lake in South America. Take a break from the drive at Puerto Río Tranquilo, on the lake's northern edge, for a boat trip to the Marble Caves, where columns of swirling blue and gray marble have been polished smooth by the lapping waters of the lake.

Finally, you'll roll into Villa O'Higgins, the appropriately far-flung village that marks the end of the road. Tradition dictates you sign off your remote road trip with a picture in front of the "Fin de la Carretera Austral" sign down by the water's edge. Mission accomplished.

Below left *Glacier Ventisquero Colgante, Parque Nacional Queulat* ***Below right*** *Mist settling over the fjordside village of Puyuhuapi*

Puerto Montt

STOP *to explore the hiking trails at beautiful* **Parque Nacional Pumalín**

HIKE *to the magnificent white-blue glacier of* **Ventisquero Colgante,** *in Parque Nacional Queulat*

SOAK *in one of the hot springs dotted around the charming village of* **Puyuhuapi**

CHILE

ARGENTINA

Pacific Ocean

MARVEL *at the marble caves at* **Lago General Carrera,** *which extends across the border into Argentina*

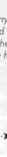

Villa O'Higgins

TAKE *the ferry across Mitchell Fjord to* **Villa O'Higgins,** *the southernmost stop on the highway*

another way

The Carretera Austral is one of South America's most challenging—and rewarding—bike rides. The weather is highly changeable, with rain, fierce headwinds, and cold temperatures likely even during summer, but that just adds to the sense of satisfaction at trail's end.

38

Ruta 40

LOCATION Argentina **START/FINISH** La Quiaca/ Cabo Virgenes **DISTANCE** 3,246 miles (5,224 km) **TIME** 3–5 weeks **ROAD CONDITIONS** Some sections unpaved **INFORMATION** Nov–Mar is best

Ruta 40 is the Andean equivalent of Route 66, an epic adventure through some of South America's most dramatic landscapes.

Stretching from the high-altitude plateaus of Jujuy in the extreme north to the barren, windswept steppe of Patagonia in the far south, Ruta 40 is Argentina's longest road. Also known as Ruta Nacional 40, RN40 or, more poetically, La Cuarenta (The Forty), it follows the path of the Andes along the country's western border with Chile. Dating back to the 1930s, this rugged route is equivalent in distance to driving from London to Sicily—and back again.

Along the way, Ruta 40 skirts one of the world's largest ice fields, journeys past the cobalt lakes and snowy peaks of the unfeasibly scenic Lake District, and reaches the breathless heights of 16,259 ft (4,956 m) above sea level at the mountain pass of Abra del Acay, a challenge for car and driver alike.

Ruta 40's biggest draw, however, is the sense of space and freedom it provides—in the far south, you can drive for hours without encountering another vehicle. It's a blissfully lonely road, indeed, at the end of the world.

another way

If Ruta 40 isn't quite long enough, you can connect onto the Pan-American Highway and continue south—via Chile and a ferry across the Strait of Magellan—to Tierra del Fuego at the very tip of South America.

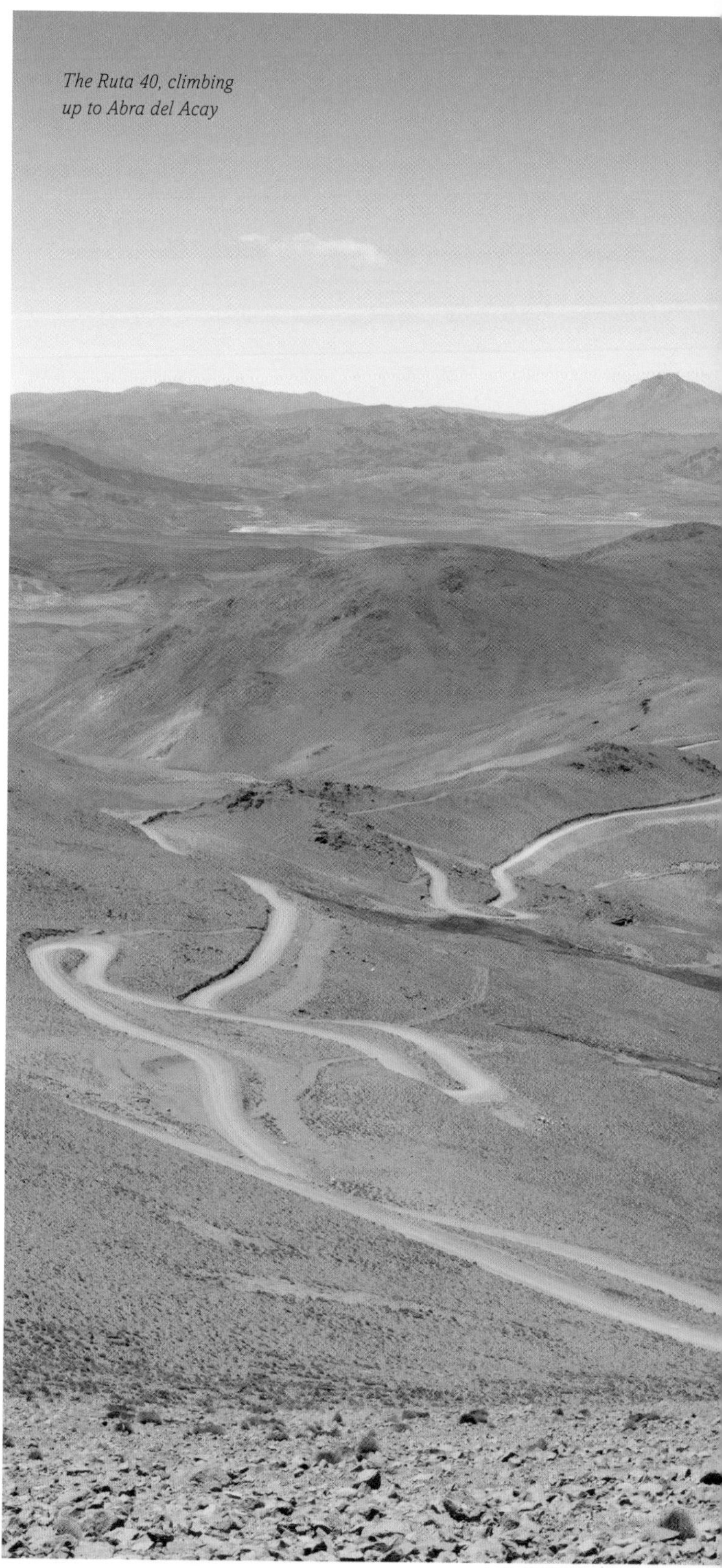

The Ruta 40, climbing up to Abra del Acay

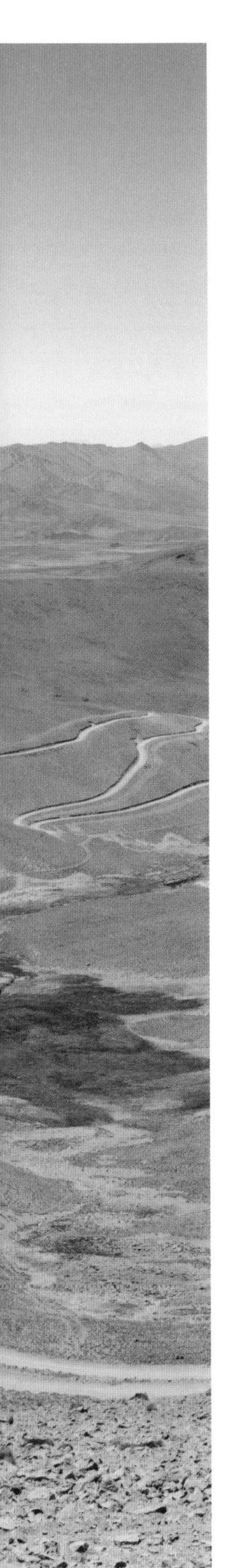

Gentoo penguins waddling out to sea in the Falkland Islands

39

The Falklands

LOCATION Falkland Islands (Islas Malvinas) **START/FINISH** Stanley/Walker Creek **DISTANCE** 87 miles (140 km) **TIME** 1–2 days **ROAD CONDITIONS** Most road surfaces are gravel or clay **INFORMATION** www.falklandislands.com

A drive beyond the Falklands' capital showcases a different side to these remote British islands in the South Atlantic.

For anyone seeking empty roads, rugged landscapes, and a bounty of bird and marine life, East Falkland has you covered. After leaving behind the capital, Stanley, and heading southwest for Walker Creek, you travel past windswept headlands and remote farmsteads, icy freshwater tarns, and bunches of yellow-flowering gorse.

While you can never completely escape the 1982 conflict—the route takes in Goose Green, site of a famous battle between British and Argentine forces—the drive shows that this is only one part of the Falkland Islands' story. Another is the surprising profusion of fauna, despite the harsh conditions, especially in winter. At Bluff Cove, you'll find a lagoon reserve with thousands of characterful gentoo penguins, plus smaller numbers of their king and Magellanic cousins. Sea Lion Island, meanwhile, is home to large colonies of the eponymous mammals, as well as grouchy elephant seals. The Falklands might be synonymous with conflict, but wildlife thrives in this island chain at the end of the earth.

You travel past wind-swept headlands and remote farmsteads

BY BIKE

Cycling has a distinguished history in the Americas. The first-ever patent for a pedal-driven bike was filed in the US, and Chileans were cycling over Andean passes as early as 1898. Today, the continents' cycle routes cross borders and traverse countries—whether you love speeding around hairpin bends, bumping along rugged trails, or cruising between vineyards, there's a trail for you.

Previous page *Approaching San Francisco's Golden Gate Bridge*

AT A GLANCE

BY BIKE

1

Empire State Trail

LOCATION US **START/FINISH** Manhattan/Buffalo **DISTANCE** 750 miles (1,207 km) **TIME** 2 weeks **DIFFICULTY** Moderate **INFORMATION** www.empiretrail.ny.gov

Set a fortnight aside for this memorable cycle and camp around America's longest multiuse trail, where you'll take in sights such as New York City, Buffalo, and the Hudson River Valley.

Cycling through New York's Hudson River Park

Buffalo, the finish point of the Empire State Trail

Encompassing around 750 miles (1,200 km) of New York State, the Empire State Trail is up there with America's ultimate cycling and camping adventures. Begin in Manhattan and set your GPS north to follow the Hudson River Greenway, a protected waterside cycle path that's used by thousands of car-free New Yorkers. You'll soon dip out of the urban sprawl near Van Cortlandt Park in favor of flat, off-road pedals alongside the disused Maybrook Line, once an important railroad connection across the Hudson River.

After a few more days in the saddle, pitching your tent at night in state forests, municipal parks, or on lakeshores, you'll skirt the beach-laden city of Albany toward Peebles Island State Park, where the path forks: point your handlebars west to Buffalo and follow family-friendly trails through historic cities like Syracuse, one of many places in Upper New York State that grew up around the Erie Canal, the so-called Mother of Cities. The stretch from Albany is around 340 miles (545 km), a week or so in the saddle, but Buffalo's art scene—and its iconic tangy wings—will surely soothe those aches.

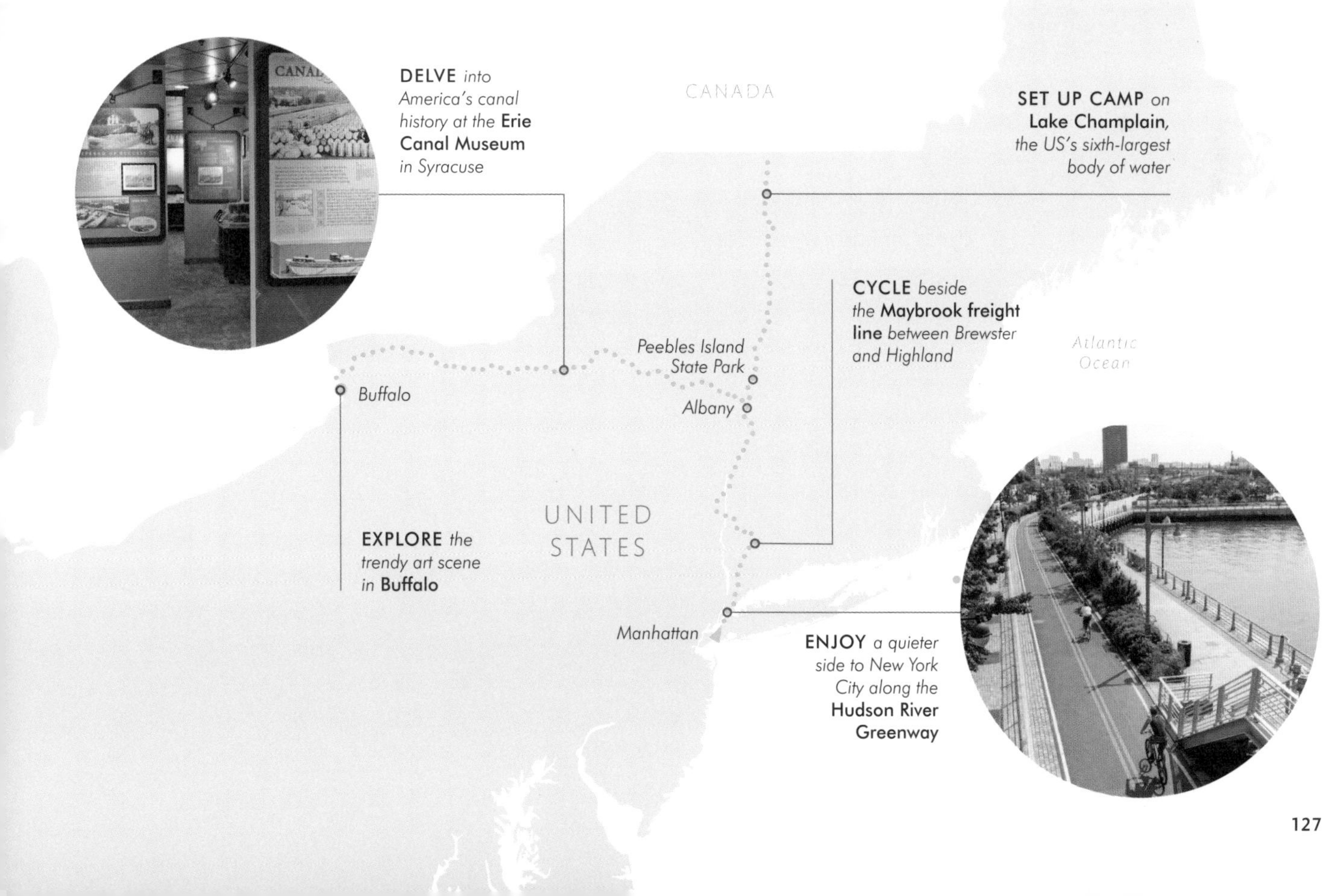

DELVE *into America's canal history at the* **Erie Canal Museum** *in Syracuse*

CANADA

SET UP CAMP *on* **Lake Champlain,** *the US's sixth-largest body of water*

CYCLE *beside the* **Maybrook freight line** *between Brewster and Highland*

Atlantic Ocean

Peebles Island State Park

Buffalo

Albany

UNITED STATES

EXPLORE *the trendy art scene in* **Buffalo**

Manhattan

ENJOY *a quieter side to New York City along the* **Hudson River Greenway**

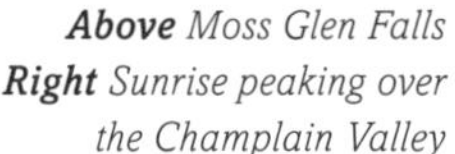

Above *Moss Glen Falls*
Right *Sunrise peaking over the Champlain Valley*

2

Champlain Triangle

LOCATION US **START/FINISH** Brandon (loop) **DISTANCE** 107 miles (172 km) **TIME** 4 days **DIFFICULTY** Easy, with some gravel sections **INFORMATION** www.walkbikeaddison.org

Coast along the peaceful byways and back roads of Addison County in Vermont's rural Champlain Valley, a winsome region sprinkled with covered wooden bridges and Dutch-gabled timber barns.

The broad, bucolic Champlain Valley, a swathe of somnolent farm belt stretching between the Green Mountains to the east and New York State's Adirondacks to the west, is quintessential New England: fertile, picturesque, and positively aflame in fall, when maples carpeting its hillsides blaze crimson and gold. It's also a dream for cyclists: Vermont hosts the second-smallest population of any US state, and its gently undulating back roads are suitably quiet, punctuated by friendly villages where historical inns offer toothsome hospitality.

To cherry-pick the area's highlights—photogenic bridges, perky market towns, waterfalls, glittering Lake Champlain—take a roughly triangular tour through Addison County. Pedal away from the Victorian clapboard houses of Brandon and roll north through leafy landscapes toward the historic towns of Middlebury and Vergennes, before pootling south to bijou Shoreham. From there, it's a pleasantly meandering ride east back to Brandon or—if you've been entranced by New England's charm—simply choose another maple-lined road and keep going.

3

East Bay Bike Path

LOCATION US **START/FINISH** Providence/Bristol
DISTANCE 14 miles (22.5 km) **TIME** 3 hours
DIFFICULTY Easy **INFORMATION** www.riparks.ri.gov

Coast through eight of Rhode Island's state parks and dig into its nautical history on this former railroad track turned multiuse waterfront path.

The East Bay Bike Path certainly packs in more than its mileage would suggest. Snaking through the heart of America's smallest state, the tranquil route around Rhode Island covers a disused railroad that once connected Bristol and Providence. Today, it flanks waterfronts formerly known as manufacturing, shipbuilding, and shipping hubs, plus plentiful green spaces often frequented by squirrels, rabbits, and opossums; lucky cyclists may even spot turtles, deer, or coyotes.

Although doable in a three-hour jaunt, the path is separated into four very manageable chunks of between 2.5 and 4 miles (4 and 6.5 km) each. Highlights include the bird haven of Squantum Woods, halfway between India Point Park and Riverside Square; the views to Rumstick Point; and the Crescent Park Carousel, an 1895 hand-carved amusement ride listed on the National Register of Historic Places. During a joyous afternoon spent wildlife spotting and railroad following, you're going to need refreshments, too—be sure to stop off at Del's in Warren for an iced lemonade.

another way

For a shorter ride, opt for the 4-mile (6 km) section of the East Bay Bike Path that runs between Warren and Bristol, taking in Rhode Island's southern chunk.

Cycling to Providence, Rhode Island, on the East Bay Bike Path

The Overseas Heritage Trail, stretching down to Key West

UNITED STATES
Biscayne Bay
Florida Bay
Key Largo
Key West
DAWDLE on the quiet and sociable car-free water crossing of **Long Key Bridge**
SAMPLE local fish on a tiki bar's wooden verandah by the water's edge
CELEBRATE the end of your ride with a sunny photo-op at the **Southernmost Point Buoy**
SEE the sea stretch to the horizon in every direction at **Seven Mile Bridge**
ENJOY the warm, clear waters with a swim, paddleboard, or dive

90 Miles to CUBA
SOUTHERNMOST POINT
CONTINENTAL U.S.A.
KEY WEST, FL

4

Overseas Heritage Trail

LOCATION US **START/FINISH** Key Largo/Key West **DISTANCE** 107 miles (172 km) **TIME** 2–4 days **DIFFICULTY** Easy **INFORMATION** www.visitflorida.com

Turquoise waters, pristine beaches, and refreshing ocean breezes: island-hop the tropical beauty of the Florida Keys on an old train line to reach the southernmost point in the US.

Tracking the route of the former Florida East Coast Railway, the Overseas Heritage Trail links together 50 of the islands that make up the idyllic Florida Keys. On it, you'll ride from Key Largo to Key West with the prevailing wind, often on smooth, paved bike paths that run parallel to scenic Highway 1, a sea-level route thick with palm trees. You'll cross seamlessly from one island to the next, traversing historical rail bridges that stretch over the languid waters. The most impressive of these is Seven Mile Bridge, an engineering marvel that makes it feel like you're cycling out at sea; unlike the drivers, you can stop, admire the view, and enjoy the cooling breeze.

Build plenty of downtime into your schedule; you'll be lured off the bike by mangrove-lined bays, seaside towns, and sandy beaches lapped by balmy waters. There are campsites for nature lovers, while luxury resorts offer a more pampered experience. Wherever you stay, there are plenty of opportunities for fishing, paddleboarding, and diving en route—and plenty of places to unwind, too, such as Islamorada's laid-back six-island village. But there's good reason to keep pedaling. At the end of the road lies the colorful buoy marking the southernmost point in the US, and Key West's promise of margaritas, conch fritters, and zesty Key lime pie.

You'll be lured off the bike by mangrove-lined bays and sandy beaches

UNITED STATES
CANADA
Owen Sound
TAKE a detour through Springboro and stay overnight at the 1815 Jonathan Wright Bed & Breakfast
VISIT Sydenham, one of the highest-populated freedom-seeker settler villages
LEARN about the railroad's history at the National Underground Railroad Freedom Center in Cincinnati
CAMP at Historic Blakeley State Park, where the last major American Civil War battle was fought
Atlantic Ocean
VISIT Rankin House, one of the very first safehouses on the railroad
Mobile
MEXICO
Gulf of Mexico

5

Underground Railroad

LOCATION US and Canada **START/FINISH** Mobile/Owen Sound **DISTANCE** 1,917 miles (3,214 km) **TIME** 1 month **DIFFICULTY** Challenging **INFORMATION** www.adventurecycling.org; best cycled in Apr/May or Sep/Oct to avoid humid summers and tropical storms

Cycle this historic path through woodlands and plantations and past heritage centers, along a route used by thousands of enslaved people during the American Civil War.

The Underground Railroad (UGRR) commemorates the network of routes that enslaved African Americans followed in their bid for freedom, both before and during the American Civil War. Beginning in Mobile, Alabama (where the last ship carrying enslaved people docked in 1860), and ending in Owen Sound, Ontario (the northernmost safe point for many freedom-seekers), the route zigzags its way across major areas of historical significance, alongside small towns and reborn cities.

Start as you mean to go on, slowly exploring the lush greenways of coastal Alabama and historic sites like Historic Blakely State Park, which precede the swathes of Civil War history soon to follow in Tennessee and Kentucky. On approaching the UGRR hotbed of the Ohio River, you'll reach magnificent Rankin House, one of the very first "railroad" stations. The homely generosity of John Rankin, a former slave-turned-ironworker himself, saved around 2,000 people. Former railroad lines like the Prairie Grass Trail in southwestern Ohio lead north to the Canadian border, where your journey ends in Ontario.

WHAT'S IN A NAME?

The Underground Railroad was neither a railroad nor some kind of tunnel system. It was given the name due to its network of people, homes, and businesses willing to risk their own lives and livelihoods to end slavery by helping transport enslaved people over long distances. Between 1810 and 1850, the UGRR led an estimated 100,000 enslaved people to freedom.

Above *The skyline of downtown Mobile, the start of the Underground Railroad north*
Right *An exhibition at the National Underground Railroad Freedom Center in Cincinnati*

6

Detroit: Back from the Brink

LOCATION US **START/FINISH** Michigan Central Station/Oudolf Garden **DISTANCE** 12 miles (19 km) **TIME** 4 hours **DIFFICULTY** Easy **INFORMATION** www.visitdetroit.com

It's not without a touch of irony that in Motor City it's now two wheels, not four, that rule. Having fallen on hard times following the collapse of its motor industry, Detroit shifted gears to embrace pedal-power, unfurling a network of cycle lanes throughout downtown.

Cycling through the city is a great way to see how Detroit has turned its fortunes around. Start at Michigan Central Station, a grand Beaux Arts train terminal that became the poster child for the city's blight but has since been transformed into a beacon of hope. It's just a few miles from here to Eastern Market, once home to Detroit's legendary techno parties; the ravers have moved out and been replaced with independent businesses, the walls of the former warehouses now splashed with street art. Finish with a peaceful moment on nearby Belle Island, where wildflower planting by a local gardening club serves as a love letter to the city.

another way

Another way to explore Detroit is by electric scooter, with the city home to plenty of rentals. Renting starts at a dollar; you'll need a driver's license to zoom across the city.

Folks enjoying the Chicago Lakefront Trail

7

Chicago Lakefront Trail

LOCATION US **START/FINISH** 71st Street, South Shore/Ardmore Avenue **DISTANCE** 18.5 miles (30 km) **TIME** 3 hours **DIFFICULTY** Easy **INFORMATION** www.divvybikes.com

For a city that bristles with skyscrapers and rumbles with trains, there's a surprising amount of wilderness in Chicago. And the Windy City's greenest spots are best reached on two wheels. The emerald in the crown of its network of cycle lanes is the Chicago Lakefront Trail, a paved path that hugs the shore of Lake Michigan. For most of its length, there's a dedicated cycling lane, well separated from the roar of Highway 41.

You could zip along the entire route in an hour and a half, but it's well worth spinning out the journey, pausing to enjoy the lake and city views along the way. For nature enthusiasts, the southern section is a treat; you'll pedal past leafy reserves that provide sanctuary for plants, animals, and migrating birds.

8

Paul Bunyan Trail

LOCATION US **START/FINISH** Brainerd/Bemidji **DISTANCE** 120 miles (180 km) **TIME** 2–3 days **DIFFICULTY** Easy **INFORMATION** www.paulbunyantrail.com

Seasons are intense in rural Minnesota—in winter, you need a snowmobile, not a bike. But for the rest of the year, the 120 flat, lavishly bridged miles (180-odd km) of the Paul Bunyan Trail offer the leisure cyclist a nature show. The car-free trail is named after a mythical giant lumberjack, a folk hero of America's logging camps, who is celebrated in statues that pop up between the dozen small towns that line the route.

Spring is a fine time to hit this saunter through tranquil lake and forest scenery, when the trailside is strewn with bright daisies, buttercups, roses, and columbines. Fall possibly pips it, though: the region, especially around the Brainerd Lakes in the trail's early stages, blazes with paintbox hues, and bracing evenings can be warmed by a shoreline hot tub in your log-cabin B&B. Summer can be hot, but tree cover offers shade. Countless lakes invite a cooling afternoon dip, too.

9

Prairie Spirit Trail

LOCATION US **START/FINISH** Ottawa/Iola **DISTANCE** 51 miles (82 km) **TIME** 1 day **DIFFICULTY** Easy **INFORMATION** www.bikeprairiespirit.com

A historic ramble through America's heartland, the Prairie Spirit Trail meanders through tallgrass prairie, farmland, and small Kansas towns where the populations number in the hundreds.

The trail follows the former Leavenworth, Lawrence & Fort Gibson Railroad, which was laid in the 1860s. Appropriately, it begins at the railroad's Ottawa passenger depot, now a museum, before taking you past rolling grasslands and over scenic bridges. Fields of wheat, corn, and soy are all around, and the tallest buildings are grain elevators. Take a lunch break in Garnett to admire the Romanesque Revival courthouse. Further south is the idyllic Anderson County Prairie Preserve, a tiny pocket of the kind of tallgrass prairie that once stretched from Texas to Canada. Home to prairie chicken (a type of grouse) and native switchgrass, this area captures the true spirit of the trail.

Lush expanse of tallgrass prairie, Kansas

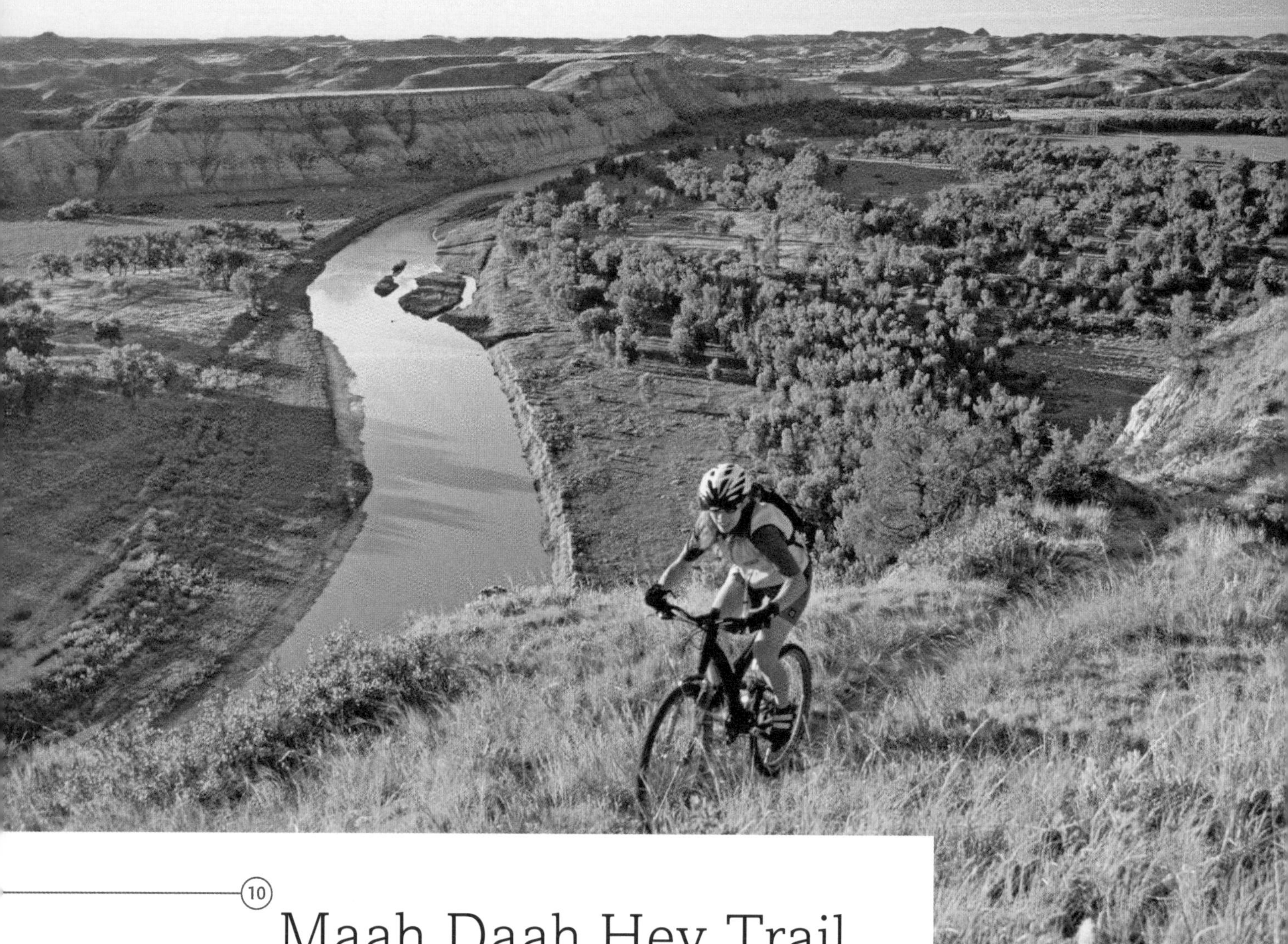

10

Maah Daah Hey Trail

LOCATION US **START/FINISH** Burning Coal Vein Campground/US Forest Service CCC Campground **DISTANCE** 144 miles (232 km) **TIME** 7 days **DIFFICULTY** Challenging **INFORMATION** www.mdhta.com; mountain bikes are not allowed in some areas of the national park

Even seasoned bikers will be challenged on this stellar route through the North Dakota Badlands, featuring otherworldly rock formations, immense drops, and Indigenous history.

Those who take to the rugged Maah Daah Hey Trail ride through landscapes lifted from a history book. Before the local Indigenous peoples were forced onto federally assigned reservations, this was their land. The trail formed part of ancient hunting and trading routes used by Indigenous peoples, including the Mandan, Hidatsa, Chippewa, and Lakota Sioux. Its name comes from the Mandan word for "grandfather," and the turtle symbols at every mile marker along the way are a Lakota

Above *Wild horses in Theodore Roosevelt National Park South Unit*
Left *Late-afternoon riding along the Maah Daah Hey Trail*

symbol that evokes determination, patience, and fortitude—all prerequisites for bikers tackling this challenging and lengthy trail.

Muster the might to take on the ride and your efforts will be thoroughly rewarded. This is your gateway to North Dakota's Badlands—an unfettered wilderness characterized by mushrooming hoodoos (thin spindles of rock that have been eroded into strange shapes), rugged hills, and wide-open skies. US President Theodore Roosevelt, who was famed for his conservation work in the Great American West, declared "It was here that the romance of my life began."

The official trail was completed in the 1990s, knitting together a bucolic patchwork of private, federal, and state lands, and then extended further in 2014: the addition of "The Deuce" section means an extra 50 mettle-testing miles (80 km). You'll slice through great swathes of protected grassland and sage brush; rush over color-splashed hills; and skirt the edge of plunging canyons on an epic journey from the South Unit of Theodore Roosevelt National Park to the North Unit. You'll not be alone, either; eagles and prairie falcons circle the heavens, while coyotes, mule deer, and white-tail deer prowl and lumber below. But while the scenery is mind-boggling, it does pay to keep your eyes on the trail:

Muster the might to take on the ride and your efforts will be thoroughly rewarded

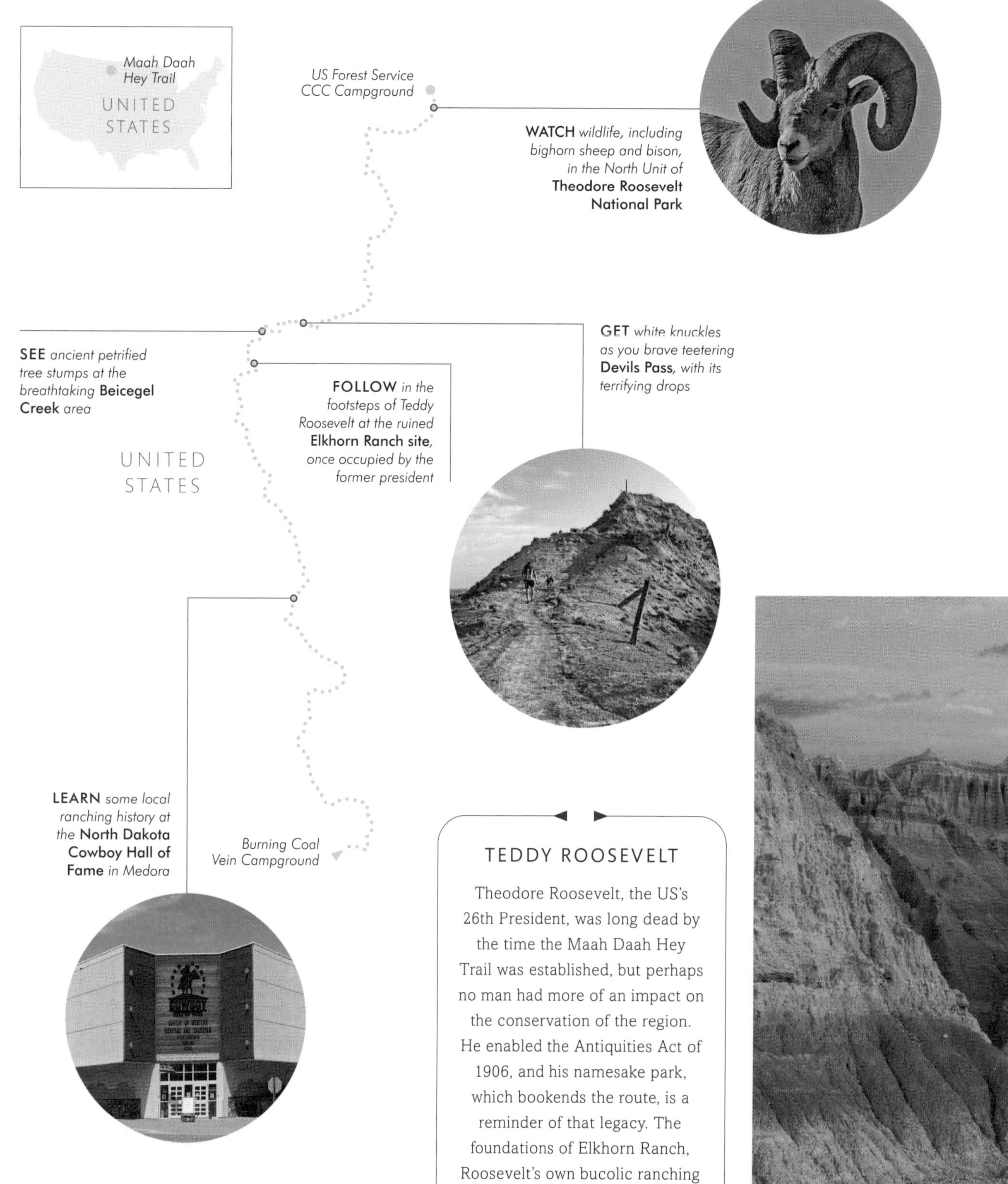
Maah Daah
Hey Trail
UNITED
STATES
US Forest Service
CCC Campground
WATCH *wildlife, including bighorn sheep and bison, in the North Unit of* **Theodore Roosevelt National Park**
SEE *ancient petrified tree stumps at the breathtaking* **Beicegel Creek** *area*
GET *white knuckles as you brave teetering* **Devils Pass,** *with its terrifying drops*
FOLLOW *in the footsteps of Teddy Roosevelt at the ruined* **Elkhorn Ranch site,** *once occupied by the former president*
UNITED
STATES
LEARN *some local ranching history at the* **North Dakota Cowboy Hall of Fame** *in Medora*
Burning Coal
Vein Campground

TEDDY ROOSEVELT

Theodore Roosevelt, the US's 26th President, was long dead by the time the Maah Daah Hey Trail was established, but perhaps no man had more of an impact on the conservation of the region. He enabled the Antiquities Act of 1906, and his namesake park, which bookends the route, is a reminder of that legacy. The foundations of Elkhorn Ranch, Roosevelt's own bucolic ranching site, can be seen along the trail.

the terrain is uneven and unpredictable and the drops are steep, sudden, and stomach flipping. Thrill-seekers will not be disappointed. Those who just want to dip a toe into the trail can make their base in Medora, a pint-size town home to the North Dakota Cowboy Hall of Fame—rustic lodges and Old West–themed hotels are plentiful in this Badlands bolthole. Otherwise, bikers can camp en route, pitching up at the primitive campgrounds that punctuate the trail.

Traversing the Maah Daah Hey isn't about checking off sights; it's about experiencing the landscape as the Indigenous peoples knew it, from thrusting crags to the snaking Missouri River. Still, some sections of the trail really sing. At Beicegel Creek, petrified tree stumps offer a window into the landscape some 65 million years ago. And then there's Devils Pass, probably the most famous, and terrifying, section of all. The narrow pass sets teeth chattering with its sheer drops—150 ft (46 m) of craggy honey-colored rock shooting toward the ground. No wonder the Maah Daah Hey is held up as one of the greatest single-track trails in the world.

another way

It is also possible to tackle the grand Maah Daah Hey Trail on foot or by horseback, in individual sections, or backpacking the whole thing. Horse-riders can also join the Maah Daah Hey Endurance Ride, held each year in June.

Above *Following a perfect ribbon of single-track*
Left *Sun rising over Badlands National Park in South Dakota*

11

George S. Mickelson Trail

LOCATION US **START/FINISH** Deadwood/ Edgemont **DISTANCE** 109 miles (175 km) **TIME** 2–5 days **DIFFICULTY** Easy to moderate **INFORMATION** www.gfp.sd.gov/parks

Winding through the Black Hills of South Dakota, the George S. Mickelson Trail condenses all ofthe Wild West's outsize lore, legends, and landscapes into 109 epic miles (175 km). The trail follows a converted rail bed, along which locomotives once moved freight, mail, and livestock—and the prospectors (and outlaws) who populated the frontier towns that popped up in the region's 1870s gold rush.

From the casino town of Deadwood—once the stage for mythologized figures like Wild Bill Hickok and Calamity Jane—the trail runs south, through colorful meadows and forests of towering ponderosa pine, and past burbling creeks and sprawling ranch land. The route also takes you through the leftovers of the region's gold-rush infrastructure: abandoned mines dot the hills, and you'll pedal through rock tunnels and over railroad bridges, some on trestles reaching high into the South Dakota sky.

WILD BILL HICKOK

Famed gunslinger Wild Bill Hickok rode into Deadwood in 1876. An avid gambler, he was seated at a poker table at Nuttal & Mann's Saloon on August 2 when Jack McCall walked up from behind and shot him. Hickok died holding two pairs: black aces over black eights, a series that ever since has been known as the "dead man's hand."

12

San Antonio Mission Trail

LOCATION US **START/FINISH** The Alamo/ Mission Espada **DISTANCE** 14 miles (22.5 km) **TIME** 3–4 hours **DIFFICULTY** Easy **INFORMATION** www.nps.gov/saan

This cycling trail connects all five of San Antonio's early 18th-century missions: The Alamo; Mission Concepción; Mission San José; Mission San Juan; and Mission Espada. Naturally, you'll want to be one of The Alamo's 2.5 million annual visitors: the historic 1836 Battle of the Alamo, where Texas sought to gain independence from Mexico, took place on this very site, and many original relics still remain at what is the state's most visited attraction. Then there's Mission San José, the largest of the five: the 300-year-old church, still with its original cloister walls, is known as the Queen of the Missions. Still, all five are worth a visit, and there are hundreds of years of history to explore on these varying sites of religion, battle, and siege. So soak it all in and pedal at your own pace.

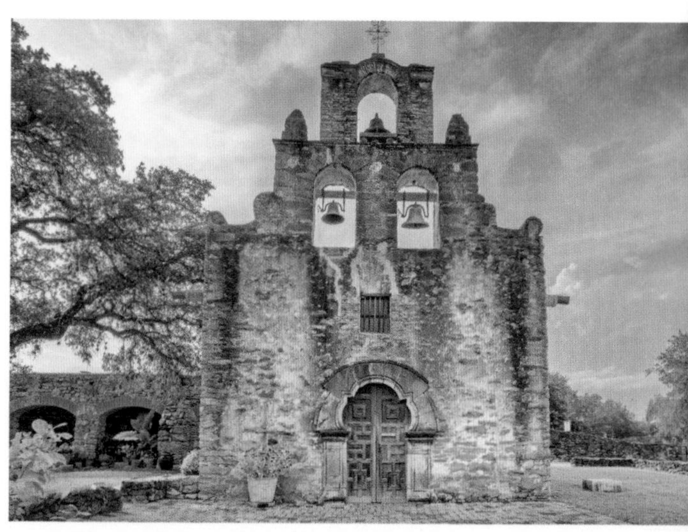

Mission Espada, one of five missions on the trail through San Antonio

Taking a break to admire the magnificent views at Slickrock

13

Iron Horse

LOCATION US **START/FINISH** Durango/ Silverton **DISTANCE** 49 miles (78 km) **TIME** 3.5 hours **DIFFICULTY** Moderate to challenging **INFORMATION** www.durango.org

In 1971, amateur cyclist Tom Mayer challenged his brother Jim—a brakeman on the Denver & Rio Grande Western Railroad between Durango and Silverton—to a race between steam engine and bicycle. Tom's two-wheeled transportation proved triumphant, and his feat went on to spawn the annual Iron Horse Classic, in which cyclists compete to beat the still-functioning steam train.

But you don't have to enter the race to enjoy this route. Just pedal away from Durango's meadows on Highway 550 and feel the screaming buildup of lactic acid over nearly 40 miles (64 km) of continuous ascent into snow-topped mountains. The rapid descent that follows may not be for the fainthearted, but it hurries you into Silverton, a mining town that has scarcely changed since the late 19th century. Look out for the old Iron Horse—a steam train from the original line—that welcomes you back to Silverton station.

14

Slickrock

LOCATION US **START/FINISH** Slickrock Parking Lot (loop) **DISTANCE** 10 miles (16 km) **TIME** 4.5 hours **DIFFICULTY** Challenging **INFORMATION** www.visitutah.com

This otherworldly 10-mile (16 km) loop around Utah's finest Navajo sandstone is at the arduous end of challenging, but the rewards are well worth it. Few bikers complete Slickrock glued to the saddle: you'll be taking on 2,500 ft (760 m) of vertical climbs, after all, so don't be too hard on yourself if you end up pushing your bike up a hill at times. First timers should head out on the practice loop to test their bike's suspension, but after that it's a several-hour rattle of twisting turns, impressive views over the Colorado River and across the Moab valley, and steep climbs up undulating ancient rock. There's not much letup here—even seasoned mountain bikers are put firmly to the test—but the sense of satisfaction that comes from completing a ride like this is unrivaled.

15

Greater Yellowstone Trail

LOCATION US **START/FINISH** Grand Teton National Park/Yellowstone National Park **DISTANCE** 180 miles (290 km) **TIME** 4–5 days **DIFFICULTY** Moderate **INFORMATION** Trail under progress; full prospective route available at www.pedbikeinfo.org/pdf/Map_Yellowstone.pdf

Though still a work in progress, the Greater Yellowstone Trail promises a spectacular ride. Pedal between two of America's most beloved national parks and beside mountain ranges, along abandoned railroad lines, and through wildlife-rich countryside.

Cycling beneath lofty peaks in Grand Teton National Park

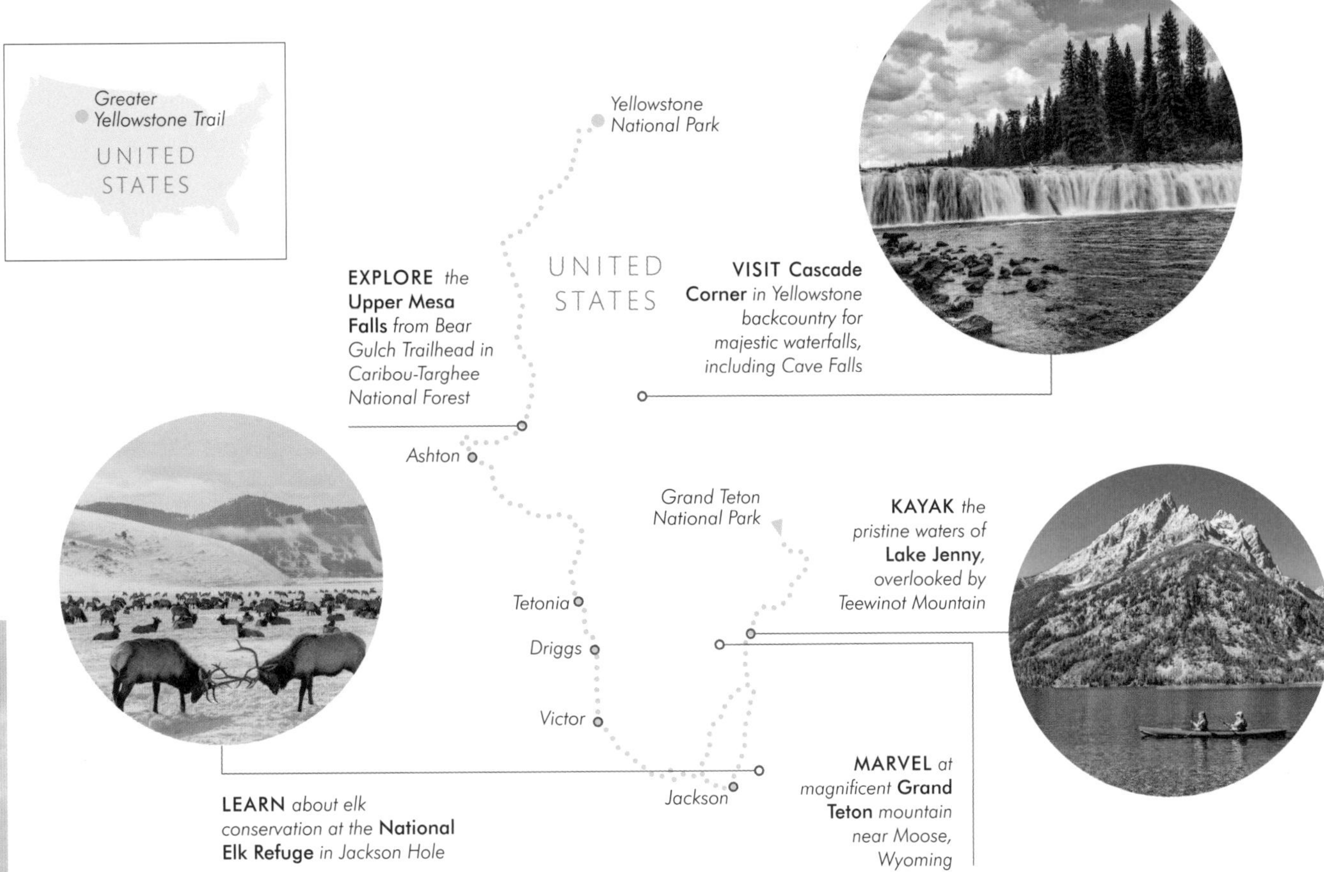
Greater
Yellowstone Trail
UNITED
STATES
Yellowstone
National Park
UNITED
STATES
EXPLORE the Upper Mesa Falls from Bear Gulch Trailhead in Caribou-Targhee National Forest
VISIT Cascade Corner in Yellowstone backcountry for majestic waterfalls, including Cave Falls
Ashton
Grand Teton
National Park
KAYAK the pristine waters of Lake Jenny, overlooked by Teewinot Mountain
Tetonia
Driggs
Victor
Jackson
MARVEL at magnificent Grand Teton mountain near Moose, Wyoming
LEARN about elk conservation at the National Elk Refuge in Jackson Hole

America's most ambitious cycling project yet, the Greater Yellowstone Trail (GYT)—which will connect two national parks (Grand Teton and Yellowstone), three states, three national forests, and one state park—is nearing completion. For now, though, cyclists can tackle many of the GYT's preexisting paved trails, which are gradually being stitched together.

For an insight into what the GYT will offer, get your pedals whirring on the completed cycle path between Jackson and Jenny Lake, Wyoming, a gorgeous 20-mile (32 km) stretch through lands home to thousands of elk. North of the tiny town of Moose, you'll be riding in the shadow of Grand Teton National Park's mightiest peaks: The Wall, Buck Mountain, and Grand Teton itself.

For a more challenging taster of the GYT, slip across the state line to ride the unpaved section between Ashton and Tetonia. The gravel can be loose and jagged on this 30.5-mile (49-km) stretch (mountain bikes are certainly required here), but the route boasts some of southeast Idaho's most stunning countryside, a hot spot for all sorts of wildlife, from deer to eagles. And you'll get to ride across several 1920s railroad trestle bridges for good measure.

More than anything, though, these two trails serve as teasers for what promises to be one of the finest multiday rides in the US. They'll no doubt leave you wanting to return to the GYT, once it's completed, to finish the (incredible) job.

another way

An existing stretch of the GYT, the 15.5-mile (25 km) rail-trail between Victor and Driggs, Idaho, runs along a former Union Pacific line. Don't miss the Spud Drive-in, an outdoor movie theater operating since 1953 with a huge potato truck.

16

Trail of the Coeur d'Alenes

LOCATION US **START/FINISH** Mullan/Plummer **DISTANCE** 73 miles (118 km) **TIME** 2–3 days **DIFFICULTY** Easy **INFORMATION** www.visitnorthidaho.com

A highlight of the cross-country Great American Rail-Trail, this bikeway wheels through jigsaw lakes, prairie towns, and Indigenous peoples' lands.

The relics of America's faded Union Pacific railroad are never far away on this meandering rail-to-trail route in the Pacific Northwest. The former railroad is now part of the Great American Rail-Trail, which unspools from Washington state to Washington, DC, muddling from crooked mountain splendor to vermillion chain lakes via flyover bridges and panoramic trestles.

Stops on the Trail of the Coeur d'Alenes reveal the story of its namesake peoples, who continue to live on the shores of Lake Coeur d'Alene and who helped accelerate the trail's creation. The route also takes in historic mining communities in Silver Valley and prairie culture in Palouse, as well as the wild wetlands of Heyburn State Park, home to moose, mule deer, and muskrats. In the well-traveled US, this is a real opportunity to take the path less ridden.

another way

The Burke-Gilman Trail is a 18-mile (29 km) section of Washington state's abandoned Great Northern, Lake Shore, and Eastern Railway corridor. Highlights include Ballard (for fishing and ice cream) and Fremont (for bike stores and beer).

Stopping by the lakeside on the Trail of the Coeur d'Alenes

Left *Mountain biking above Lake Tahoe*
Below *Playing in the sparkling waters at Sand Harbor*

17

Lake Tahoe

LOCATION US **START/FINISH** Stateline (loop) **DISTANCE** 73 miles (118 km)
TIME 1 day **DIFFICULTY** Moderate **INFORMATION** www.biketahoe.org

It's clear why this route has been dubbed America's most beautiful bike ride. Tracing the sparkling shore of Tahoe, North America's largest alpine lake, it offers soul-stirring views and restful detours.

Shimmering coves and evergreen forests line the road around Lake Tahoe, which leads cyclists from Nevada to California and back again. This state-straddling circuit is big on views: the lake's dazzling blue expanse on one side of the road, razor-edged cliffs and sugar pines on the other.

Starting in Stateline in Nevada, the road heads southwest and almost immediately crosses over into California, wiggling between Cascade Lake and Lake Tahoe until a zigzagging ascent. Your exertions from the climb are soon rewarded by views of Emerald Bay, whose glassy waters look almost tropical against the rocky beach.

It's an easier cruise onward to turquoise Rubicon Bay and Tahoe City, with its pleasant beach and excellent spread of cafés, bars, and restaurants. The toughest climb is on the eastern shore, up to Spooner Lake. There's a park entrance fee, but it's worth it if you want to secure your bike and wander a while by the aspen-fringed shores. After all, you're only one more easy-going hour of cycling away from the finish line.

A cyclist approaching Golden Gate Bridge

(19)

Stanley Park Seawall

LOCATION Canada **START/FINISH** Eastern side of Stanley Park Dr./Lagoon Dr. **DISTANCE** 6 miles (10 km) **TIME** 1 hour **DIFFICULTY** Easy **INFORMATION** www.vancouver.ca

Encircling the entire periphery of Vancouver's most beloved green space, the Stanley Park Seawall is an absolute pleasure to tour by bike and affords spectacular views of the city and its surroundings. The paved, flat path first leads you by way of Brockton Point, home to a collection of eye-catching totem poles; as you pedal, look down to where the rocky shores meet the glittering Burrard Inlet, the depths of which are a known feeding spot for orcas. Reaching the seawall's northern edge, you'll come to the park's most dramatic view: Lions Gate Bridge, spanning high across the water to the North Shore, a region backed by sharp-ridged mountains. Third Beach, and shortly after, Second Beach, soon come into view, marking the end of the route, their sandy strips ideal for watching a peach-hued sunset.

(18)

Golden Gate Bridge

LOCATION US **START/FINISH** Fisherman's Wharf/ Sausalito **DISTANCE** 8 miles (13 km) **TIME** 1.5 hours **DIFFICULTY** Easy **INFORMATION** www.blazingsaddles.com

While some bucket-list rides require certain levels of skill or fitness, this pinch-me pedal across the iconic Golden Gate Bridge is a doddle. Beginning your mini odyssey at buzzy Fisherman's Wharf, you'll climb through Great Meadow Park (if you're on an e-bike, it'll make a difference here) before dropping down toward Marina Boulevard, where the famous landmark comes into sight. You'll soon be approaching the 1.7-mile (2.7 km) long bridge, in all its international-orange—and often misty—glory; don't worry about cars, as there's a specified cycle lane. Take your time and stop, where it's safe to do so, to admire the views. After completing one of life's shortest but most rewarding cycles, it's an open-road, downhill roll toward Sausalito, where you can finish up your ride "sittin' on the dock of the bay, watchin' the tide roll away"—it was in a houseboat here in 1967 that Otis Redding wrote the well-known song.

Pedaling along the shorefront in Stanley Park

Quails' Gate winery, in the Okanagan Valley

20

Okanagan Wineries

LOCATION Canada **START/FINISH** Kelowna/Osoyoos **DISTANCE** 77 miles (123 km) **TIME** 4–6 days **DIFFICULTY** Easy **INFORMATION** www.totabc.org; www.tourismkelowna.com

Watch out California: Sonoma and Napa Valley have a new rival. Located in the Southern Interior of British Columbia, the Okanagan Valley is home to 200-plus wineries, making it the most planted region in western Canada. It's also a scenic journey just to get here, traveling through the Thompson and Fraser valleys, where the terroir is so diverse that it's like going from Bordeaux to Burgundy to Champagne.

Most bike rides start in Kelowna at one of the region's big three wineries: Mission Hill, Summerhill Pyramid, or Quails' Gate (a favorite of former US President Barack Obama). From there, it's a southerly ride toward fruit towns Penticton, Oliver, and, finally, Osoyoos on the US border. Tasting stops could include Phantom Creek, Hidden Terrace, Burrowing Owl, Tantalus, and Covert Farms; temper your plan with stays at roadside winery guesthouses along the way.

21

Confederation Trail

LOCATION Canada **START/FINISH** Tignish/Elmira **DISTANCE** 170 miles (274 km) **TIME** 1 week **DIFFICULTY** Easy **INFORMATION** www.tourismpei.com

Built on the former PEI Railway corridor between Tignish and Elmira, the Confederation Trail draws thousands of cyclists to Canada's smallest province each year. Why? The easy riding, for one; the trail is well maintained and signed, and the gradient rarely exceeds 2 percent, which makes it perfect for beginner cyclists and family adventures. The serene setting is another—you can't help but tune out the world and tune in to the smells of spruce and pine, the distant lapping of the sea, and your own thoughts. Then there's the easy access to off-trail experiences. You can spend the morning pedaling and the afternoon trying your hand at clamming, walking among the rare parabolic dunes of Greenwich National Park, or gorging on chocolate-covered potato chips, a Prince Edward Island delicacy and the perfect post-pedal pick-me-up.

another way

For an easy extension, follow the 6-mile (10 km) branch trail down to Souris, where you can stroll along the boardwalk and visit the quaint seaside shops before hitting the beach at Basin Head Provincial Park.

(22)

P'tit Train du Nord

LOCATION Canada **START/FINISH** Mont-Laurier/Saint-Jérôme
DISTANCE 145 miles (234 km) **TIME** 4 days **DIFFICULTY** Easy
INFORMATION www.ptittraindunord.com

Pack your saddlebags and pedal your way along the "Little Train of the North," a route through the heart of the forested Laurentian Mountains.

The P'tit Train du Nord follows a former railroad line originally constructed in the 1890s for transporting freight and, later, tourists on their skiing vacations. A host of villages and towns developed along its tracks, but as cars rose in popularity, the demand for the train declined. The route was eventually refitted into the multiuse trail it is today.

As you ride, you'll weave through forests and cross pretty wooden bridges that span sparkling rivers. Other parts of the trail curve past placid lakes, with a slip of beach tempting you to set down your bike and dip in your toes. And just as you'll start to feel peckish, a quaint little tourist town will hone into view, its heritage train station converted into a gourmet bistro with sunny outdoor terrace. After finishing off a plate of poutine (fries smothered in cheese curds and thick gravy), the signature dish of Quebec, you can browse the local boutiques for vintage treasures and handmade crafts before setting off on the next leg of the adventure.

> You'll weave through forests and cross pretty wooden bridges

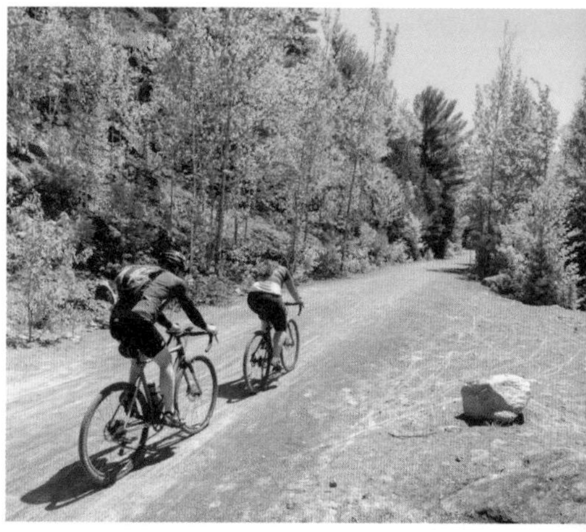

Above *Cycling the P'tit Train du Nord*
Left *Saint Joseph Lake, one of the many lakes in the forested Laurentian Mountains*

Spray rising off Niagara's famous Horseshoe Falls

23

Great Lakes Waterfront Trail

LOCATION Canada **START/FINISH** Niagara Falls/South Glengarry **DISTANCE** 536 miles (862 km) **TIME** 10 days **DIFFICULTY** Easy **INFORMATION** www.waterfronttrail.org

Stretching from Niagara Falls to the Quebec border, this route takes you past world-famous waterfalls, powerful rivers, and one very great lake.

You're never far from the water on this picturesque ride, which follows the opening section of the Great Lakes Waterfront Trail. Beginning at the iconic Niagara Falls, pause to feel the mist on your face before pootling alongside the wide Niagara River toward Lake Ontario. You'll spend much of your ride tracing the shoreline of this vast body of water, passing by Toronto's skyscrapers, an incredible 28 beaches, and biodiverse wetlands, where you can stop to spot beavers. At the mouth of the Rouge River, you'll bike up to bluffs overlooking Lake Ontario—from here, it's easy to see why the Iroquois called it the "Lake of Sparkling Waters." The last section of the ride tracks the St. Lawrence River, offering views of the emerald islands that rise out of its inky waters. As you roll toward the border, you'll find it hard to resist cycling the rest of the trail.

another way

Take a side trip to Toronto Island, just a few minutes from downtown. Hop on the ferry to cycle this pretty island's boardwalk and enjoy great views of the city.

A lonely road weaving through Baja California

24

Transpeninsular Highway

LOCATION Mexico **START/FINISH** Tijuana/Cabo San Lucas **DISTANCE** 1,060 miles (1,705 km) **TIME** 1 month **DIFFICULTY** Easy to moderate **INFORMATION** Lack of hard shoulders can be a challenge when traffic is busy (in Tijuana, Ensenada, and La Paz)

This bike ride through the desert landscapes of Baja California takes in beaches, Spanish missions, fishing villages, and cacti-studded mountains.

Like a long, bony finger extending south along the Pacific coast of Mexico, Baja California is an arid, isolated land traversed by just one road. Highway 1—aka the Carretera Transpeninsular, or Transpeninsular Highway—runs more than 1,000 miles (1,700 km) from the US border to the southern tip of Baja, where huge resorts loom out of the sand. There are few settlements along the way, and even these are separated by long stretches of desert, where only coyotes, vultures, and lizards venture.

The first section to Ensenada is the busiest—take some time to enjoy the fish markets, celebrated seafood tacos, and breezy promenade of this seaside town before cycling one of the longest, loneliest segments of the highway. South of El Rosario, the route cuts deep inland, a seemingly endless ribbon of tarmac through a dusty red landscape peppered with yucca, date palms, and giant cardón cacti, their huge trunks poking out of the rocks like spiky crowns.

At Guerrero Negro, pause your pedaling to take in some whale-watching in the nearby lagoons—hordes of California gray whales congregate here from December to April to give birth. South of here, the flat desert plains of Baja California Sur stretch to the horizon, but the emptiness is punctured by some of the most fascinating towns on the peninsula.

> Bahía Concepción's dazzling white-sand beaches are hard to resist

The palm-fringed oasis of San Ignacio contains a handsome central plaza and beautiful 18th-century Spanish mission, San Ignacio Kadakaamán, as well as a museum of Baja cave art—thousands of years old, these images of humans, animals, and mysterious geometric symbols were created by Baja's original inhabitants.

At Santa Rosalía, the highway follows the Gulf of California for the first time, far more placid than the Pacific. Santa Rosalía itself is an old copper-mining community, with a church said to have been designed by Gustave Eiffel and an old French-style bakery. Further along the Gulf coast, enchanting Mulegé is another oasis-like town with white adobe houses and an old Spanish mission, but the best section of the highway lies just beyond it: Bahía Concepción's dazzling white-sand beaches are hard to resist, its blue-green

Bahía Concepción, opening into the Sea of Cortez

waters especially refreshing after a long, dusty ride. Take some time to enjoy bone-white Playa El Coyote, or Playa El Requesón, a stunning sandbar poking into the bay. Loreto makes for another good pit stop, with one of the oldest Spanish missions in the region and some excellent restaurants.

From here, it's another long cycle through the desert, laced with dried-up washes and canyons, to the state capital, La Paz, where the traffic will come as a shock. You're nearly there; take the direct route through charming Todos Santos to Cabo San Lucas, the end of the line. Beyond the resorts and beach bars lies the majestic stone arch at Land's End itself, a jagged ridge plunging into the Pacific.

MUNCH *on the best fish tacos in the world in Ensenada's authentic* **Mercado Negro**

UNITED STATES

Tijuana

Gulf of California

SURF *the Pacific swells off the beaches of* **El Pescadero,** *just south of Todos Santos*

WATCH *majestic gray whales nurse their calves in* **Guerrero Negro's** *lagoon*

MEXICO

WONDER *at ancient cave art tucked away in the rolling hills near* **San Ignacio**

Pacific Ocean

Cabo San Lucas

EXPLORE *the beautiful 18th-century Spanish colonial mission in* **Loreto**

another way

For a real adventure, get off-road on the wilder Baja Divide cycle route. This slices through the deserts and mountains at the heart of the peninsula—it's 95 percent unpaved and is for experts only.

25

Hummingbird Highway

LOCATION Belize **START/FINISH** Belmopan/Dangriga
DISTANCE 53 miles (86 km) **TIME** 1–2 days
DIFFICULTY Easy **INFORMATION** www.travelbelize.org

Lined with lush orchards, towering mountains, and sinuous rivers, this humble thoroughfare is deserving of its reputation as Belize's most beautiful road.

In a country where cycling is the unofficial national sport, there's no better way to feel at home in Belize than when perched on a bike seat. And what better place to saddle up than the iconic Hummingbird Highway? Connecting the capital city of Belmopan to the Caribbean coast town of Dangriga, the road is named after the country's profusion of hummingbirds—if you're lucky, you'll spot some as you're pedaling along.

This is more of a quiet country road than a highway, lined by small villages and the simple delights of nature. Gently rolling hills make it easy to settle into a rhythm, so there's plenty of time to enjoy the scenery: sweet-smelling citrus plantations, the looming peaks of the Maya Mountains, and tangled jungle foliage. As you coast down the final section into Dangriga, some of the best beaches in Belize will appear on the horizon, the perfect finale to the highway's end.

BELIZE'S OTHER BLUE HOLE

The Blue Hole, Belize's most famous natural attraction, is a flooded cavern in the Belize Barrier Reef that stretches 410 ft (125 m) to the ocean floor. But it's not the country's only one. About 18.5 miles (30 km) south along the Hummingbird Highway from Belmopan lies Herman's Blue Hole National Park, home to a sparkling natural pool formed by a collapsed sinkhole.

Left *The Hummingbird Highway*
Below *A rufous-tailed hummingbird*

Cyclists tackling the bumpy track to Viñales

26

Havana to Viñales

LOCATION Cuba **START/FINISH** Havana/Viñales **DISTANCE** 112 miles (180 km) **TIME** 3–5 days **DIFFICULTY** Moderate **INFORMATION** Viazul buses (www.viazul.wetransp.com) accept bikes for a surcharge

Travel from one extreme to the other on this seldom-used back route, pedaling from Cuba's clamorous capital to the nation's rural west.

There's no greater showcase of Cuba's varied landscape and culture than on the short-distance potholed road between hectic metropolis Havana and bucolic backwater Viñales. The route splices together the capital's revolutionary monuments and spirited salsa clubs with a tranquil countryside of banana plantations and bird-rich hills.

Pedaling the little-trafficked coastal road gives you a window into a side of the country that few foreigners see. Leaving Havana through its leafy western suburbs, you'll travel alongside the glimmering Gulf of Mexico to Mariel, Bahia Honda, and La Mulata, before cutting inland to Viñales at La Palma. While most people take the direct A4 road, you'll be following a route that's backdropped by countryside *fincas* and oxen pulling plows through tobacco fields. The emerald-green end point of Viñales sits among karst *mogotes*, in a scenic area that's riddled with caves—and more bumpy cycle tracks that are just ripe for exploring.

another way

You can extend the coastal cycle by taking hilly but utterly worthwhile diversions inland. Pedal through the forest-clad mountains around eco-village Las Terrazas or visit the mountain resort of Soroa.

Above *Catedral de Nuestra Señora de la Asunción, Santiago de Cuba*
Left *Cycling the coast road from La Mula to Santiago de Cuba*

You'll share the road with locals perched on a range of oft-repaired bikes

CLIMB *the steps to the sunflowery* **Celia Sanchez memorial***—dedicated to a local revolutionary—in Manzanillo*
CUBA
STOP *for snacks and supplies at* **La Mula***, a ramshackle municipal campsite and resort*
HIT THE ROAD *at dawn to see* **Santiago de Cuba's** *energetic morning life*
Manzanillo
BRACE YOURSELF *for the short, steep hills of* **La Plata***, on the way to Pilón*
Santiago de Cuba
Caribbean Sea

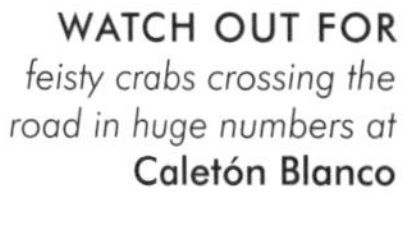
WATCH OUT FOR *feisty crabs crossing the road in huge numbers at* **Caletón Blanco**

27

Cuba's Coast Road

LOCATION Cuba **START/FINISH** Santiago de Cuba/Manzanillo **DISTANCE** 172 miles (278 km) **TIME** 1 week **DIFFICULTY** Moderate **INFORMATION** www.rutabikes.com

A world away from Cuba's resorts is this forgotten old highway, where bicycles rule the road. Ride between towering cliffs and a glittering sea, through isolated, welcoming communities.

Bookended by Santiago de Cuba and Manzanillo, this route leads through small-town and tiny-village Cuba, where visitors are rare, accommodations informal, and bicycles practically the only mode of transportation.

Most of the way is smooth, except for a few short, dramatic stretches of improvised dirt road. The middle section, from Chivirico to Pilón, is about as far off the beaten track as you can cycle without requiring a helicopter. Here, the coastal highway is impassable to almost all vehicles, but it's easily cyclable and for around 100 miles (160 km) you'll share the road with locals perched on a range of much-patched and oft-repaired bikes. There are no shops or stalls in the remote central section, but elsewhere roadside kiosks provide plenty of chances to refuel. Enjoy fresh sugar-cane juice, fruit shakes, and snacks—even cigars and rum, if you want to fully embrace the local lifestyle.

After the brief tropical twilight turns hot day into warm evening, family-run *paladares* (restaurants in private houses) offer comfort for aching muscles and empty stomachs. Expect heaped plates of chicken, beans, rice, and fresh fruit, and perhaps also lobster if you're lucky. You may be cycling beyond the back of beyond, but nowhere has ever felt such a home from home.

another way

If it's short, scenic circular rides you're after, base yourself in Viñales, west of Havana. Explore the lush landscape of tropical plantations, caves, lakes, and villages on largely flat country lanes that wind between pretty sugarloaf hills.

Steam rising from the crater of Soufrière volcano on the island of Guadeloupe

28

Guadeloupe Circuit

LOCATION Guadeloupe **START/FINISH** Pointe-à-Pitre (return) **DISTANCE** Up to 780 miles (1,256 km) **TIME** 1–9 days **DIFFICULTY** Moderate to challenging **INFORMATION** www.guadeloupecyclisme.com

Guadeloupe is obsessed with cycling. Its flagship Tour de Guadeloupe has been running since 1948 and sees semipro riders cover 780 miles (1,256 km) over nine days in August. The stages take in the forests, plains, and coastal roads of Grande-Terre island and the more mountainous terrain of larger Basse-Terre. It's not just about cycling, though—it's a cultural event that the whole island celebrates.

You could have a go at completing your own Tour, or settle for something a bit more manageable. Try a loop from Saint-François, taking in sugar-cane plantations, a 19th-century rum distillery, and the paradisiacal shores between Sainte-Rose and Mahaut before tackling the Col des Mamelles, one of the Tour's key climbs. Or if you're feeling brave, hit the road leading up active Soufrière volcano, which dead-ends in misty rainforest; with grades of up to 20 percent, it's a mighty challenge.

29

Double Rivers Waterfall Ride

LOCATION Trinidad and Tobago **START/FINISH** Brasso Seco (return) **DISTANCE** 7 miles (11 km) **TIME** 2 hours **DIFFICULTY** Moderate **INFORMATION** www.brassosecoparia.com

A pulse-raising ride through the rainforest-clad Northern Range is one of Trinidad's lesser-known charms. From Brasso Seco, a shaded track heads eastward, hugging the hillside, toward Double River Falls. Initially meandering through old cocoa and coffee plantations, the undulating trail offers tantalizing views of distant treetops. After crossing creeks and sliding through mud, you'll eventually have to abandon the bike for a hike, clambering over moss-covered boulders up a narrow ravine. But the rewards are well worth the sweat and gears: greeting you is an impressive cascade, tumbling into an inviting pool—just perfect for a dip. You might be sharing the moment with fun-loving locals or soaking up utter tranquility, broken only by the sound of birdsong.

30

Encarnacion to Iguazú

LOCATION Paraguay and Brazil **START/FINISH** Encarnacion/Foz do Iguaçu **DISTANCE** 215 miles (350 km) **TIME** 3–5 days **DIFFICULTY** Moderate **INFORMATION** www.trentobike.org

The dusty red roads, deep green fields, and long slopes of Paraguay are little explored, even by intrepid cyclists—but don't miss out. Forge your own path on this cycle between Encarnacion's touristy beach bars and Iguazú to the north.

The route is a blank rural canvas of an adventure, ad-libbing between the wide shoulder of Route 6's main road—where you can stop off at the atmospheric UNESCO-listed Jesuit ruins in Trinidad and Tavarangue—and dirt tracks that weave past remote farms and Indigenous communities. The route shadows the Paraná River all the way to the border with Brazil. Crossing over to Foz do Iguaçu, Brazil's service town for the famous waterfall, jolts you back to big-city globalization.

another way

For a quick and easy taste of cycling in Paraguay, rent a bike and roam Encarnacion's riverfront bars and restaurants—and maybe enjoy a sunset dip in the Paraná's clean, fresh waters.

31

Ruta de los Siete Lagos

LOCATION Argentina **START/FINISH** Villa la Angostura/San Martin de los Andes **DISTANCE** 70 miles (112 km) **TIME** 1–2 days **DIFFICULTY** Moderate **INFORMATION** Can close in winter

Taking you through Patagonia's idyllic Lake District region, the Ruta de los Siete Lagos (Route of the Seven Lakes) is famed as one of Argentina's most spectacular drives. But it's a journey that's even better by bike—this is scenery that demands to be pored over, and only on two wheels can you give it the attention it deserves.

Winding through two national parks, you'll be surrounded by breathtaking Andean vistas, complete with snowy peaks and crystal-clear rivers. It's an easygoing cycle, and there are plenty of opportunities to immerse yourself in the picture-perfect scenery, from a cooling dip in one of the mirror-like lakes—enchanting Lago Escondido is perhaps the most beautiful—to a hike through rainforest chiming with birdsong. Taking it slow has never been more appealing.

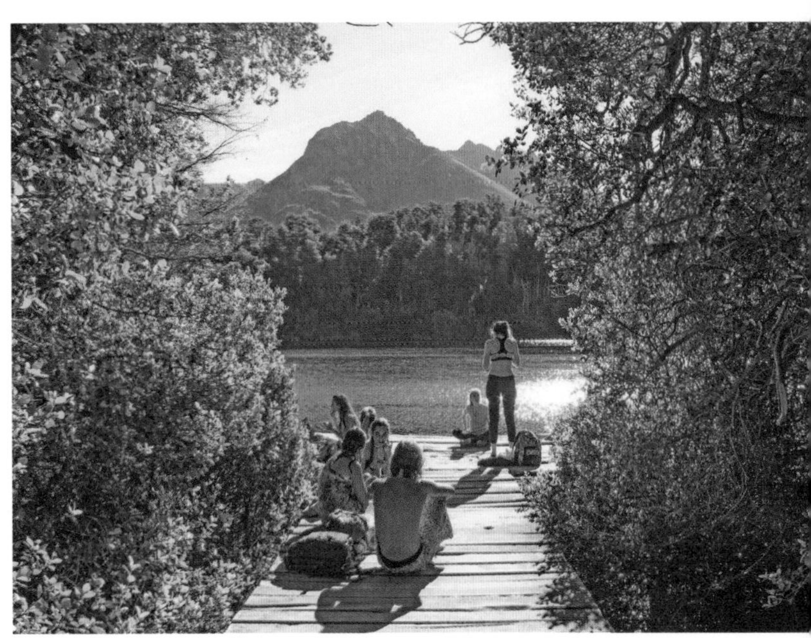

Soaking up the view at Lago Escondido on the Ruta de los Siete Lagos

The winding service road up to Valle Nevado

32

Valle Nevado

LOCATION Chile **START/FINISH** Santiago (return) **DISTANCE** 80 miles (130 km) **TIME** 7–10 hours **DIFFICULTY** Challenging; very long 8,000 ft (2,500 m) climb to altitude **INFORMATION** www.pedalnorth.com/valle-nevado-chile

This is one of the world's greatest cycling roads, featuring 58 hairpins and mighty views of Aconcagua, plus a mammoth descent back down to Santiago.

The service road up to the resort of Valle Nevado (Snowy Valley) offers cyclists an extraordinary mountain-climbing experience. It's busy with ski traffic in winter, so come between October and April to enjoy this serpentine ride to the max.

The long haul begins at the eastern city limits of Lo Barnechea. The first half of the route tracks a river valley, after which the tarmac zigzags up the sides of endless brown, cactus-strewn foothills. It's all on a grand scale, with the Andes looming ahead: Aconcagua, the Americas' highest peak, fills the sky. As the air thins out, pause for breath at the viewpoint, which looks down over three huge valleys. As you near the top, the ski center appears, high among the treeless, biscuit-colored mountains; mountain bikers utilize the lifts to push on even higher still.

Apart from a kiosk soon after the start, there are no facilities on the long ascent, so plenty of water and snacks are a must. Sunscreen and a jacket, too; it's hot, shadeless work up and a windy—but invigorating—ride downhill back to Santiago.

another way

The 29-switchback, 7,700 ft (2,350 m) descent down the staircase-like RN7 highway is an extreme cycling experience, vaulting the Andes from Uspallata, Argentina to Los Andes, Chile.

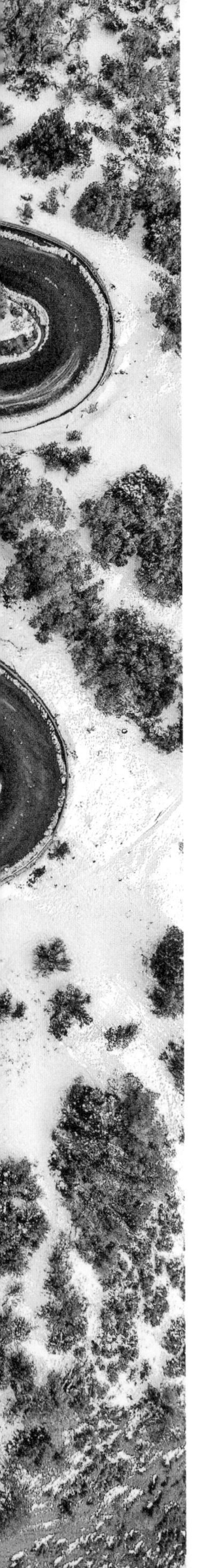

33

Death Road

LOCATION Bolivia **START/FINISH** La Paz/Coroico **DISTANCE** 40 miles (64 km) **TIME** 5–6 hours **DIFFICULTY** Moderate **INFORMATION** Make sure you are fully acclimatized to the altitude in La Paz before attempting the ride

Running from the altiplano to the steamy forests of the Yungas, the ominously named Death Road provides cyclists with a dramatic change of scenery.

Built by Paraguayan prisoners of war in the 1930s, the Yungas Road plunges from the high-altitude city of La Paz to the tranquil resort town of Coroico, which clings to a mountainside some 11,800 ft (3,600 m) below. In the 1990s, hundreds of people died in accidents here every year, giving rise to the macabre nickname Camino de la Muerte—Death Road. A bypass has since been built around the most dangerous segment, but intrepid cyclists (and many motorists) continue to travel down the original route.

The scenery is spectacular—a series of emerald-green hills—but your eyes must stay firmly on the road ahead. Some sections are just 10 ft (3 m) wide, with sheer drops on one side; regular roadside shrines tell the sombre story of those that didn't make it. A barrage of oncoming traffic, large potholes, and mini waterfalls splashing across the road provide further challenges, but the sense of satisfaction on reaching Coroico in one piece is immense.

THE YUNGAS

Coroico is the gateway to the Yungas, a transition zone between the Andes and the Amazon. Crisscrossed with ancient trading routes, the region is remarkably fertile—coca has been used by Indigenous peoples here for millennia. The rivers of the Yungas are also rich in gold, and myths about lost or hidden treasure have long drawn fortune hunters.

Cyclists carefully navigating Bolivia's Death Road

34

Trans Ecuador Mountain Bike Route

LOCATION Ecuador **START/FINISH** Tulcán/Cuenca **DISTANCE** 657 miles (1,060 km) **TIME** 2–4 weeks, depending on the version **DIFFICULTY** Challenging **INFORMATION** www.bikepacking.com; best Jun–mid-Sep

Flanked by nearly 50 towering volcanoes, the Trans Ecuador Mountain Bike Route crosses national parks and market towns on a sublime journey through the country's Andean highlands.

Above *Cathedral of the Immaculate Conception*
Left *Following a track in the shadow of Cotopaxi*

Following in the footsteps of explorer-pioneer Alexander von Humboldt, the Trans Ecuador Mountain Bike Route (TEMBR) comes in two versions. The original is tough singletrack; for hard-core mountain bikers. This friendlier alternative is on tracks and back roads, and, unlike its predecessor, is all very rideable.

Not that it's easy. The terrain is mountainous—the route isn't also known as the Avenue of Volcanoes for nothing—the weather can be tempestuous, the climbs are hard-fought, and the surfaces range from rural asphalt to cobbles to gravel. But you'll get to gaze on a showcase of both volcanic grandeur (conical colossi such as Cotopaxi and Chimborazo) and cultural vivacity (local markets are a technicolor hubbub of people, crafts, and intriguing foods). Dry season (Jun–mid-Sep) is the time to come, although it can still rain long and hard; there's a reason the land is so lush and green. Misty weather is magical, as rugged dirt roads reveal themselves elusively, rising and falling across the landscape like ocean breakers.

This is a ride of unique experiences. The off-piste is defined by *páramo*, the high, humid grassy tundra only found in Ecuador, Colombia, and Venezuela; while tens of thousands of *frailejónes*—a shrubby perennial—cover every square foot of El Angel Ecological Reserve, growing among tussock grasses 10,000 ft (3,000 m) up. As tall as people, and sporting velvet-leaved hairstyles, these characterful plants catch moisture in the air and feed it into the earth.

You'll gaze on a showcase of volcanic grandeur and cultural vivacity

Above *Llamas in the Andes near Cuenca*
Right *Climbers hiking up Cotopaxi*

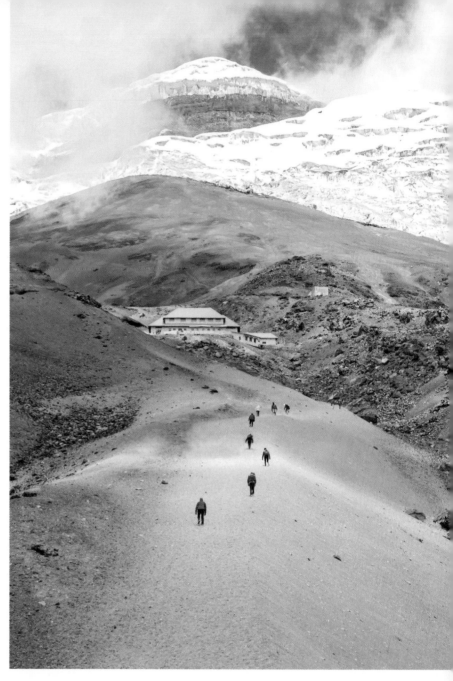

HUMBOLDT: ECOLOGICAL PIONEER

The phrase "Avenue of the Volcanoes" was coined by Alexander von Humboldt (1769–1859), the renowned Prussian naturalist who explored South America from 1799 to 1804. Humboldt's writings revealed the nature of the continent to European scientists. Inspired by his observations, he was a founding father of environmentalism and is credited with being the first person to recognize human impact on climate change.

Down in Ecuador's textile hub of Otavalo, the market is a vibrant parade of Quechuan handicrafts. Just don't get too comfortable in this inviting tourist hub; you'll soon be climbing out on cobbled and sometimes turfy back roads in search of Cotopaxi's perfect funnel outline. Towering high above the tree line, Ecuador's most iconic volcano dominates a national park that's speckled with delicate miniature flora. Its quiet and captivating wilderness gives way to fertile highlands around the emerald-hued crater lake of Quilotoa, where steep-sided hills are home to shepherds, sheep, and llamas, and patchwork quilts of quinoa and potato fields.

On the path to Chimborazo, the final volcano on your route, the small settlement of Salinas de Guaranda is home to thriving grassroots tourism and local independent businesses, including its own chocolate factory. The country's highest peak, Chimborazo is—thanks to an equatorial bulge—the place on earth that is farthest from the center. And also, therefore, closest to the sun. A high point, literally, to bring your ride nearly to a close. Cuenca awaits, its elegant colonial spires, domes, and colonnades providing the perfect grand-finale to the TEMBR experience.

another way

Los Tres Volcanes is a five-day, 258-mile (415 km) bikepacking route that connects Ecuador's classic sights: picture-postcard Cotopaxi; the impressive crater lake of Quilotoa; and lofty Chimborazo.

Pacific Ocean

COLOMBIA

Tulcán

BROWSE *richly colored clothes and textiles in* **Otavalo's** *daily market; Saturday's is biggest*

WATCH *daredevil climbers through the campground's telescope at* **Cotopaxi Lodge**

HIKE *the four-hour circuit of* **Quilotoa Lake,** *with its crater of awesome breadth*

ECUADOR

TRY *local delicacies and fresh regional produce at* **Guamote's** *super Thursday-morning market*

Cuenca

RELAX *in* **Cuenca** *and soak up the city's artistic and musical vibe*

PERU

35

Colca Canyon

LOCATION Peru **START/FINISH** Chivay/Cabanaconde **DISTANCE** 40 miles (65 km) **TIME** 1 day (one-way) **DIFFICULTY** Moderate **INFORMATION** www.peru.travel/en/attractions/colca-canyon

Ride through little-visited villages in an Andes-scale valley and, up top, enjoy dronelike views down the dizzyingly deep canyon.

The gaping Colca Canyon is a landscape of Andean magnitude, where everything either soars or plummets. Seasoned mountain bikers get their thrills on the adventurous off-roading and plunging freewheel rides in neighboring Colca Valley, but most everyday cyclists prefer the day-ride between Chivay and Cabanaconde, which follows gravel roads along the Colca Canyon's rim. The southern route is where the tourist buses go, especially early morning; opt for the quieter northern alternative, which passes through the old Spanish-era villages of Coporaque, Ichupampa, and Lari, with their elegantly simple whitewashed churches and pretty squares dwarfed by the surrounding hills. The ride culminates in a series of viewpoints, notably the Mirador Cruz del Condor, perched precariously above the canyon floor, where the massive birds of prey circle in the blue mountain air.

another way

The 500-mile (805 km) Cones and Canyons route from Arequipa is an extreme adventure for self-sufficient bikepackers. Ride mostly fair gravel tracks through vast mountainscapes, remote villages, and both the Colca and (even bigger) Cotohuasi canyons.

Views of the Colca Canyon from the Cruz del Condor

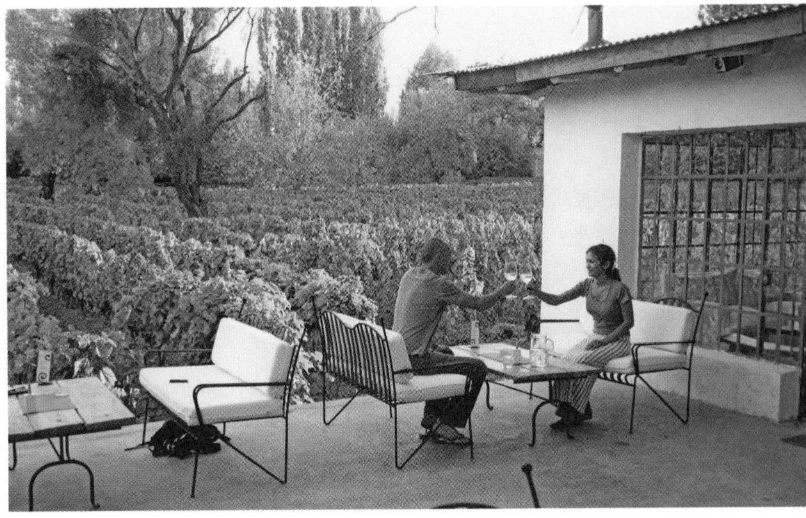

Above *Relaxing at a vineyard in Mendoza* ***Top left*** *The Andes framing Mendozan vineyards*

36

Wine Routes of Mendoza

LOCATION Argentina **START/FINISH** Coquimbito (loop) **DISTANCE** 5–15 miles (10–25 km) **TIME** 1 day **DIFFICULTY** Easy **INFORMATION** www.winetourism.com/wine-region/mendoza

Embark on a leisurely wine-and-dine trundle through Mendoza's vineyards, stopping to sample some of Argentina's renowned Malbecs along the way.

Most of Argentina's prodigious wine output comes from Mendoza, a lively student town and province of sunny, rolling countryside—the region is home to 800 wineries. Many are strung along the town's edge, at Coquimbito, where you can rent a cheap-and-cheerful town bike and make up your own spontaneous tasting tour. Dozens of wineries, from small family businesses to large commercial producers such as Trapiche and Trivento, offer tours, food, and tastings, many of them walk-ins.

Coquimbito's Calle Urquiza is a typical Argentinian suburban road, all straight lines and low-rise concrete houses, relieved by a separate cycle path. But running off it are quiet, tree-lined lanes, with endless rows of vines trundling across the terrain and wine *bodegas* only a grape-seed's-throw apart. Plan to stop at one or two to sit out on a shady terrace (no doubt with superb mountain views) and enjoy wine-food pairings that highlight Malbec's delicious soft, velvety plum and chocolate flavors.

MALBEC

The Malbec grape came to Argentina from France in the 1880s, but the different conditions in each country produce very different tastes. France's vineyards are on plateaux or modest hillsides and benefit from a moderate climate, producing a black-cherry taste. Argentina's Mendozan vineyards, meanwhile, enjoy year-round sun from their lofty Andean slopes or vast plains, resulting in chocolaty flavors.

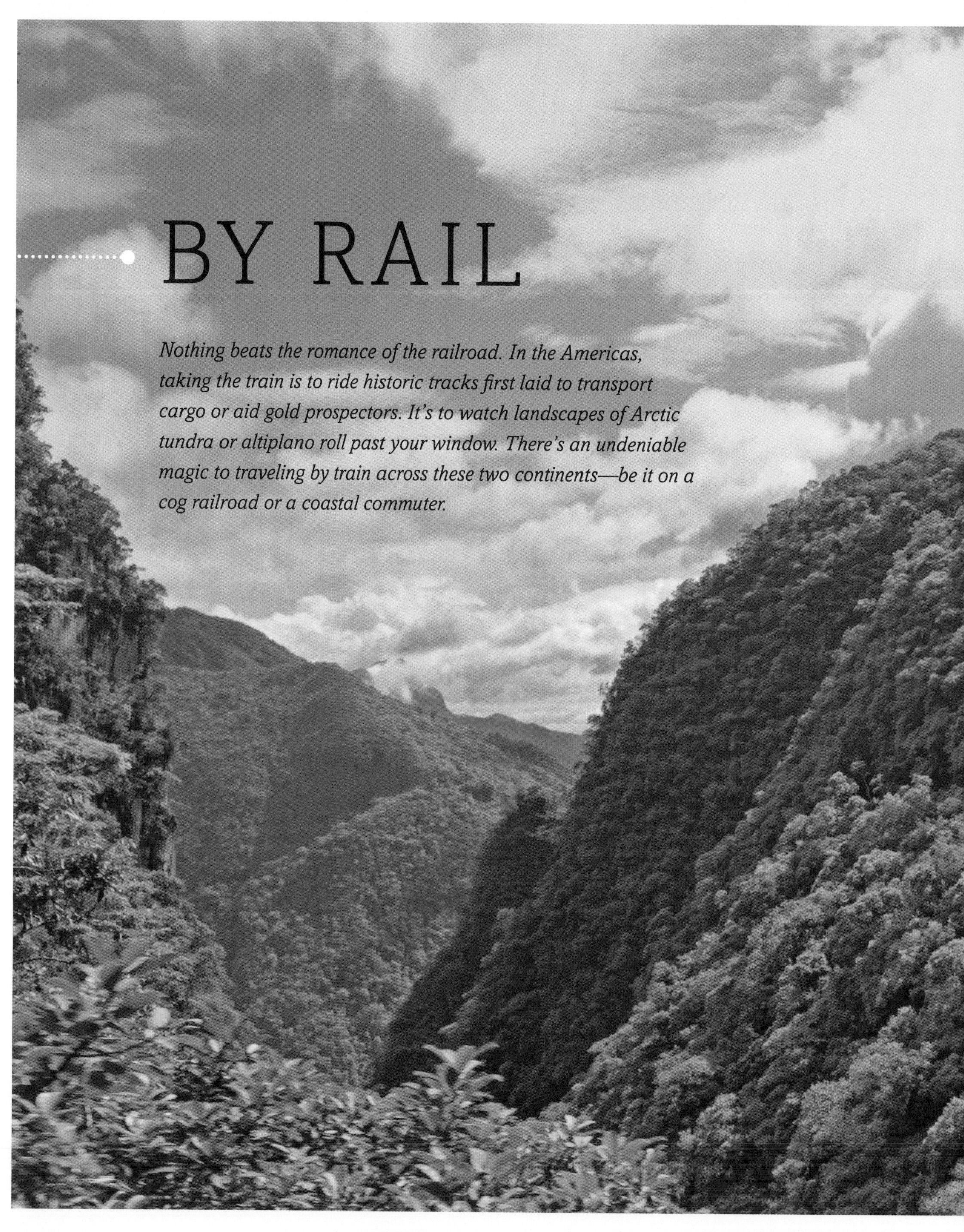

BY RAIL

Nothing beats the romance of the railroad. In the Americas, taking the train is to ride historic tracks first laid to transport cargo or aid gold prospectors. It's to watch landscapes of Arctic tundra or altiplano roll past your window. There's an undeniable magic to traveling by train across these two continents—be it on a cog railroad or a coastal commuter.

KEY TO MAP

.... Long route

• End point

Previous page *The Serra Verde Express trundling through Brazil's jungle*

AT A GLANCE

BY RAIL

The Denali Star Train, *running through its namesake national park*

1

Denali Star Train

LOCATION US **START/FINISH** Anchorage/Fairbanks **DISTANCE** 356 miles (573 km) **TIME** 12 hours **INFORMATION** Tickets must be booked in advance at www.alaskarailroad.com

Ride the rails through the remarkable landscapes of Alaska, taking in the views and wildlife-spotting from glass-domed panoramic rail cars.

The *Denali Star Train* between Anchorage and Fairbanks takes in some of the finest scenery in Alaska: thick boreal forest, yawning skies, and Denali itself, the train's namesake and the tallest mountain in North America.

Civilization is quickly forgotten on this journey. The suburbs of Anchorage melt away into a dark green blur of conifers, cut through by the cerulean sweep of the Indian River and dotted with occasional clearings where hardy souls have endeavored to build a life in a log cabin. They share these forests with moose, caribou, and curly horned Dall sheep (all of which you're likely to spot), black and grizzly bears (which you may catch a glimpse of if luck is on your side), and wolves (which will no doubt stay hidden among the firs and the ponderosa pines). The most spectacular sight comes as the train rattles over the Hurricane Gulch Bridge, a 900 ft (274 m) marvel of arched steel rising above a deep V-shaped valley smothered in conifers.

While outside is all wilderness, you'll feel anything but wild within your cozy car, sipping a complimentary drink and enjoying the sights as train tour guides bring this legendary landscape to life.

EXPERIENCE *summer's midnight sun in northerly* ***Fairbanks,*** *the train's final stop and your journey's end*

Fairbanks

UNITED STATES (Alaska)

DISEMBARK *in* **Denali National Park** *to admire Mount Denali, North America's highest peak*

MARVEL *at the ingenuity of Alaskan engineers as you cross the railroad bridge over* **Hurricane Gulch**

JUMP OFF *in* **Talkeetna** *to enjoy some mountain biking, skiing, or river rafting*

ENJOY *the fine seafood restaurants and world-class museums of* **Anchorage** *before boarding the train*

Anchorage

Gulf of Alaska

ALASKA'S BEARS

Alaska is the only US state where all three North American bear species exist and is home to 98 percent of the country's bear population. Brown bears, including the fearsome grizzly, live mainly along the southern coast. Black bears are much smaller and tend to inhabit forests, while polar bears roam Alaska's northern coastal reaches.

2

California Zephyr

LOCATION US **START/FINISH** Chicago/San Francisco **DISTANCE** 2,438 miles (3,924 km) **TIME** 2 days **INFORMATION** www.amtrak.com/california-zephyr-train

Slicing through the mythical landscapes of the American West, the California Zephyr *links Chicago and San Francisco by way of the awe-inspiring Rockies and the snowcapped High Sierras.*

Few train rides offer such natural beauty as the *California Zephyr*—almost every landscape on the continent is represented on its course through the heart of America. From Chicago, this not-to-be-missed train rattles first over the Great Plains and on to Iowa and Nebraska, plowing through an ocean of wheat fields dotted with red barns, grain elevators, and tractors. Expect mighty rivers, too—the train crosses the Mississippi on a rusty bridge south of Burlington, and the swirling Missouri at Omaha—and mountain sections that provide the route's most memorable views.

Above *The* California Zephyr
Left *Canyonlands National Park, Utah*

Beyond Denver, the train ratchets up the famous Big Ten Curve before diving under snowy ridges and snaking through the dizzying canyons, spruce forests, and cascading rapids of the Rockies' Front Range. The slopes of Winter Park, a major ski resort, are smothered with snow in the winter months, while in summer, emerald green trees stretch up to bright blue skies. The train continues down the Fraser River Valley to Granby, where it begins to follow the mighty Colorado River across the western slopes of the Rockies; as you trundle past Hot Sulphur Springs Resort, open the windows and you might detect the sulfuric scent of the springs, wafting in with the fragrant pine mountain air. The Colorado valley soon becomes narrower, slicing through a drier landscape of sparsely covered hills. Look out for whitewater rafters paddling below you on this rougher stretch of river. As the train glides west, the valley narrows further, the rocks becoming redder and more weathered, with crumbling mesas and buttresses rising high above the tracks. At Dotsero, the railroad begins to trail the I-70 Highway as it scythes along a deep section of the Colorado River into Glenwood Springs and out of the Rockies altogether. Beyond this beautifully sited spa town lies the arid deserts of Utah.

HELL ON WHEELS

Completed in 1869, the route of the *California Zephyr* was America's first transcontinental railroad. Its tracks were laid by a crew of immigrants, Civil War veterans, and formerly enslaved laborers, who worked in terrible conditions. Hundreds died, and mobile camps on the route were soon dubbed "Hell on Wheels."

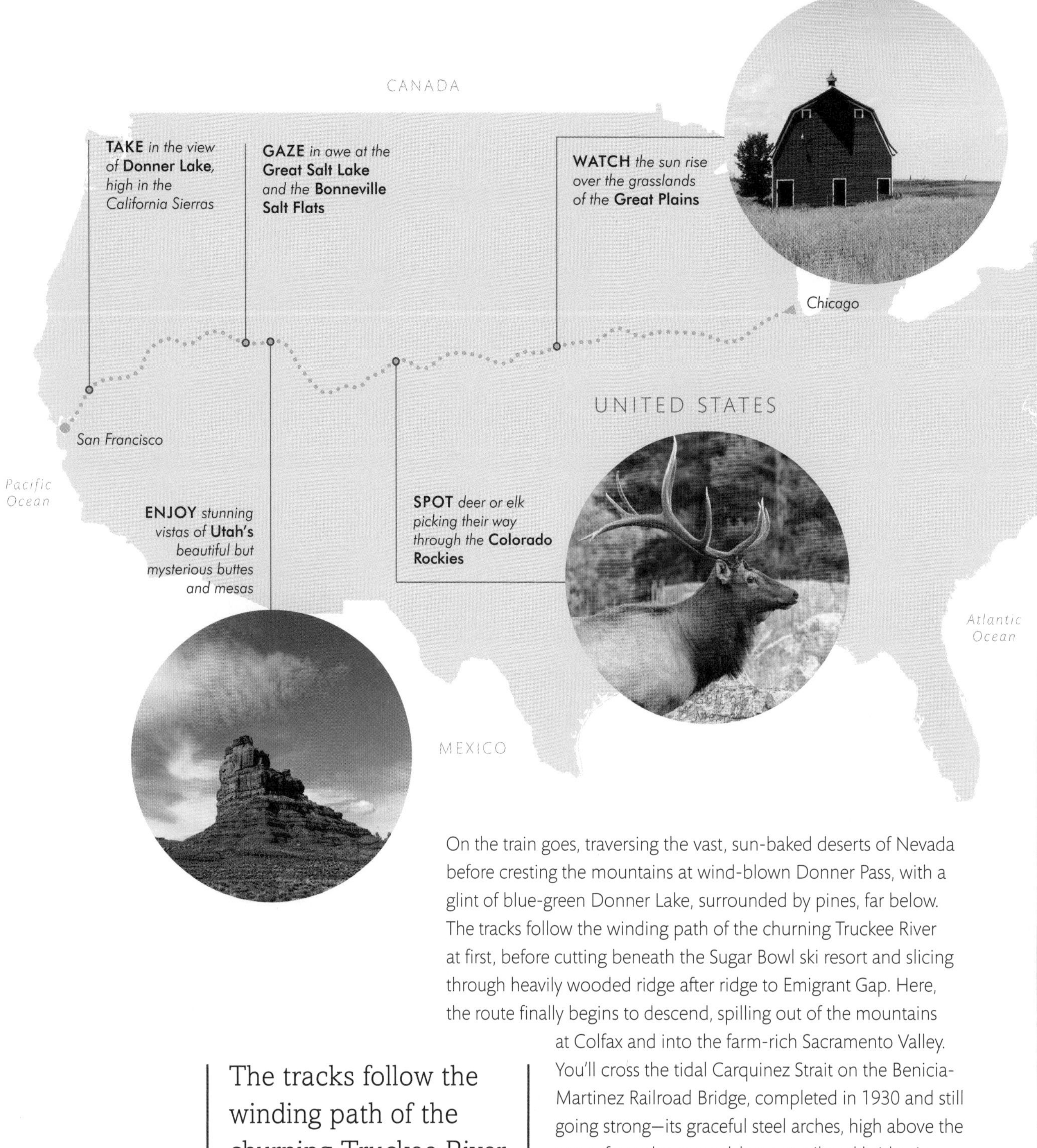
CANADA
TAKE *in the view of* **Donner Lake,** *high in the California Sierras*
GAZE *in awe at the* **Great Salt Lake** *and the* **Bonneville Salt Flats**
WATCH *the sun rise over the grasslands of the* **Great Plains**
Chicago
UNITED STATES
San Francisco
Pacific Ocean
ENJOY *stunning vistas of* **Utah's** *beautiful but mysterious buttes and mesas*
SPOT *deer or elk picking their way through the* **Colorado Rockies**
Atlantic Ocean
MEXICO

On the train goes, traversing the vast, sun-baked deserts of Nevada before cresting the mountains at wind-blown Donner Pass, with a glint of blue-green Donner Lake, surrounded by pines, far below. The tracks follow the winding path of the churning Truckee River at first, before cutting beneath the Sugar Bowl ski resort and slicing through heavily wooded ridge after ridge to Emigrant Gap. Here, the route finally begins to descend, spilling out of the mountains at Colfax and into the farm-rich Sacramento Valley. You'll cross the tidal Carquinez Strait on the Benicia-Martinez Railroad Bridge, completed in 1930 and still going strong—its graceful steel arches, high above the water, form the second-longest railroad bridge in North America. On sunny days, Mount Diablo looms in the background, while yachts and freight ships tack through the strait on their way to San Pablo Bay and the ocean. On the final approach to Oakland, the track edges around glistening San Francisco Bay, the Golden Gate heralding the Pacific beyond and this beautiful journey's end.

> The tracks follow the winding path of the churning Truckee River

another way

Amtrak operates two other transcontinental rail routes from Chicago: the northwestern Empire Builder *to Portland and Seattle via St. Paul, and the* Southwest Chief *to Los Angeles via Kansas City and Albuquerque.*

Right *Donner Summit Bridge, California*
Below *The dazzling colors of Utah's Great Salt Lake*

3

Coast Starlight

LOCATION US **START/FINISH** Los Angeles/Seattle **DISTANCE** 1,377 miles (2,216 km) **TIME** 2 days **INFORMATION** www.amtrak.com

This train ride takes in some of the US's most dazzling scenery, from the sun-drenched Southern California shoreline to the snowy peaks of the Cascade Range.

Leaving Los Angeles behind, the *Coast Starlight* traces the Pacific coastline for some 350 miles (563 km), scooting north to Oakland and, ultimately, Seattle. From departure in sunny Southern California, the passenger train passes by the mist-swathed piers of Santa Barbara and remote beaches at Jalama before heading inland to skirt the fields of lettuce and strawberries that patchwork between Paso Robles and Salinas. At Oakland, you get a tantalizing glimpse of San Francisco across the bay, before the train drives inland once more.

North of Redding, pine forests and snowy mountains fill the horizon, among them the giant cone of Mount Shasta—all the more impressive through the curved windows of the train's observation carriage. After a brief stop in Klamath Falls, the train twists its way through the heart of the volcanic Cascade Mountains. On the homeward run, it feels as if you're floating on Puget Sound, the inlet that connects Seattle to the ocean. Finally, fir trees fall away and the skyscrapers of Washington's "Emerald City" rise up ahead.

The skyline of downtown Seattle

another way

Take in the Southern California coastline instead aboard the Pacific Surfliner, *which connects some of sunny SoCal's best surf spots along the 361-mile (564 km) stretch between Los Angeles and San Diego.*

The Cass Scenic Railroad, chugging through thick Appalachian woodland

4

Cass Scenic Railroad

LOCATION US **START/FINISH** Cass Scenic Railroad State Park **DISTANCE** 11 miles (18 km) **TIME** 4.5 hours **INFORMATION** www.mountainrailwv.com; trains typically run Wed–Sun

Embark on an old-time journey through the Appalachian peaks on a charming vintage logging train, which trundles through woodland toward a rugged mountain summit.

At the turn of the 20th century, the village of Cass, founded by the West Virginia Pulp and Paper Company, ran on coal and lumber; in 1901, a railroad was built to haul timber from the thick Appalachian woodland to the mill in town. Fast-forward more than a century and Shay locomotives still rattle along the tracks—but now they are filled with wide-eyed tourists rather than the fruits of the forest, with logging cars having been converted into passenger space.

At just 11 miles (18 km) one way, the ride on this scenic railroad is short but very sweet. You'll ride through woods filled with spruce trees and drink in gratifying panoramas of the Appalachian Mountains as they unfold before you, bursts of ocher, orange, and marigold when fall takes hold. The final destination is Bald Knob, a summit of Back Allegheny Mountain and one of the highest points in West Virginia—from here, a sea of tree-carpeted bluffs ripples out before you.

The Grand Canyon Railway train sliding into a handsome wooden station

5

Grand Canyon Railway

LOCATION US **START/FINISH** Williams/Grand Canyon **DISTANCE** 65 miles (105 km) **TIME** 2 hours 15 minutes **INFORMATION** www.thetrain.com; advance booking essential

Vintage elegance, Wild West shootouts, and even a rootin'-tootin' cowboy band await on board the Grand Canyon Railway, an unforgettable way to take in the spectacular countryside that surrounds the US's headline natural attraction. Many visitors to the Grand Canyon content themselves with a brief stop to snap a few photos, but riding this vintage train from Williams, Arizona, promises a more diverse experience, as sweeping prairies, parched desert, and the pine and aspen trees of Kaibab National Forest flash by your window.

With different train cars modeled on designs from the 1920s, 1950s, and other golden decades of rail travel, you can choose your level of luxury. A mock shootout makes for some exciting entertainment before departure, while "cowboy" musicians serenade you along the way—by the time you arrive on the canyon's South Rim, you're fully immersed in the spirit of the Old West.

6

Durango & Silverton Narrow Gauge Railroad

LOCATION US **START/FINISH** Durango/Silverton (return) **DISTANCE** 90.5 miles (145.5km) **TIME** 9 hours **INFORMATION** www.durangotrain.com

One of North America's most historic railroads, the Durango & Silverton Narrow Gauge Railroad showcases Colorado's San Juan National Forest in all its natural splendor. You'll chug through gorgeous landscapes like the Cascade Canyon, a 15,000-year-old glacial canyon in Grand Teton National Park, and the Animas Valley, where native wildlife like buck deer and great blue heron thrive along its gushing river.

This is a real slice of North American history: dating back to 1881, the railroad is one of the continent's oldest. Yes, those vintage cars help make this journey a cut above your average train trip, but what truly makes it a unique adventure is the track itself. With a gauge width of just 36 in (91 cm), almost two-thirds of the standard size, this steam train takes sharper turns than a regular train, making for a thrilling ride.

7

Rockies to the Red Rocks

LOCATION US **START/FINISH** Denver/Moab **DISTANCE** 350 miles (563 km) **TIME** 2 days **INFORMATION** www.rockymountaineer.com/train-routes/rockies-red-rocks; route is seasonal

When it comes to otherworldly landscapes, the American Southwest rarely disappoints. Some of its very best Martian scenery is on dazzling display on this train journey from Colorado's capital Denver to the Utah town of Moab.

The Rocky Mountaineer has long-running routes in Canada, but this Southwestern odyssey represents the operator's debut foray into the United States. It is an itinerary that beats a steep, switchbacked path into the Rocky Mountains, whisking passengers past snow-dusted ski resorts and through soaring tunnels, before rocketing toward blazing red rock country, with a stop in a quaint mountain hot-springs city along the way. Expect dizzying views of the Colorado River and a feast of sandstone cliffs, with Moab the final flourish.

Glenwood Springs, on the Rockies to the Red Rocks route between Denver and Moab

8

Boone and Scenic Valley Railroad

LOCATION US **START/FINISH** Boone/Fraser **DISTANCE** 11 miles (18 km) **TIME** 1 hour 45 minutes **INFORMATION** www.bsvrr.com; operates spring to late fall, Thu–Sun

Trains have clattered along this Iowa railroad since 1893, when the line was used to ferry goods from coal-rich Fraser, eventually expanding to destinations such as Des Moines and Fort Dodge.

Passenger services began on the old line in 1983, and scenic rides now ease out from the pint-size town of Boone, rattling through deer-filled forests, vaulting across the Des Moines River, and finishing up in the historic mining town of Fraser. Bass Point Creek Bridge, a striking steel confection that soars 156 ft (48 m), was constructed between 1912 and 1913 and is still the star of the route—it shoots above the timberline, offering woodland views that are particularly impressive in the fall.

another way

If you're looking for an extra hit of adrenaline, eschew the train in favor of a rail bike. The motor-assisted, open-air vehicles grant riders unparalleled views over the Des Moines River Valley.

9

Mount Washington Cog Railway

LOCATION US **START/FINISH** Marshfield Base Station/Mount Washington summit **DISTANCE** 3 miles (5 km) **TIME** 1 hour 45 minutes **INFORMATION** www.thecog.com; summit shuts mid-Oct to early May

Offering an ascent up the highest peak in the US Northeast, this is the world's first mountain-climbing cog railroad.

In the 1860s, engineer Sylvester Marsh had a dream: to build a cog railroad up Mount Washington. It was initially met with disbelief: the terrain was steep (the railroad has an average grade of 25 percent) and the weather wild—Mount Washington has some of the world's worst, with volatile storms, battering wind, and thick snow. Marsh ignored the naysayers, though, and the first section opened in 1868, with the final vault to the mountain's weather-beaten summit finished the following year.

Fast-forward more than a century and a half and both biodiesel locomotives and coal-powered steam engines push to Mount Washington's dizzying 6,288 ft (1,917-m) climax. Along the way, trains cross the Ammonoosuc River and Jacob's Ladder, a high trestle bridge that marks the steepest section of the railroad. From the top, you can drink in views over the White Mountains, which fan out craggy and snow-dusted.

The cog railroad train, climbing up Mount Washington

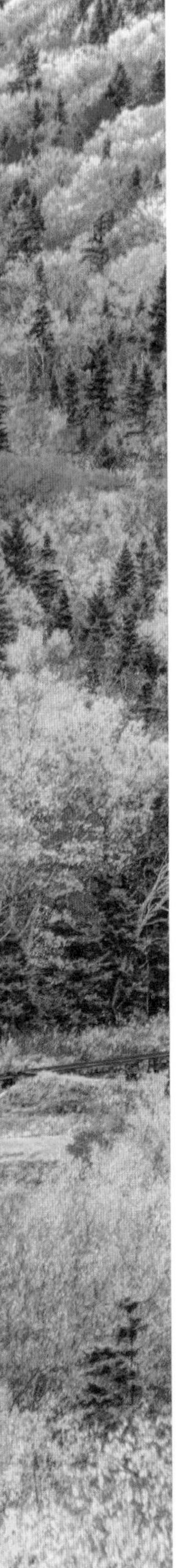

(10)

White Pass & Yukon Route Railroad

LOCATION US and Canada **START/FINISH** Skagway/Carcross **DISTANCE** 68 miles (109 km) **TIME** 1 day **INFORMATION** www.wpyr.com; open May–Sep

Blasted out of solid rock in just two years, this mind-blowing railroad forges a historic and scenic route through North America's wild northern frontier.

When gold was discovered in the Klondike in 1896, the hopeful fortune-hunters hiked in along the treacherous Chilkoot Trail *(p34)*, but between 1898 and 1900, a narrow-gauge railroad was built to make their journey a little easier.

Building a railroad through such inhospitable terrain was a challenge, however. The White Pass & Yukon Route Railroad features numerous tunnels and sharp, precipitous bends, climbs almost 3,280 ft (1,000 m) in its first 20 miles (32 km) and tops out at 2,864 ft (873 m) White Pass, which marks the US/Canada border.

You can still make this hair-raising journey today, but in comfy vintage train cars, pulled by steam and diesel engines. They leave from the Alaskan port of Skagway, hugging the mountainsides, snaking over high trestle bridges and chugging past pristine landscapes. Through the window, misty waterfalls can be seen streaming down the cliffsides, while blankets of wildflowers bloom brightly across the meadows and deer forage around the edges of mineral-blue lakes.

GOLD RUSH CEMETERY

Many prospectors didn't make it back home. Skagway's Gold Rush Cemetery, just north of town (and passed on the train), is the last resting place of 174 souls, most interred between 1898 and 1908. Inmates include local scoundrel Jefferson "Soapy" Smith, who died in a gunfight with Frank Reid (also buried here).

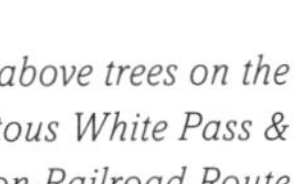

Skirting above trees on the precipitous White Pass & Yukon Railroad Route

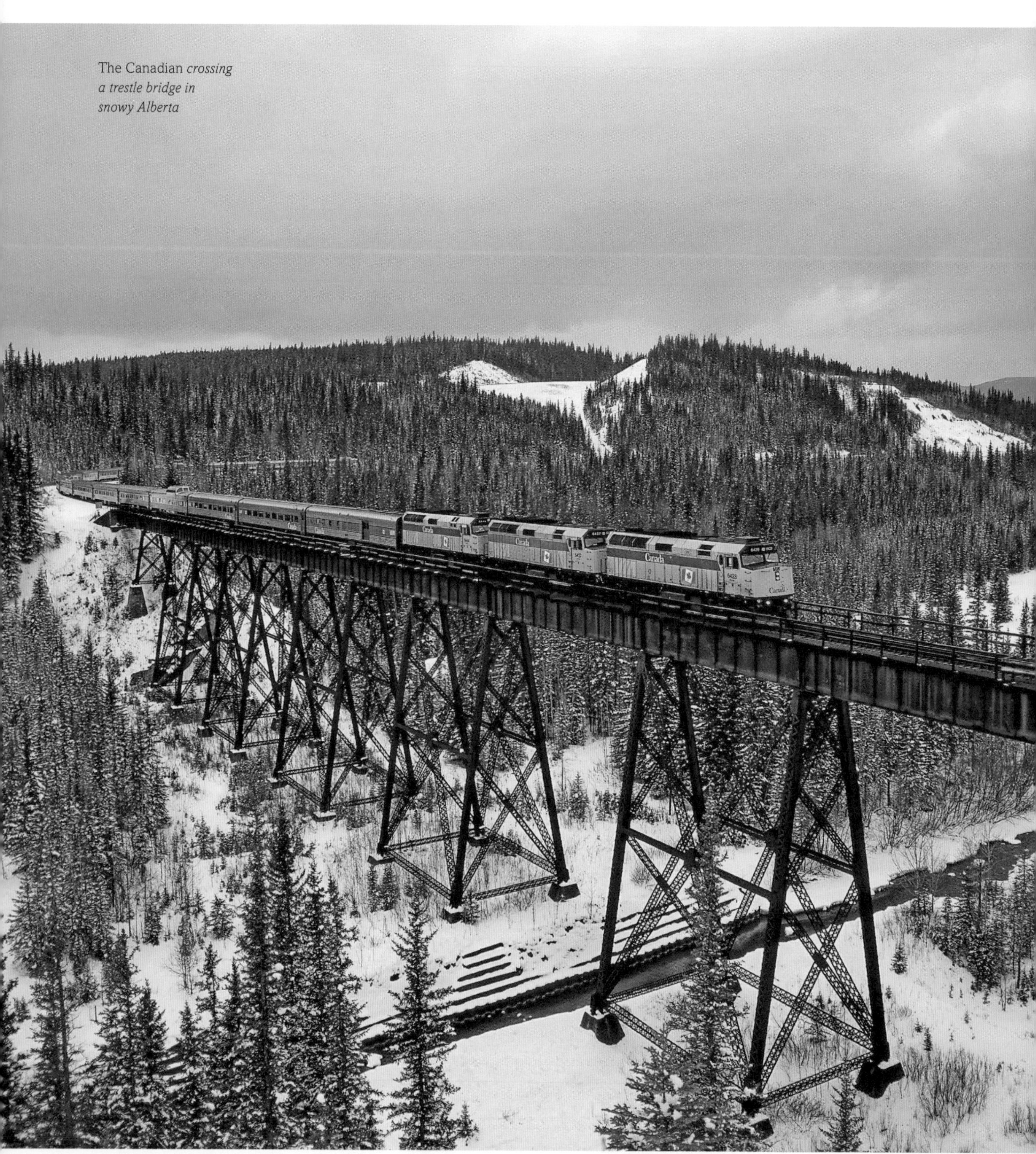

The Canadian *crossing a trestle bridge in snowy Alberta*

11

Canada—Coast to Coast

LOCATION Canada **START/FINISH** Halifax/Vancouver **DISTANCE** 3,945 miles (6,350 km) **TIME** 1–2 weeks **INFORMATION** www.viarail.ca; *The Ocean* runs thrice weekly, *The Canadian* twice a week

Travel right across Canada, from the ports of Nova Scotia to the wide Pacific Ocean, aboard epic long-distance trains and you'll be following in the rail-tracks of the country's pioneering settlers.

Railroads made Canada. More than simply a means of transportation, they were an exercise in nation-building, uniting remote reaches of this enormous landmass, linking the coast to the wild interior and proving that humankind could tame Mother Nature. Constructing them wasn't easy. Engineers had to figure out how to blast through the virtually indestructible four-billion-year-old rock of the Canadian Shield and how to surmount the Rocky Mountains. But figure it out they did. By 1885, tracks spanned the country.

Of course, First Nations peoples had been widespread across Canada for millennia. But it was the railroads that exploded the population, delivering arrivals from Europe and beyond to all corners of this fledgling country; between 1928 and 1971, nearly a million immigrants and refugees passed through the Pier 21 facility in Halifax, Nova Scotia, Canada's equivalent of New York's Ellis Island. Here, the hopeful new settlers were fed and processed before boarding basic cars or, if they were well-to-do, the fancier *Ocean Limited* service, to journey to their new homes. They would have had no idea what lay ahead.

It was the railroads that exploded the population, delivering arrivals

By linking together a few of today's VIA Rail trains, it's possible to recreate the historic continent-crossing trips of those early pioneers. *The Ocean*, as it's now known, leaves from the station near Pier 21 (now a fantastic museum) and heads south through Nova Scotia's forests, lakes, and Cobequid Mountains. It enters New Brunswick, stopping at Moncton—once the headquarters of Canada's Intercolonial Railway, which controlled services across the Maritimes—then crosses into Quebec, following the wide, whale-frequented St. Lawrence River and finishing in lively Montreal. It takes around 22 hours to cover this 836-mile (1,346 km) route.

To continue west, you'll need to make the quick train-hop from Montreal to Toronto (doable in about five hours), where you can pick up *The Canadian*. Running all the way to Vancouver, this is not just a train service; it's a window onto the entire country—quite literally, in fact, as its perspex-roofed Skyline cars provide passengers with uninterrupted views. It's a comfortable ride, too, especially if

another way

Those short on time could ride the Rocky Mountaineer *instead. The classic two-day route of this scenic train links Vancouver and Banff via Kicking Horse Pass, tackled by an ingenious sweep of spiral tunnels.*

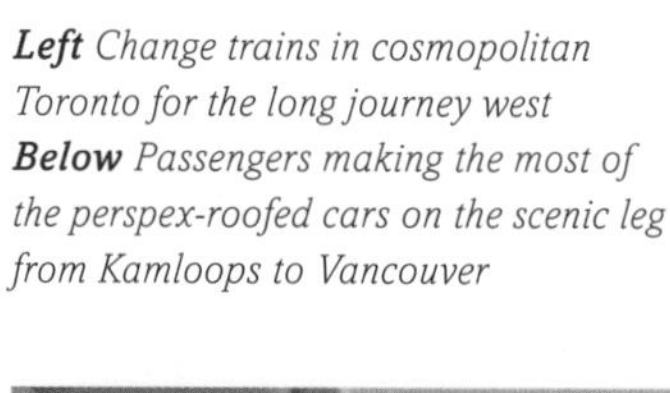

Left *Change trains in cosmopolitan Toronto for the long journey west*
Below *Passengers making the most of the perspex-roofed cars on the scenic leg from Kamloops to Vancouver*

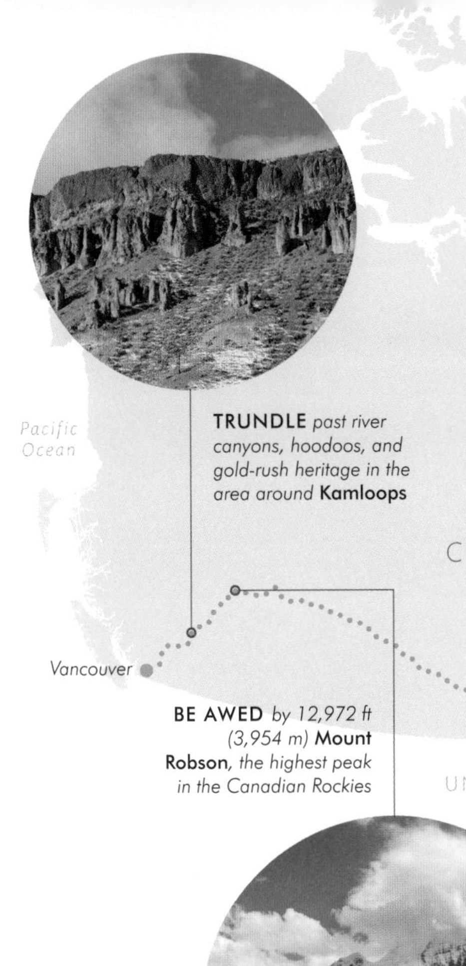

Pacific Ocean
TRUNDLE past river canyons, hoodoos, and gold-rush heritage in the area around Kamloops
STOP in Winnipeg to visit the excellent Winnipeg Art Gallery, home to a vast collection of Inuit art
DELVE into decades of poignant immigration history at Halifax's Pier 21 Museum
CANADA
Atlantic Ocean
Vancouver
Halifax
BE AWED by 12,972 ft (3,954 m) Mount Robson, the highest peak in the Canadian Rockies
UNITED STATES
GAZE UP at the glittering towers of Toronto, one of the world's most multicultural cities

you opt for Sleeper Plus or Prestige class, which include cozy beds, à la carte dining, live music, and wine tastings on board.

Traveling 2,775 km (4,466 km) over the course of four nights, the stainless-steel coaches of *The Canadian* pull out of Toronto and soon swap the city's soaring skyscrapers for Ontario's near-infinite sprawl of boreal forest, exposed rock, lakes, and rivers. The train traverses the flat plains of Manitoba and the waving grasslands of Saskatchewan, which are dotted with grain silos—the "cathedrals of the prairies." Beyond that is Alberta and, eventually, the Rockies. Suddenly, snow peaks seem to be everywhere. The railroad crosses into British Columbia at Yellowhead Pass, then descends to Kamloops and the dusty Fraser Canyon before finally reaching Vancouver and the Pacific Ocean: an inspiring end to the journey.

RIDING THE CANADIAN

The Canadian runs year-round. Timetables are planned so the scenery is excellent both ways, although riding east–west feels more in keeping with the spirit of those early settlers. It's possible to break your trip—in Jasper, say (for the Rockies), or Winnipeg (for more of Manitoba). Otherwise, the train stops long enough for a leg stretch at major stations.

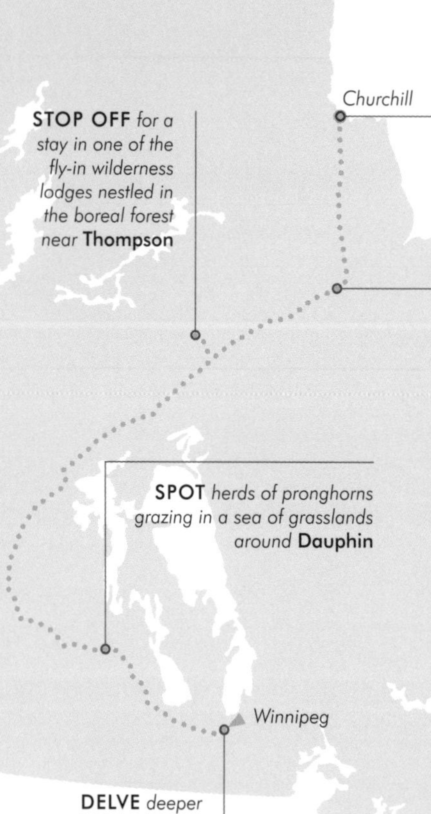

KAYAK *the shores of the* **Hudson Bay**, *home to beluga whales during the summer months*

STOP OFF *for a stay in one of the fly-in wilderness lodges nestled in the boreal forest near* **Thompson**

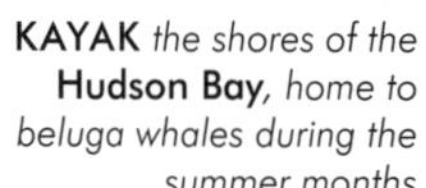

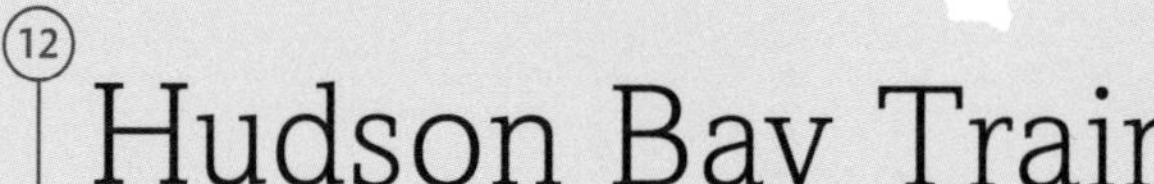

DELVE *deeper into the history of* **Winnipeg**, *which rose from strategic hunting grounds to modern city*
UNITED STATES

(12)

Hudson Bay Train

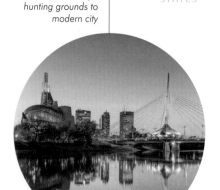

LOCATION Canada **START/FINISH** Winnipeg/Churchill **DISTANCE** 1,055 miles (1,697 km) **TIME** 3 days **INFORMATION** www.viarail.ca

Embark on a multiday rail journey through the stunning Canadian wilderness to reach a remote northern settlement where polar bears outnumber local residents.

Rolling along sturdy steel tracks that were originally laid over a century ago, the *Hudson Bay Train* was once solely focused on the transportation of resources such as ore, lumber, and wheat. While it still carries these vital goods today, the line also doubles as a passenger service to the otherwise hard-to-reach town of Churchill—the only other way in is by air.

Setting out from the city of Winnipeg, the train whisks you past the edge of the Canadian Shield before whistling through the vast, flat expanse of the Prairies, where yellow canola fields are occasionally punctuated by aging grain elevators. Day two brings verdant farmers' fields and clusters of small, rural communities, which soon give way to spruce and pine, icy creeks, and muskeg, a rugged land of swamps and bogs—and few roads. In the evening, spend time stargazing out of your car window and searching for a glimpse of the green- and purple-hued dance of the Northern Lights.

OBSERVE *the Northern Lights in the midnight sky after departing the outpost of* **Gillam**

SPOT *herds of pronghorns grazing in a sea of grasslands around* **Dauphin**

By morning, the forested terrain has transitioned to barren-looking tundra, which explodes with pink and yellow wildflowers during the short summer season. It's here, by the banks of the Hudson Bay, that the tiny town of Churchill sprang up. Disembark: a world of outdoor adventures awaits. Just don't stray too far from town on foot—you're at the fringes of the Canadian Arctic here, where the polar bear is king.

POLAR BEAR CAPITAL

Churchill is the so-called Polar Bear Capital of the World. The bears live out on the pack ice for most of the year, when tourists take to huge tundra buggies to spot them hunting for seals. During the summer melt, however, the bears come ashore—and Churchill is right on their annual migratory route. Bears that get too bold around town are placed in a holding facility (known as the polar bear jail) before being airlifted by helicopter back out into the region's wilder realms.

Above *The Northern Lights, swirling through the Canadian sky*
Below *A polar bear hunting on pack ice near the town of Churchill*

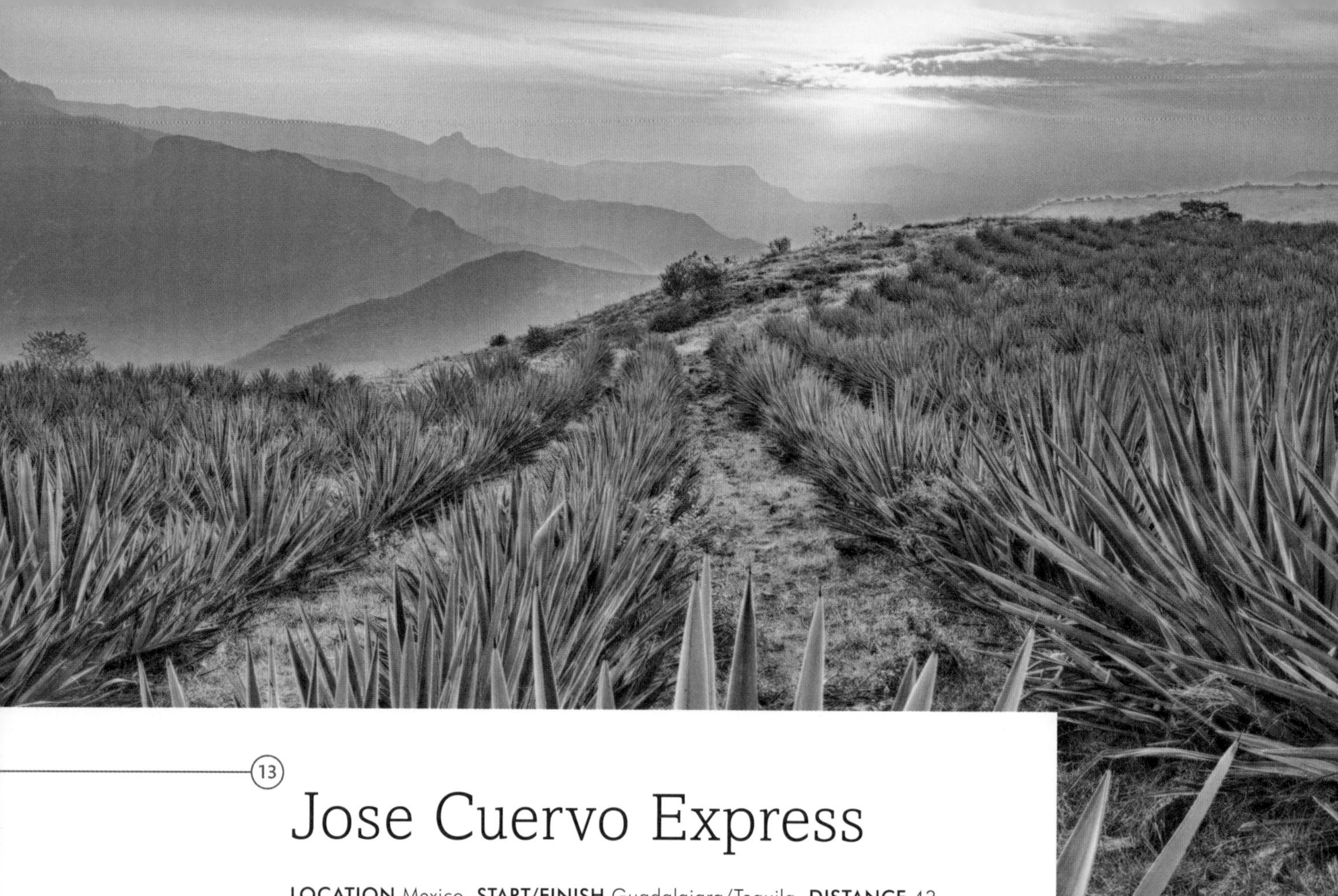

13

Jose Cuervo Express

LOCATION Mexico **START/FINISH** Guadalajara/Tequila **DISTANCE** 43 miles (69 km) **TIME** 1 hour 15 minutes **INFORMATION** www.mundocuervo.com/eng; tickets must be booked in advance

Ride the only vintage train in Mexico to the historic town of Tequila, enjoying mariachi bands and tequila tastings on board as you make your way west from Guadalajara.

If you enjoy a tipple, then the thought of visiting the Mexican town of Tequila—home of its storied namesake spirit—might feel more like a pilgrimage. The town is still the center of world tequila production and is dotted with distilleries, including that of Jose Cuervo, whose vintage train is the undisputed best way to get here in the first place.

The aquamarine leaves of blue agave—the spiky plant used in tequila production—sprout in vast fields from the red volcanic soil of Jalisco as the so-called Tequila Train barrels away from Guadalajara, Mexico's second city. Don't spend too long gazing out at the landscape, though—the view inside the train is just as beautiful, particularly in the premium Diamond car, where a gorgeous embossed metal ceiling, wooden fittings, and plush carpets evoke the golden age of luxury parlor train travel.

There's entertainment to be enjoyed, too, in the form of rousing mariachi brass music and *lotería*, a riotous Mexican version of bingo. And, of course, there's tequila. You'll have the chance to savor Jose Cuervo's range of spirits during an educational tequila-tasting experience on board, and, on disembarking, to take a tour of the distillery and learn how the vast, pineapple-like hearts of the blue agave plant are turned into a drink that is now beloved worldwide. It's worth staying a while in historic Tequila itself, famed around these parts for its colorful architecture and equestrian and mariachi traditions as much as its Jalisco firewater.

Above *Tequila tasting in the cellars at Jose Cuervo's distillery*
Left *Day breaking over a field of blue agave plants near the town of Tequila*

TEQUILA

Tequila is the local variation of mezcal, a spirit distilled from the agave plant. Tequila is made from blue agave, whose spiky leaves surround a succulent heart called a *piña*. These *piñas* are baked in brick ovens and mashed to extract their juice, which is fermented to produce a clear, "silver" tequila. This is either sold as is or aged in barrels to produce "golden" tequila.

VISIT *the agave fields outside Tequila for a demonstration by the jimadores, who harvest the spiky plant*

DISCOVER *more about the history of the town and the drink at the* **Museo Nacional del Tequila**

MAKE TIME *to explore Guadalajara's magnificent* **Catedral de Guadalajara**

TOUR *the beautifully preserved stone halls, brick ovens, and vast wooden barrels of* **Jose Cuervo's distillery**

SETTLE *into your journey aboard the* **Jose Cuervo Express** *with a tequila cocktail and some mariachi music*

14

Chepe Train

LOCATION Mexico **START/FINISH** Los Mochis/ Divisadero **DISTANCE** 194 miles (312 km) **TIME** 2 days **INFORMATION** www.chepe.mx/en

Leading into the heart of Mexico, the *Chepe Train* winds through the forested mountain valleys of the Copper Canyon. Leaving Los Mochis and the west coast behind, it ascends into the Sierra Madre; it doesn't take long to realize how the canyon got its name: the landscape transforms into a maze of show-stopping valleys, their slopes a copper-green riot of mountain and tree. This is train travel on a Hollywood scale; viaducts span yawning chasms and tunnels burrow through immovable mountains.

Jump off at the city of El Fuerte to roam the Iglesia de Dolores, the ruins of an old Jesuit church. Back on board, it's cameras at the ready as plunging valleys and hanging bridges pass by on the approach to the Divisadero viewpoint. The Rarámuri, an Indigenous group famed for their long-distance running, live here; keep your eyes peeled for the canyons they call home, where the Río Urique snakes to the horizon.

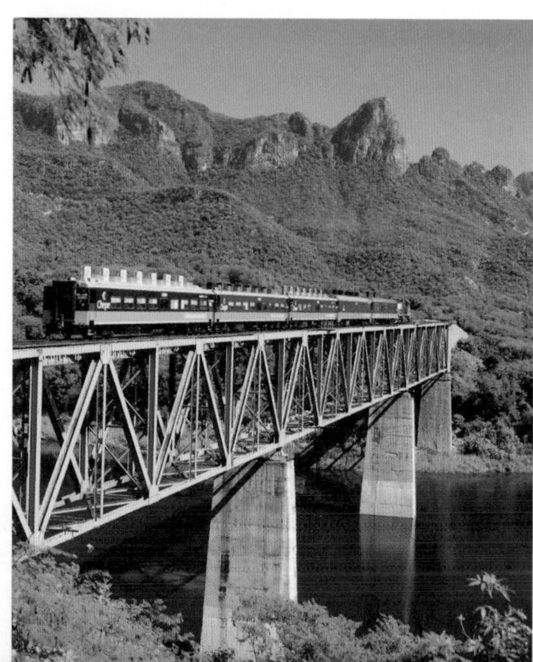

The Chepe Train, *traveling across a bridge in the Copper Canyon*

15

St. Kitts Scenic Railway

LOCATION St. Kitts & Nevis **START/FINISH** Basseterre (return) **DISTANCE** 30 miles (48 km) **TIME** 3 hours **INFORMATION** www.stkittsscenicrailway.com; around 11.5 miles (18 km) by bus

The narrow-gauge railroad that loops around St. Kitts was built in 1912 to transport the Caribbean island's "white gold" from the plantations to the capital Basseterre. Sugar cane was planted here from the 1640s, and by 1775, the island had 200 estates. Now the sugar industry's days are over, the railroad's jaunty double-decker cars carry passengers instead.

It's a wonderful way to see St. Kitts—the top deck is open-air and the waiters serve rum punch. Services start from Needsmust Station and run counterclockwise, tracing the shore. Waves pound the cliffs on one side and lush highlands rise up to Mount Liamuiga on the other, while you trundle via box-girder bridges, palm-frilled villages, and old plantations. At La Vallee, in the island's north, passengers must disembark—the line is no longer usable along the west coast, so the full loop (via Brimstone Hill Fortress) is completed by an equally scenic bus.

BRIMSTONE HILL FORTRESS

UNESCO-listed Brimstone Hill Fortress was built for the British by enslaved Africans in the 17th and 18th centuries. The fort was abandoned in 1853 but has been remarkably well preserved. Walk the ramparts to admire the military architecture and the breathtaking Caribbean views.

Train tracks crisscrossing the sheer-sided Nariz del Diablo

16

Nariz del Diablo

LOCATION Ecuador **START/FINISH** Alausí/ Sibambe **DISTANCE** 7.5 miles (12 km) **TIME** 3 hours **INFORMATION** www.ecuador.travel/en

Completed in the early 1900s, Ecuador's Trans-Andean Railway involved such a huge investment of time, money, and human lives that it was dubbed the "Most Difficult Railway in the World." For the hardest section, between Alausí and Sibambe, workers had to cut tight switchbacks into the rock to get past the Nariz del Diablo (Devil's Nose), a near-vertical outcrop rising above the Chanchán River. A singular feat of engineering, this track is now a thrill-seeker's dream.

To ride these historic rails, board a wooden carriage in the town of Alausí and take in verdant valley views as the train clickety-clacks down the mountain on strikingly sharp gradients. Use the stopover in Sibambe to trek up into the hills for a scenic shot of the Devil's Nose from across the valley, before hiking back and doing the daredevil ride all over again.

17

Belmond Andean Explorer

LOCATION Peru **START/FINISH** Cusco/Arequipa **DISTANCE** 386 miles (622 km) **TIME** 3 days **INFORMATION** www.belmond.com

The marks of civilization melt away as the *Belmond Andean Explorer* trundles out of Cusco, roads and rooftops replaced by scenes of wild natural beauty: thunderous rivers, ragged peaks, sweeping plains.

On board, the sumptuous interiors of South America's most luxurious sleeper train reflect the magnificence of the landscape. But one view crowns them all: sunrise on the shoreline of Lake Titicaca. At these high altitudes, the distinction between water and sky becomes flimsy and indistinguishable.

As the train begins its final descent, the journey offers up one last spectacular vista: the whitestone colonial city of Arequipa—the train's final stop—shimmering in the afternoon sunlight, watched over by a triumvirate of looming volcanoes.

18

Ferrocarril Central Andino

LOCATION Peru **START/FINISH** Lima/Huancayo **DISTANCE** 206 miles (333 km)
TIME 14 hours **INFORMATION** www.ferrocarrilcentral.com.pe

From crashing Pacific Ocean to craggy Andean plain, this train journey climbs through a spate of Peru's most exquisite mountain scenery on the greatest elevation change of any railroad line on earth.

Sticky coastal metropolis Lima and chilly Andean city Huancayo are chalk and cheese; one a place of pummeling surf, grand buildings, and a dining scene rivaling South America's best, the other embodying centuries-old Peruvian mountain tradition with its ancient craft villages and Quechua people dressed in rainbow-hued clothes. Yet they are connected via one of history's most audacious railroad projects: a line, linking Lima's important Pacific port of Callao with the country's lucrative mining centers, that travels from near sea level in the country's capital up and over 13,125 ft (4,000 m) summits in the heart of the Andes.

As the carriages approach their breath-sapping high point, enjoy a photo stop

Beginning at central Lima's ornate Beaux Arts Desamparados station, the train trundles across Peru. At San Bartolomé, the engine is hand-swiveled by turnstile to navigate the harsh Andean contours above; at Galera (15,686 ft/4,781 m), you'll be able to say you've passed through the world's highest publicly accessible passenger railroad station—as the cars approach their breath-sapping high point, enjoy a quick but incredible photo stop and drink it all in. The train then rattles through the fertile high-altitude valley of the Río Mantaro, with its wonderful handicrafts villages, before finally reaching Huancayo.

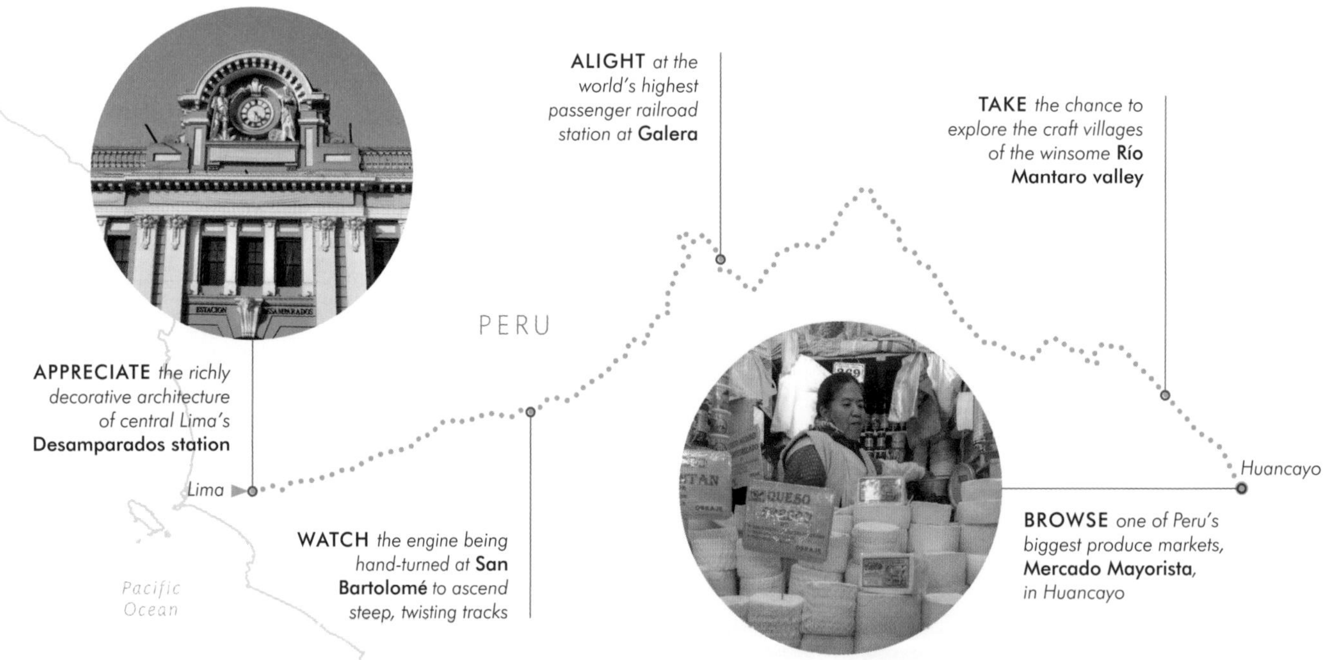

APPRECIATE *the richly decorative architecture of central Lima's* **Desamparados station**

WATCH *the engine being hand-turned at* **San Bartolomé** *to ascend steep, twisting tracks*

ALIGHT *at the world's highest passenger railroad station at* **Galera**

TAKE *the chance to explore the craft villages of the winsome* **Río Mantaro valley**

BROWSE *one of Peru's biggest produce markets,* **Mercado Mayorista,** *in Huancayo*

The Ferrocarril Central Andino *traversing the Andes between Lima and Huancayo*

(19)

Serra Verde Express

LOCATION Brazil **START/FINISH** Curitiba/Morretes **DISTANCE** 69 miles (110 km) **TIME** 4 hours **INFORMATION** www.serraverdeexpress.com.br

Encapsulating all of South America's scenic splendor, the Serra Verde Express *offers jaw-dropping views of granite peaks, jungle-clad gorges, and sparkling waterfalls.*

Inaugurated in 1884, the route of the *Serra Verde Express* was hailed as one of Brazil's greatest engineering marvels, its 14 tunnels and 30 bridges spanning once inaccessible terrain. Originally made to transport the region's rich farm produce to the port of Paranaguá, it is now one of the continent's last great rail journeys.

Setting out from Curitiba, the train rumbles past crumbling suburban villas and across pastures grazed by humpbacked zebu cattle. You emerge from the route's first tunnel into a different world: a tropical forest of blue hydrangeas and fluttering parrots. Few passengers alight at the sleepy stations along the way, but many hop off at the Santuário de Nossa Senhora do Cadeado viewpoint, to photograph the plunging mountain gorges. Arriving in Morretes, everyone spills out of the train ready, after all that adventure, for a blow-out lunch: the town is famous for its *barreado*, a hearty beef stew cooked in a clay pot.

You emerge into a different world: a tropical forest of blue hydrangeas and fluttering parrots

The Serra Verde Express, *trundling through cloud forest on the way to Morretes*

The immense salt flats near Uyuni

20

Expreso del Sur

LOCATION Bolivia **START/FINISH** Oruro/Villazón **DISTANCE** 373 miles (600 km) **TIME** 1 day **INFORMATION** Southbound trains arrive late at night in Uyuni and Tupiza: make sure you book accommodations in advance

As it cuts across the high and inhospitable Altiplano, the Expreso del Sur *skirts the otherworldly landscapes of the Salar de Uyuni, the planet's biggest salt flat.*

One of the last surviving railroad services in Bolivia, the *Expreso del Sur* (*Southern Express*) runs along a line built in the late 19th century to transport the country's vast mineral and nitrate wealth to Pacific ports in what is now Chile. Today, it carries passengers from the mining city of Oruro to the town of Villazón on the border with Argentina, a high-altitude route packed with jaw-dropping scenery.

Most travelers ride the train as far as the remote towns of Uyuni or, a few hours farther south, Tupiza. The former is the gateway to its namesake salt flat, a mesmerizingly white expanse roughly the size of Jamaica. Surrounded by chalk-smudge peaks and dotted with islands of giant cacti, the *salar* looks like something from another planet.

Tupiza, meanwhile, is the jumping-off point for trips across the Cordillera de Chichas, whose badlands resemble the Wild West—appropriate given this was the spot that notorious US outlaws Butch Cassidy and the Sundance Kid were finally gunned down in 1908.

CEMENTERIO DE TRENES

A haunting sight just outside Uyuni, the "Train Cemetery" is home to an array of rusting steam engines, goods wagons, and passenger cars. They were abandoned in the 1940s following the Great Depression and the collapse of the region's nitrate industry.

Club de Regatas La Marina, Tigre

21

Tren de la Costa

LOCATION Argentina **START/FINISH** Buenos Aires/Tigre **DISTANCE** 9.5 miles (15.5 km) **TIME** 30 minutes (one way) **INFORMATION** www.trendelacosta.com.ar

The Tren de la Costa *carries passengers from Argentina's sprawling capital to a resort on the delta of the second-largest river system in South America.*

Traveling on the narrow-gauge *Train of the Coast* from the Buenos Aires suburb of Olivos to the island-town of Tigre feels like stepping back a hundred years. While the trains are modern, the cute, red-brick stations you pass en route have a charming retro look that harks back to the line's early 20th-century heyday, when it shuttled *porteños* (Buenos Aires residents) to Tigre's fashionable casino and clubs.

When the trendy set moved on from Tigre, the route fell out of use, eventually closing in the 1960s, before being revived three decades later when Argentina's railroads were privatized. The stations were renovated and given their own theme: for example, Estación Borges, named after Argentina's influential author Jorge Luis Borges, has an open-air sculpture gallery and a literary café, while Estación Barrancas has an antiques market. Although Tigre may be the end of the railroad line, the journey across Argentina doesn't have to stop there. The lively resort—today a mix of the elegant and the gaudy—is also the jumping-off point for boat trips into the labyrinthine waterways and forest-clad islands of the steamy Paraná Delta.

another way

If you're staying in downtown Buenos Aires, a cheaper and more convenient—though less atmospheric—way to reach Tigre is to catch a regular commuter train from centrally located Retiro station.

22

Tren del Fin del Mundo

LOCATION Argentina **START/FINISH** Estación Fin del Mundo/Parque Nacional Tierra del Fuego **DISTANCE** 4.5 miles (7 km) **TIME** 1 hour **INFORMATION** www.trendelfindelmundo.com.ar

The southernmost railroad on earth, the Tren del Fin del Mundo *chugs through the wilderness of Tierra del Fuego, providing a fascinating insight into the region's tumultuous history.*

In the early 20th century, prisoners in the far-flung city of Ushuaia—then a penal colony known as the "Siberia of the South"—were enlisted to build a railroad line to transport timber for the rapidly growing settlement at the very foot of mainland South America. Following their backbreaking labor in harsh conditions, the first *Tren de los Presos* (Prisoners' Train) steamed along the tracks in 1909.

Today, Ushuaia is a thriving port city and Antarctic cruise hub, the prison has been turned into a museum, and the railroad carries passengers to and from Parque Nacional Tierra del Fuego, a haven for hiking and bird-watching.

The narrow-gauge line, now known as the *Tren del Fin del Mundo* (End of the World Train), is a decidedly slick experience; there is an overblown narration on board, actors dressed in yellow-and-blue prison uniforms greet passengers at the intervening stations, and there are plenty of opportunities to buy souvenirs. But alongside the frivolity, the railroad provides a snapshot of the region's remarkable history, while immersing you in some captivating scenery—subantarctic tundra, beech forests, boglands, and towering, snow-streaked mountains.

EAGER BEAVERS

The train periodically passes patches of denuded forest, caused by the descendants of beavers introduced to the region in the 1940s. It proved a disaster. The hoped-for fur trade never took off and the beavers reproduced prolifically, spread widely and are thought to have damaged 25 percent of the region's forests.

The Tren del Fin del Mundo, *Parque Nacional Tierra del Fuego*

BY WATER

Snow-sided fjords and floating gardens. Penguins and pink river dolphins. From the Caribbean to Cape Horn, the scale and variety of the Americas' waters are astounding. Take an expedition ship to Antarctica or a paddle steamer up the Mississippi, raft the Río Cangrejal in Honduras or ferry-hop through the Grenadines. Taking to the water brings out the tranquil side of travel.

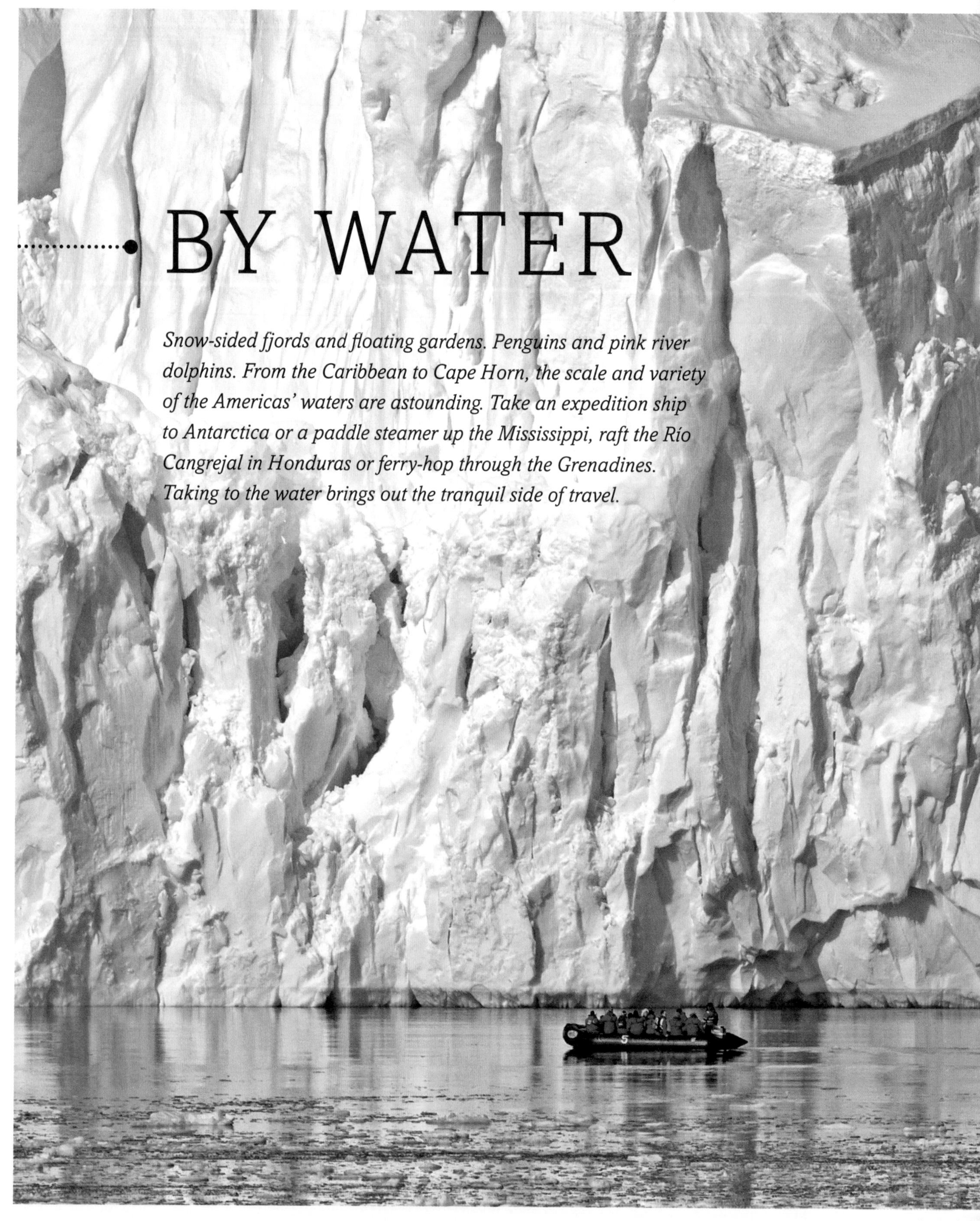

KEY TO MAP

.... Long route

• End point

Previous page *Touring Paradise Bay, in the Antarctic*

AT A GLANCE

BY WATER

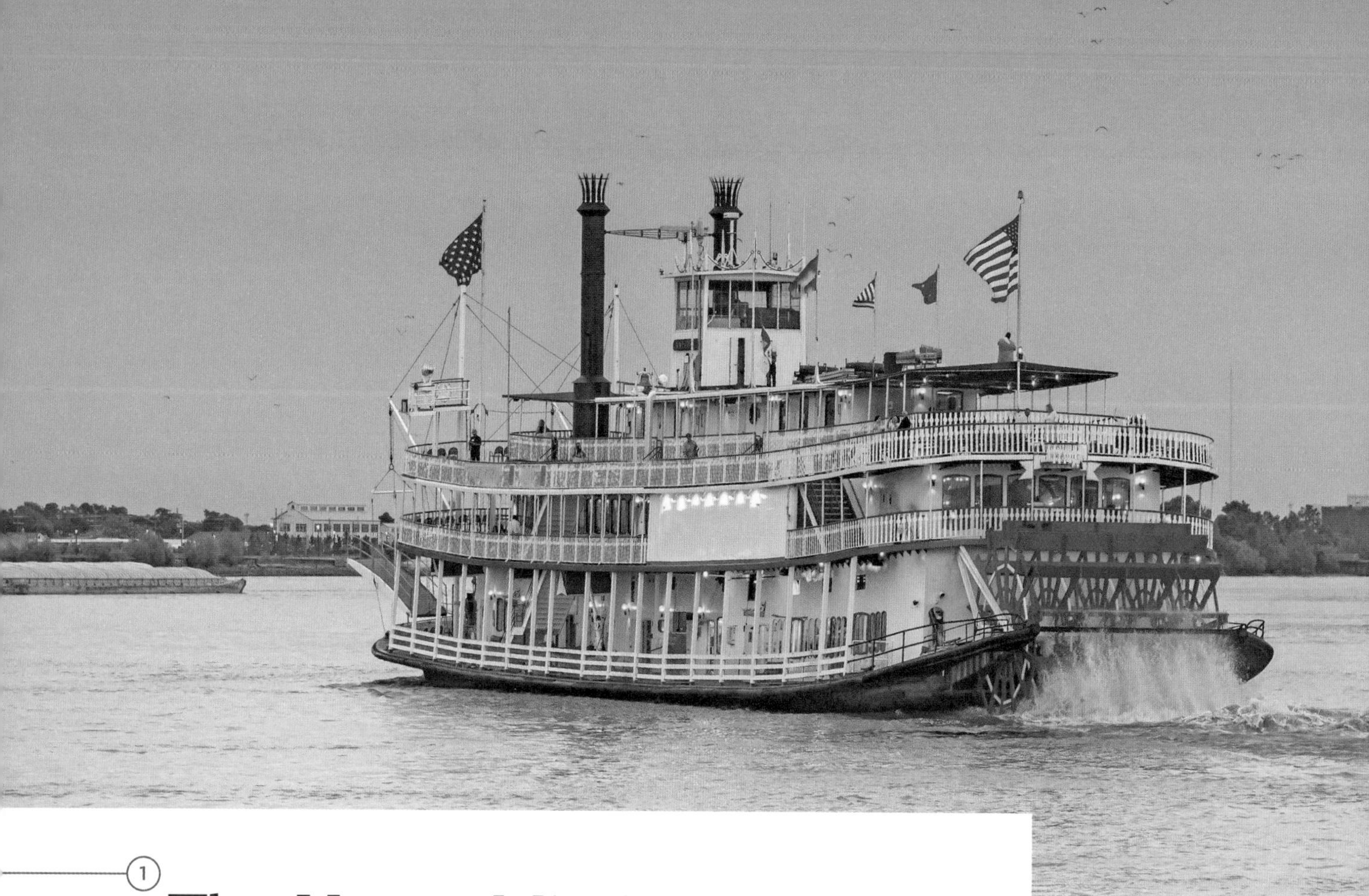

A traditional paddle steamer cruising on the Mississippi River

1

The Upper Mississippi: St. Louis to Red Wing

LOCATION US **START/FINISH** St. Louis/Red Wing **DISTANCE** 542 miles (872 km) **TIME** 9 days **INFORMATION** www.aqvoyages.com

Rewind time and roll deep into the heart of America's Midwest on the country's lifeblood: the Mississippi River. You'll find historic towns full of unsung charm and literary legends on the way.

No river embodies America quite like the mighty Mississippi, the silver seam stitching together the very fabric of the country. America's second-longest river twists for 2,340 miles (3,766 km) from Lake Itasca in Minnesota to the Gulf of Mexico. Local hero Mark Twain eloquently described it as "reposeful as a dreamland" in his 1883 memoir *Life on the Mississippi*. And there's no better way to explore its languid rhythms, timeless towns, and fertile farmland than aboard a century-old paddle steamer, winging you back to a more elegant and unhurried age of travel.

> You'll be rolling on the river that shaped a literary nation

As the big wheel keeps on turning, you'll be rolling on the river that shaped a literary nation—Mark Twain, F. Scott Fitzgerald, and T. S. Eliot were all born on these muddy banks. Itineraries vary, but

The Upper Mississippi:
St. Louis to Red Wing
UNITED STATES
Red Wing
TAP INTO *the craftsmanship of early pioneers in the historic city of* **Red Wing**
HOP ON *the* **Fenelon Place Elevator,** *the world's shortest, steepest funicular, in Dubuque*
UNITED STATES
HEAD UP TO *the observation deck to spot bald eagles, pelicans, and herons on the river*
SLIP INTO *the pages of a Mark Twain novel at the author's boyhood home of* **Hannibal**
KICK OFF *your paddle-steamer cruise in* **St. Louis,** *where the Gateway Arch glimmers*
St. Louis

this one dives in at the Midwest's deep end, starting in St. Louis, with its soaring silver Gateway Arch, and making ports of call in sleepy towns like Alton (birthplace of jazz star Miles Davis), genteel Hannibal (of Mark Twain boyhood-home fame), historic Dubuque, and beautifully preserved Red Wing in Minnesota. All of them are worth a wander, but Hannibal, the so-called America's Hometown, is particularly interesting–visit the Mark Twain Boyhood Home and Museum for an insight into the author who captured imaginations with works like *The Adventures of Tom Sawyer* (1876) and *The Adventures of Huckleberry Finn* (1884).

But you'll recall the moments on deck with equal fondness: the jaunty sound of the calliope as the paddle steamer passes through a lock; lazy days spent lounging in a rocking chair, observing bald eagles wheeling in flawless blue skies; fiery sunsets giving way to starry skies; and a dark, silent river that holds some of America's greatest stories and secrets.

MARK TWAIN

Samuel Langhorne Clemens—better known as Mark Twain—was born in Hannibal on the Mississippi in 1835. In *Old Times on the Mississippi* (1875), he described it as a "white town drowsing in the sunshine of a summer's morning." And with its parade of historic houses and slow pace of life, it has changed little over time.

2

Isle Royale National Park

LOCATION US **START/FINISH** McCargoe Cove/Malone Bay **DISTANCE** 22 miles (35 km) **TIME** 4 days **INFORMATION** Permit required to overnight in Isle Royale National Park; route involves portage; park accessed via ferry

Enter a watery oasis on this paddling-and-portage trail that joins a glittering necklace of lakes in Isle Royale National Park with back-to-basics campgrounds offering kayakers refuge along the way.

Michigan's Isle Royale National Park is a world of water, enveloping the 210 sq mile (544 sq km) island that floats in mammoth Lake Superior. It makes sense, then, that the best way to explore is by kayak, forgoing the trails that zigzag the moose-roamed island.

Seasoned paddlers can take to a watery network of trails, with the route from McCargoe Cove to Malone Bay one of the most popular. This journey joins up a patchwork of shimmering inland water bodies, from Chickenbone Lake to Siskiwit Lake. Begin at McCargoe Cove Campground, where bucolic sites swaddled by trees nose up to the water's edge. Once your paddle hits the water, time seems endless. Paddlers inch past rugged banks peppered with mountain ash and balsam firs, heaving themselves out of the water at the various portage points—you carry your kayak through the forest, pitching up at primitive campgrounds, before taking to the water once more, until you hit the final pull-out point in Malone Bay.

Paddling in Isle Royale National Park

(3)

Lake Michigan

LOCATION US **START/FINISH** Traverse City/Green Bay **DISTANCE** Varies depending on route, weather, and whims, but roughly 258 miles (415 km) **TIME** 1–4 weeks **INFORMATION** Gunkholing requires moderate sailing experience; sailing conditions on Lake Michigan are best in spring and summer

It's time for gunkholing: a slow sail following only the wind and your whims. Drop anchor in remote coves and go off-grid for a while.

Gunkholing is the American pastime of sailing from place to place, cruising into coves and up estuaries in search of hidey-holes to get away from it all. Its name derives from the mud (or gunk) that collects on the hulls of boats when anchor is dropped in one of these hidden bays at low tide.

Of course, the last thing a gunkholer wants is someone telling them where to go, but with its deep forests and sparsely populated coast, northern Lake Michigan is ripe for plotting an itinerary full of gunkholing best bits. Tack west from Michigan's Traverse City to remote Beaver Island, where Mormon leader James Strang declared himself king in the mid-1800s. Discover Indigenous peoples' burial grounds and abandoned religious settlements on the uninhabited islands of Garden and High. And explore the bucolic peninsula of Wisconsin's Door County, whose jagged coastline provides plenty of secluded spots where you can fall asleep to the haunting call of loons. First time gunkholing? This journey will ensure that it won't be your last.

Top *Sailing boats coming into dock in Door County* ***Above*** *Holland Harbor Light, Lake Michigan*

another way

Other top places to gunkhole in North America include Maryland's Chesapeake Bay; Washington state's Puget Sound; the coast of Maine; Florida's southwestern coast; and the North Channel of Lake Huron in Canada.

Summer sloop sailing off the Nantucket coast

4

Nantucket

LOCATION US **START/FINISH** New Bedford/ Nantucket **DISTANCE** 80 miles (50 km) **TIME** 1–2 days **INFORMATION** www.visitma.com

The dune-fronted island of Nantucket, cast adrift off Cape Cod on the Massachusetts coast, was once the start of many a whaler's adventure and the island prospered wildly from the industry—hence, the bonanza of cedar-shingle oceanfront mansions you can still see here today. Nantucket is more sedate these days, a place where you can spend the summer flip-flopping between beachcombing and watching boats glide in on the surf.

You can get a taste of the old times, though, on a high-sea adventure of your own, setting sail in a sloop and cruising past candy-striped lighthouses and the Muskeget and Tuckernuck islands, with their wave-tossed skerries. The mainsail billowing in the breeze as you skip across the whitecaps feels pure Nantucket, and in a summer southwester, the waters can get bumpy enough for a quite exhilarating sail.

5

Etowah River Water Trail

LOCATION US **START/FINISH** Etowah River Park/Kelly Bridge **DISTANCE** 9 miles (14 km) **TIME** 4 hours **INFORMATION** www.exploregeorgia.org

The Etowah River is an enigma. Country songs have been penned about it—musician Jerry Reed crooned about "Ko-Ko Joe," a curious man who lived on a bend of the winding waterway—and it has long been sacred to the region's Indigenous peoples, who feasted on its bounty of fish.

Today, ancient fishing weirs still punctuate the Etowah River Water Trail, which snakes out for a total of 163 miles (262 km). The stretch from Etowah River Park to Kelly Bridge in Georgia serves the best of the waterway on a silver platter. It slices through the Dawson Forest, thick with sycamore and hemlock trees that drape over the water like lace curtains; all the while, kingfishers flutter in the canopy and catfish lurk in the depths below.

MISSISSIPPIAN CULTURE

The intriguing Etowah River and its banks protect vestiges of ancient Mississippian culture, which flourished from around 1000 to 1550 AD. The Etowah Indian Mounds State Historic Site is the most intact relic of this period, featuring a 63 ft (19 m) earthen knoll that is thought to have been used to raise the home of the peoples' priest-chief.

6

Tchefuncte River

LOCATION US **START/FINISH** Fairview-Riverside State Park (return) **DISTANCE** 9 miles (14 km) **TIME** 3 hours **INFORMATION** www.louisianatoursandadventures.com

Twisting through a Spanish-moss-cloaked swathe of southern Louisiana, the Tchefuncte River wends its way toward Lake Pontchartrain. It's a picture-postcard example of the stirring, swampy landscapes of the South—think bayous lined with cypress trees and a blanket of grassy marshland. In total, the river flows out for some 70 miles (113 km), but you can experience the waterway in all its glory on short boat rides that putter out and back from Fairview-Riverside State Park. Set off from the park's boat launch and inch toward the majestic Tchefuncte River Lighthouse, a landmark of the region. Time your journey for sunset, when the beacon contrasts with tangerine skies and the river is liquid gold.

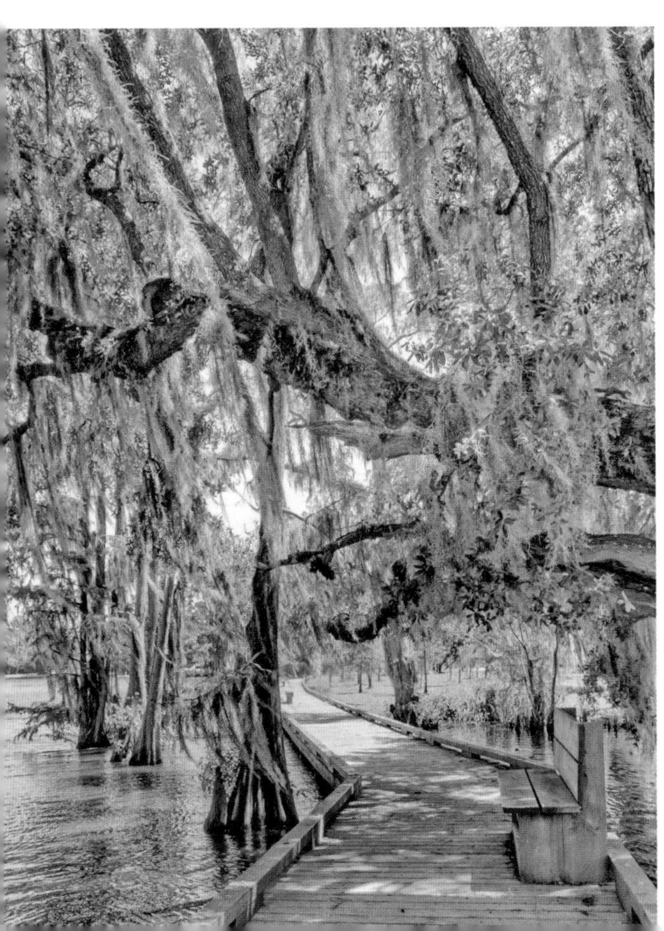

Oak cloaked with Spanish moss, Tchefuncte River

7

Mississippi River

LOCATION US **START/FINISH** Montezuma Landing/Clarksdale **DISTANCE** 18 miles (29 km) **TIME** 1 day **INFORMATION** www.island63.com

To truly understand the Mississippi River, you need to leave its banks and explore this storied waterway by canoe. Don't go it alone, though: someone who knows "Ole Miss" like the back of his hand is John Ruskey, a charismatic waterborne adventurer who leads paddling trips with the Quapaw Canoe Company in Clarksdale, Mississippi.

Pushing off at Montezuma Landing, you'll zigzag across gravy-colored waters, dodging giant tanker ships and handsome paddle steamers along the way while keeping an eye out for alligators lounging by the swampy shoreline. Floating past tumbledown cotton warehouses, you'll tether your canoes on sandy islands, where over a picnic of cold cuts Captain Ruskey serenades his paddlers with a folksy number or two on his guitar. Then it's back to Mississippi—keeping an eye out for those 'gators again.

another way

Blues fans should book onto the Muddy Waters Wilderness trip, which retraces the late, great musician's life. You'll visit his plantation birthplace and paddle along the Mississippi landscape that shaped his musical genius.

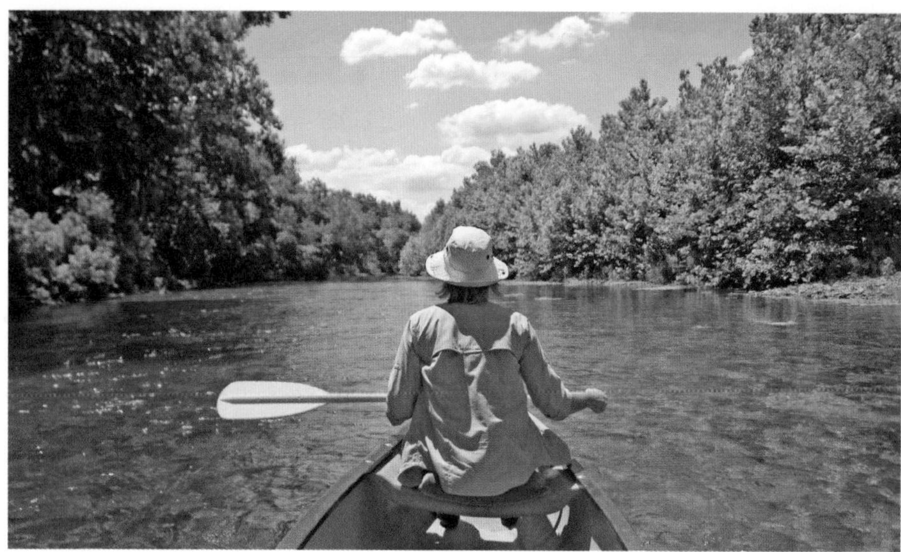

Paddling along the Current River in the Ozark National Scenic Riverways

8

Ozark National Scenic Riverways

LOCATION US **START/FINISH** Powder Mill/Van Buren **DISTANCE** 28 miles (45 km) **TIME** 10 hours **INFORMATION** www.nps.gov/ozar

Glide beneath oak-covered bluffs and between forested riverbanks on a paddle down the snaking Current River.

The Ozark National Scenic Riverways protects 134 miles (216 km) of the Current and Jacks Fork rivers: two wild waterways that slice through the cavern-studded karst bluffs of the hypnotizing Ozark Mountains of southeast Missouri.

A paddling trip from Powder Mill to Van Buren on the Current River makes an ideal introduction to this beautiful national preserve. You'll wend your way between soaring crags, pausing at natural wonders such as the charming Blue Spring, a couple of miles into the journey; the water body was called "Spring of the Summer Sky" by the Indigenous population because its color is so blue. Enveloped by the Mark Twain National Forest, Watercress Spring Campground is a beacon for weary paddlers, or you can venture a little farther on into the city of Van Buren, where a couple of comfortable inns and lodges provide a treat at the end of the trip.

THE OZARKS ON SCREEN

The Ozarks rose to prominence when it became the star of the hit Netflix show of the same name in 2017. The series followed Jason Bateman's Marty Byrde, who moved his family to this bucolic slice of Missouri after getting embroiled with a Mexican drug cartel. It was actually filmed in Georgia, whose bluffs and wiggling waterways put on a convincing performance.

9

Colorado River

LOCATION US **START/FINISH** Lees Ferry/Lake Mead
DISTANCE 277 miles (443 km) **TIME** 6–18 days
INFORMATION www.nps.gov/grca; rafting season Apr–Oct

Take in the might of the Grand Canyon from the valley floor, as you ride the frothing rapids of the Colorado River.

The age and enormity of Arizona's Grand Canyon is almost unfathomable, the oldest layers of its ravishing red-gold-purple-black rock being almost two billion years old. And the most intimate way to see all this is by river raft—indeed, traveling by water is the only way to reach the canyon's remotest spots.

The Colorado carves its way right through Grand Canyon National Park, and it's possible to raft a wild 277-mile (443 km) section of this mighty emerald-hued river. It's a breathtaking paddle, via 160-odd rapids that range from small flutters to white-knuckle Class Vs—not least the terrifying drop of Lava Falls—but if you join a guided commercial trip, they'll steer you safely through. At night, having pitched up on a beach at the end of a hard day's paddling, you can enjoy the stillness of the canyon, the tinkling of the river the only sound around.

another way

You don't have to raft the full canyon. Operators run shorter itineraries focusing on the Upper Canyon (4–8 days), Lower Canyon (4–12 days), or the Whitmore Wash–Pearce Ferry stretch (3–5 days).

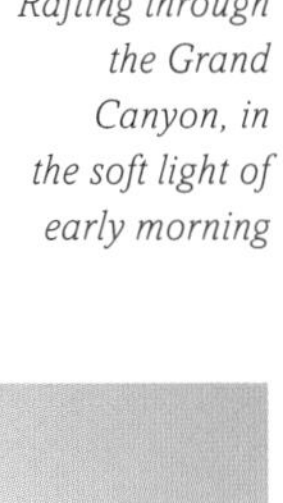

Rafting through the Grand Canyon, in the soft light of early morning

Whiz through mangrove corridors and natural canals

Top *An airboat zipping through the Everglades' wildlife-rich wetlands*
Right *An alligator hiding among mangrove roots*

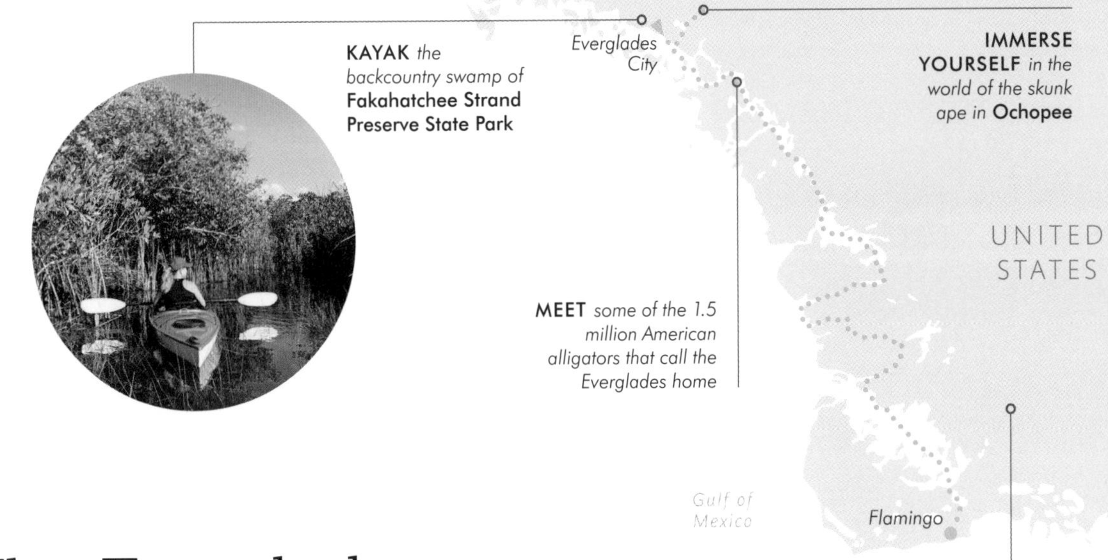
KAYAK the backcountry swamp of Fakahatchee Strand Preserve State Park
Everglades City
IMMERSE YOURSELF in the world of the skunk ape in Ochopee
UNITED STATES
MEET some of the 1.5 million American alligators that call the Everglades home
Gulf of Mexico
Flamingo
Florida Bay

10

The Everglades

LOCATION US **START/FINISH** Everglades City/Flamingo **DISTANCE** 130 miles (210 km) **TIME** 2 days **INFORMATION** www.visitflorida.com

Air-boating across the surface of the largest wilderness east of the Mississippi offers opportunity to spot the flora and fauna of Florida's most spectacular national park.

The Everglades is the Amazon of North America, a shallow, seasonally flooded depression that provides a refuge for all sorts of vegetation and wildlife: tufts of royal palms, tropical hardwood hammocks, and a florid bounty of orchids, plus turtles, snakes, and manatees.

And American alligators, of course, which are most commonly found sunning themselves in swamps or by the roadside on the Everglades Parkway, also known as Alligator Alley. Seeing the reptile is one of the main draws of trips out into this vast salt-marsh prairie, and a hair-mussing airboat is the ultimate way to do it. Your captain will whiz you through mangrove corridors and natural canals, created by slow-moving waters that seep south from the Orlando and Kissimmee river basins to southern Florida's Gulf coastline. It's a portal to an otherworldly realm.

Confusingly, the Everglades is also home to the American crocodile. Get close enough and you'll spot the difference—it's all in the nose, with alligators having a U-shaped snout and crocodiles bearing pointier jaws. Legend also tells of the mythical skunk ape, a southern relative of the sasquatch, a mangrove-dwelling woolly ape more Creature from the Black Lagoon than Tarzan. It's unlikely you'll come across one, but with so many of nature's curious critters on display in these wetlands, you'll be happy that life is often better than fiction.

KEEP AN EYE OUT *for turtles, snakes, and manatees swimming between the hardwood hammocks at* **Mahogany Hammock**

another way

No boat? No worries. Take a knee-deep walk into the heart of the Everglades instead on a walking tour of Fakahatchee Strand Preserve State Park, a thread of accessible back-country swampland.

11

Santa Catalina Island

LOCATION US **START/FINISH** Los Angeles/San Pedro **DISTANCE** 44 miles (71 km) **TIME** 2 or 3 days **INFORMATION** www.catalinaexpress.com; www.kayakcatalinaisland.com

Kayak the tranquil coastline of this natural island paradise just off the Los Angeles coast, where you'll find ample opportunities for crystal-clear sea snorkels.

A short boat ride from buzzy Los Angeles, rugged Santa Catalina Island is privately owned by the Catalina Island Conservancy, whose work ensures that nearly 90 percent of its land is free from development—an unheard of statistic in these parts. Island life is slow here; most cars are banned and there's a 14-year waiting list for residents wishing to own one. Kayaking, then, is the best way to get around—and for more reasons than one.

Santa Catalina's eastern (leeward) side is a good place to start, especially if you're a beginner, as you can slowly make your way along the coast, dipping in and out of sheltered bays like Avalon and Isthmus Cove. Paddling the island's lush 52-mile (84 km) circumference will take several days if you're going to tackle it all, but there's no need to rush—the mainland's laid-back SoCal vibe extends offshore as well, and there are five designated campsites to overnight at. The translucent seas attract oodles of sea life, so the more time you're on the water, the more likely you are to see leopard sharks and bat rays. Just don't forget your snorkel.

Avalon Bay, on the eastern side of Santa Catalina Island

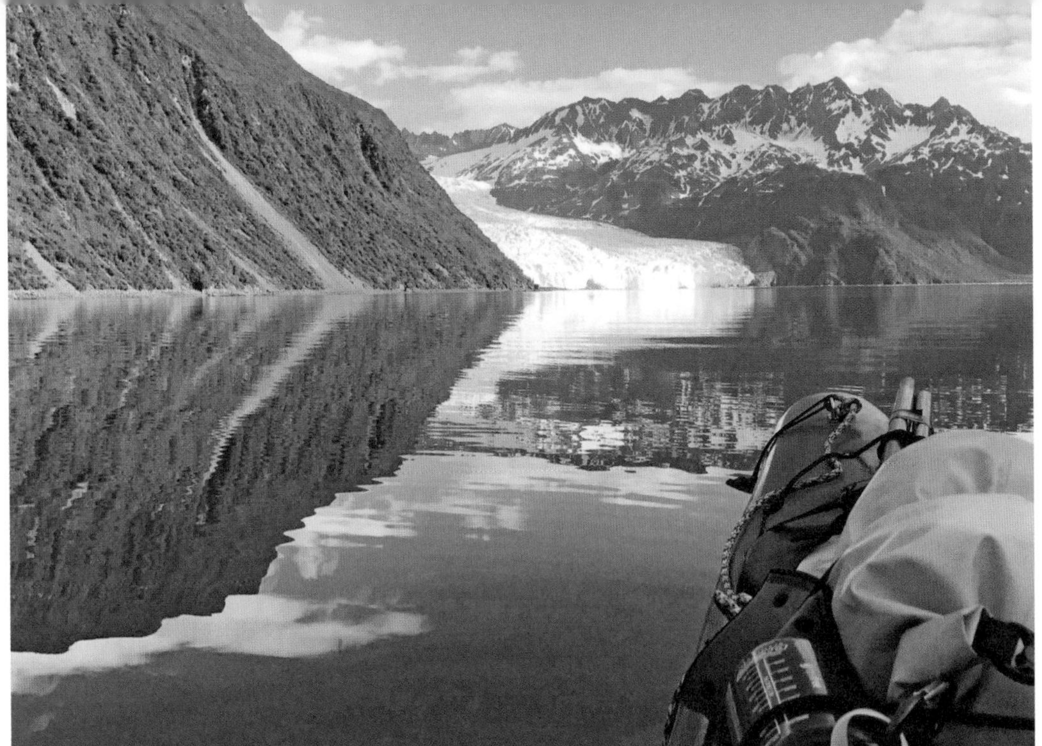

Kayaking toward the Aialik Glacier, in Kenai Fjords National Park

12

Kenai Fjords National Park

LOCATION US **START/FINISH** Seward/Aialik Bay **DISTANCE** 50 miles (80 km) **TIME** 1–2 days **INFORMATION** www.nps.gov/kefj

Kayak through a bay deluged with icebergs, before coming face-to-face with spectacular Aialik Glacier, its menacing ice chunks dropping off into the vast bay.

What does it feel like to be dwarfed by a 600 ft (183 m) ice mountain from the seat of a sea kayak? Cheek-to-cheek with the Aialik Glacier, so near that the air frosts and clings to your face, you'll quickly learn two things. First, it's best not to get too close; when the glacier calves, it creates mini tidal waves strong enough to sink a ship. Second, it pays to paddle clear of the bobbing icebergs; deceptively dangerous and unpredictable underwater, some of them are the size of trucks.

To find out for yourself, head out on a paddle through Alaska's Kenai Fjords National Park, west of Seward. Superlatives abound in Aialik Bay, at the heart of the park, not least for the Harding Icefield, which covers 700 sq miles (1,125 sq km) of Alaska's Kenai Mountain range. It's so big, in fact, it's the largest ice sheet in the US. Wilderness on this scale certainly puts you in your place.

another way

Trips on the Klondike Express, *the fastest (and largest) catamaran in Alaska, head out from the town of Whittier into sublime Prince William Sound, visiting a whopping 26 glaciers along the way.*

13

The Inside Passage

LOCATION US and Canada **START/FINISH** Skagway/Vancouver **DISTANCE** 1,181 miles (1,900 km) **TIME** 1 week **INFORMATION** www.travelalaska.com; www.hellobc.com

Much of the Inside Passage remains untouched wilderness, its small ports and harbors cut off from the rest of North America. Exploring it all by cruise ship is just the ticket.

Adrift somewhere in the Inside Passage, between the coast of southeast Alaska and northwest British Columbia, there's pandemonium. An orca and calf have been spotted off the starboard side, all sploshing tail flukes, nursing calls, and frothy spume in their wake. Observers jostle with binoculars and smartphones, eager for the best views and photographs. Behind them lies a shifting background of seismogram-shaped mountains, as magical as any landscape painting.

This is a snapshot of time spent cruising the Inside Passage, the spectacular sea channel of islands sandwiched between the fjordlands of the Pacific Northwest. Trafficked by freighters, tugs, and fishing crafts for decades, the route is now equally popular with travelers eager to capture a sense of life on these outer-edge islands, many of which are inhabited only by grizzly or black bears.

Left *Cruising beneath the mighty peaks of Misty Fjords National Monument* ***Right*** *Orcas off Vancouver Island*

Seen on a map, it's a coast that traditionally spreads north from Puget Sound in Washington state to the Alaskan panhandle, but the main event nowadays is the coastal midriff of islands, sea inlets, and historic harbor towns. Fittingly, cruise and catamaran operators focus the bulk of their itineraries between the Johnstone Strait off northeast Vancouver Island and the ABC Islands (Admiralty, Baranof, and Chichagof) in the northern part of the Alexander Archipelago, where marine life is at its most awe-inspiring and active. In a region where there are few roads and only impenetrable hemlock and sitka spruce forests, it's also by far the best place to cram in as many coastal highlights as possible.

After you've been spoiled with orca, dolphin, and whale encounters—from May to October, the cetaceans are a dime a dozen—you can make the most of time spent on land at the Inside

Left *Skagway's main street, lined with colorful timber buildings*
Below *Kayaking in Misty Fjords National Monument*

UNITED STATES (ALASKA)

CANADA

RIDE *the* **White Pass & Yukon Route Railroad** *to recapture the spirit of the Klondike-era gold rush*

Skagway

GO *on a grizzly bear tracking safari in Alaska's lesser-seen* **ABC Islands**

Pacific Ocean

LEARN *more about the ancient cultures of the Haida Gwaii people at* **SG̲ang Gwaay Llnagaay**

Vancouver

UNITED STATES

SPOT *breaching dolphins and whales while cruising* **Johnstone Strait**

HIKE *to a vast tidewater glacier at* **Misty Fjords National Monument**

Passage's most curious port towns. In the north, Skagway is a Wild West fan's dream destination, with clapboard saloons, half-timbered gold rush–era buildings, and the historic White Pass & Yukon Route Railroad *(p183)* that rattles deep into the vast interior. To the south, in Ketchikan, you can take in the awe-inspiring Misty Fjords National Monument, which environmentalist and grandfather of the National Park movement John Muir compared to Yosemite.

Entering British Columbia, it's next the turn of Haida Gwaii, a string of remarkable islands that archaeologists believe could be the first place humans set foot in North America *(p222)*. Today, the Haida peoples' legacy lives on in animal-crested totem poles and at SG̲ang Gwaay Llnagaay, an abandoned 19th-century village turned UNESCO World Heritage Site.

The Inside Passage represents what North America has come to mean for many: an age-old frontier land, vast and free, yet a place that promises to make the wildest of dreams come true.

another way

If you're short on time, the Georgia Strait between Vancouver and Victoria gives a glimpse of what lies in store along the Inside Passage—whale-watching trips and rigid inflatable boat excursions seek out some of its fabulous marine life.

An orca breaching in the waters of Clayoquot Sound

(14) Yukon River Quest

LOCATION Canada **START/FINISH** Whitehorse/Dawson City **DISTANCE** 444 miles (715 km) **TIME** 4 days **INFORMATION** www.yukonriverquest.com

The Yukon River Quest is a paddle race like no other: 444 miles (715 km) through the heart of Canada's wild northwest. You can tackle the swirling waters of the Yukon on your own, of course, but the organization of a well-run annual summer event adds a welcome safety net in a region where the elements are rarely in your favor; the weather can be punishing here, and the ever-present wilderness is beautiful but dangerous—this is bear country, after all. The rewards for taking part are obvious as soon as you start paddling: a silent mass of black spruce, thick conifers, and deserted river beaches your only real company as you work your way downriver to the finish line in Dawson.

another way

The 83-mile (133 km) Muskoka River X is the world's longest one-day expedition paddle race, following in the paddle strokes of the First Nations families who plied this route through Ontario—along two rivers and across four lakes—in the 1800s.

(15) Clayoquot Sound

LOCATION Canada **START/FINISH** Tofino (return) **DISTANCE** 30 miles (50 km) **TIME** 1 day **INFORMATION** www.tourismtofino.com

For most people, Vancouver Island's Tofino is ripe for a summer vacation, an end-of-the-road place where the tumbling Pacific, forested mountains, and lumber-washed beaches collide to create a fantasy destination for surfers and beach-bike riders. But a more intrepid experience awaits at Clayoquot Sound, further north.

Your passport to adventure is a sea kayak, for paddling amid a flurry of dolphins and spritzing orcas out in the estuary, or a high-performance inflatable, to access the narrow nooks and half-moon bays farther inland. The classic trip is a black-bear watching safari around the time-warp tide lines of uninhabited Meares Island. To a soundtrack of muted squeals, you can watch black bears swaggering down to the shoreline at low tide to crack barnacles and tongue-scoop mussels. It will just be your little boat, the epic Canadian wilderness and the matted-hair bears, emerging from the spruce forests like enormous ursine apparitions.

16

Desolation Sound

LOCATION Canada **START/FINISH** Lund/Port McNeill **DISTANCE** 135 miles (220 km) **TIME** 7–10 days **INFORMATION** www.hellobc.com

Of all the animals in Desolation Sound, the channel between Vancouver Island and the Great Bear Rainforest, the most emblematic is the ghostlike spirit (or kermode) bear, a distinctive white-coated species that is thought to be the world's rarest ursine. Your best chance of spotting one? From the prow of a boat or catamaran while sailing among the half-drowned islands of the coast's brackish inlets.

But to cover distance in Desolation Sound—to Toba Inlet, perhaps, Cortes Island, or Homfray Channel—is not only to experience seemingly limitless forest and emotive wildlife but to learn more about the legends of the First Nations who have lived on this coast for 10,000 years. Aboard, your skipper will regale you with stories of the way things once were, narrating your surroundings as you sail. Meanwhile, out in the bays, sea lions mosh and the spray from 44-ton humpbacks lingers in the air like wisps of smoke.

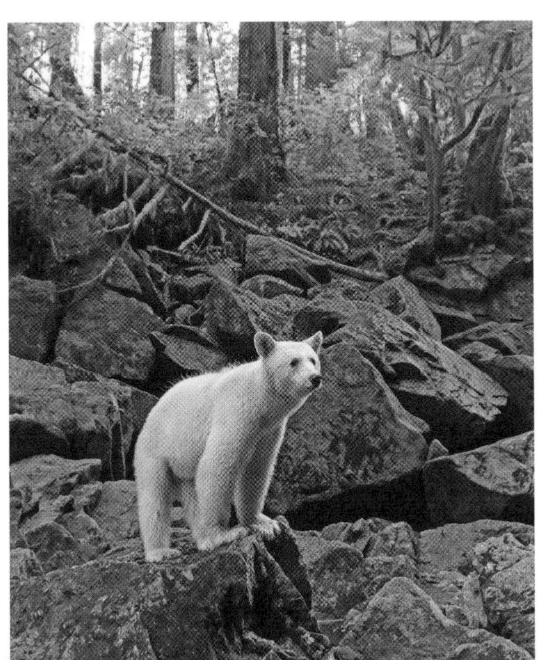

The Great Bear Rainforest, home to the rare white-coated spirit bear

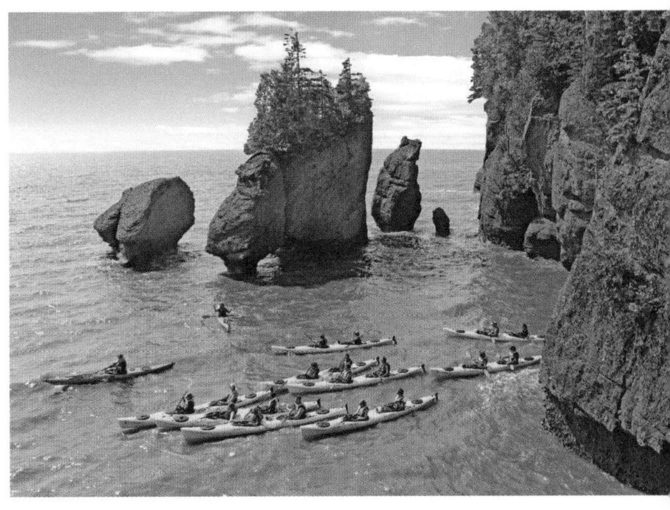

Kayakers admiring the view by the Hopewell Rocks in the Bay of Fundy

17

The Bay of Fundy

LOCATION Canada **START/FINISH** Advocate Harbour (return) **DISTANCE** From 5 miles (8 km) **TIME** 1–3 days **INFORMATION** www.novascotia.com; check tide times first

The Bay of Fundy is the Everest of the maritime world. This inlet between the provinces of Nova Scotia and New Brunswick has the planet's biggest tidal range—between its high and low extremes, the water level varies by up to 52 ft (16 m). And while that's impressive in itself, what the tidal range reveals is even more so. Every six hours, with the turn of the tides, caves, beaches, and sea stacks are exposed and then consumed. Every minute shows a different world.

For a front row seat to this watery wonder, take to a kayak. There are many possible put-ins, but Cape Chignecto Provincial Park is an excellent shoreline to explore. Starting out from spots like Advocate Harbour, you'll encounter bald eagles and gray seals, Mi'kmaq folklore, ancient red cliffs, and rocks that seem to sink and soar with the inexorable lap of each wave. This really is the pinnacle of East Canada kayaking.

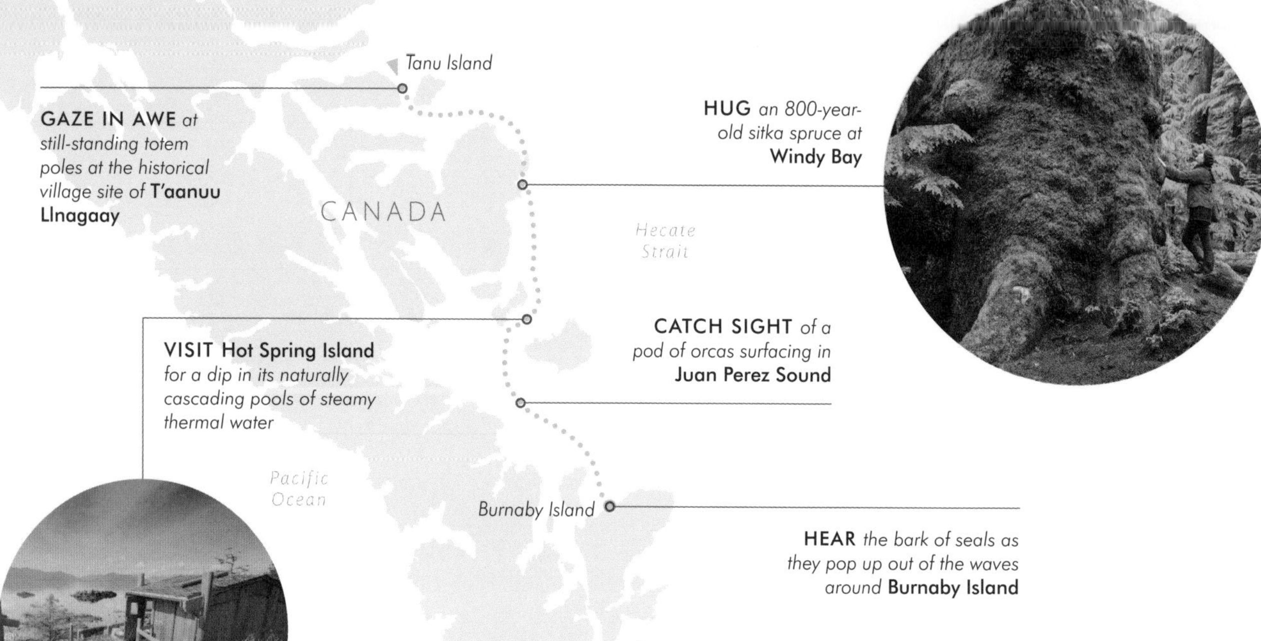
Tanu Island
GAZE IN AWE at still-standing totem poles at the historical village site of T'aanuu Llnagaay
CANADA
HUG an 800-year-old sitka spruce at Windy Bay
Hecate Strait
CATCH SIGHT of a pod of orcas surfacing in Juan Perez Sound
VISIT Hot Spring Island for a dip in its naturally cascading pools of steamy thermal water
Pacific Ocean
Burnaby Island
HEAR the bark of seals as they pop up out of the waves around Burnaby Island

18

Around the "Canadian Galápagos"

LOCATION Canada **START/FINISH** Tanu Island/Burnaby Island **DISTANCE** 31 miles (50 km) **TIME** 1 week **INFORMATION** www.gohaidagwaii.ca; advance reservations required for Gwaii Haanas

Embark on a superb sea-kayak expedition, navigating a remote archipelago where pristine waters meet ancient rainforests, all saturated in wildlife and rich with First Nations history.

Off the coast of British Columbia lie the islands of Haida Gwaii, known as the Canadian Galápagos due to their unique flora and fauna. Only a few are inhabited, leaving the other 200 or so in a natural state where wildlife thrives.

Devote at least a week to paddling through the islands' Gwaii Haanas National Park Reserve, where the incredible clarity of the water provides views right down to the ocean floor: sea anemones sway to the rhythm of the currents and giant Pacific octopuses tend to their shell gardens. You might spot black bears on the shorelines of some of the larger islands, feasting on crabs in tidal pools; high above, bald eagles patrol the skies. On land, you can head into thick groves of spruce and cedar, some with trunks as wide as a car. Sheltered beneath this canopy of green, the remains of Haida villages lie under a carpet of moss, slowly succumbing to natural decay; time it right and you might meet a Haida Watchman, a guardian of these historic memorials. As you set up camp each evening, listen for the sounds of a humpback's exhalation just offshore. Just think, tomorrow promises even more.

THE HAIDA

Haida Gwaii is the heartland of the Haida First Nations, whose ancestral lineage can be traced back to the end of the last Ice Age. As glaciers retreated and land corridors opened for migration, North America's first humans arrived via the Bering Strait. Archaeological sites have been found throughout Haida Gwaii; many more lie deep underwater, after glacial melt flooded the region.

Kayaking beneath the forested mountains of Haida Gwaii

19

Floating Gardens of Xochimilco

LOCATION Mexico **START/FINISH** Embarcadero Belem/Belem de las Flores **DISTANCE** 2.5–6.5 miles (4–10 km) **TIME** 1–4 hours **INFORMATION** www.visit-mexico.mx

Set on the southern periphery of one of the planet's biggest metropolises, Mexico City's Xochimilco waterways once connected the area's pre-Hispanic settlements. Today, hawkers vend their wares on vessels doubling as market stalls and verdure drapes the canals, creating a countrified vibe that feels light-years from Mexico City's frenetic downtown.

Explore them on one of the vibrantly decorated boats that wait at Embarcadero Belem. The best route by *trajinera* (tourist boat) visits Parque Ecológico de Xochimilco, which is formed by a number of *chinampas*—"floating" gardens built on artificially made islands of interwoven reeds, created to produce supplies of fresh food since the age of the Aztec Empire. On board, meanwhile, you'll be served food and serenaded with mariachi music while you ply the network of canals that have garnered Xochimilco the moniker "Venice of Mexico."

The New River to Lamanaii

LOCATION Belize **START/FINISH** Orange Walk (return) **DISTANCE** 26 miles (42 km) **TIME** 6 hours **INFORMATION** www.travelbelize.org

Given its imposing location on the banks of a freshwater lagoon, it's no surprise that the ancient Maya named this once-important port city Lamanaii, meaning "submerged crocodile." Take an hour-long boat trip from Orange Walk down the New River to its ruins and you will get to see these creatures for yourself, hiding in the mangroves along the river's edge. Spider monkeys are also often spotted swinging through the trees that hang over the waters' edge, along with river turtles, green iguana, and some of the 100-plus species of birds that live in the rainforest here.

Lamanaii itself is the longest-occupied settlement in the Maya world, inhabited from about 1500 BCE to well after the arrival of Spanish missionaries. It's a dramatic site—almost overshadowed by the journey to get here.

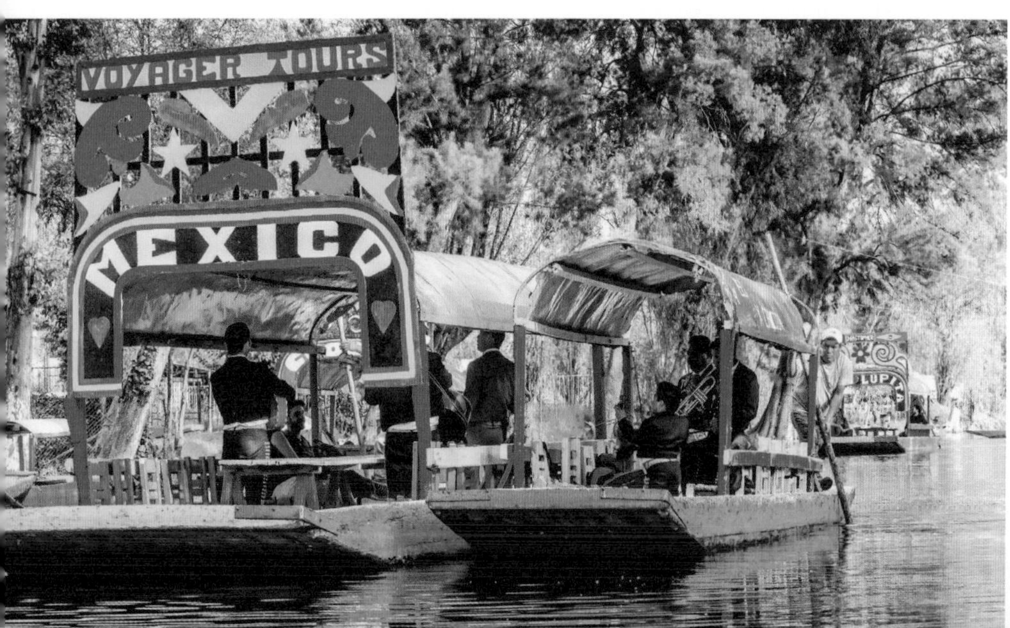

Colorful boats—with traditional mariachi bands—plying the canals of Xochimilco

Rafters riding rapids on the Río Cangrejal

21 Río Cangrejal

LOCATION Honduras **START/FINISH** Trips depart from La Ceiba **DISTANCE** 5 miles (8 km) **TIME** 4 hours **INFORMATION** www.honduras.travel/en

Just 40 minutes from the Caribbean port city of La Ceiba, the Río Cangrejal (Crab River) is a stone-strewn river valley that cuts through the dense rainforest of Parque Nacional Pico Bonito. The riotous Class II to IV rapids found here offer the ideal conditions for rafting, for total beginners and whitewater veterans alike.

Grab a paddle and brace yourself for one of the wildest river rides in Central America. It's an adrenaline-pumping session of splash-happy action, bumping into and over huge boulders and swirling around whirlpools with names like La Lavadora (the Washing Machine). As the river broadens and calms, you can stop paddling and surrender to the current. Gaze up at the surrounding forest towering from the riverbank to seek out brightly colored birds and playful monkeys as you luxuriate in the wonders of this pristine wilderness.

22 Río Sambú

LOCATION Panama **START/FINISH** La Palma/Sambú-Puerto Indio **DISTANCE** 40 miles (65 km) **TIME** 3–4 hours **INFORMATION** www.jungletrek.com; www.traveldarienpanama.com

The trip up the sinuous Río Sambú and into the legendary Darién rainforest is one of those journeys where getting there is more exciting than the destination itself. After leaving the ramshackle jungle town of La Palma, the anticipation builds as your motorized skiff skims across the bay, before sweeping into the river. Immediately, the boat slows, and the water becomes mirror still. Towering mangroves guard the river's entrance, where elegant white ibis cautiously probe the mudflats. As the snaking Sambú pushes on through the emerald undergrowth, keep your eyes and ears open for capuchin monkeys cavorting in the treetops, parrots squabbling, and the iridescent flash of an Amazon kingfisher. Eventually, wood-and-thatch homes peek out from the vegetation, and tethered dugouts bob into view, announcing your arrival at the twin settlement of Sambú-Puerto Indio. Marking the gateway to a dozen Indigenous Emberá and Wounaan communities, this is also the place to arrange further adventures, deeper into the Darién.

another way

During, or just after, the rains, when water levels are high enough, hire a local guide to forge farther up the Río Sambú by motorized dugout, as far as the remote Emberá community of Pavarandó.

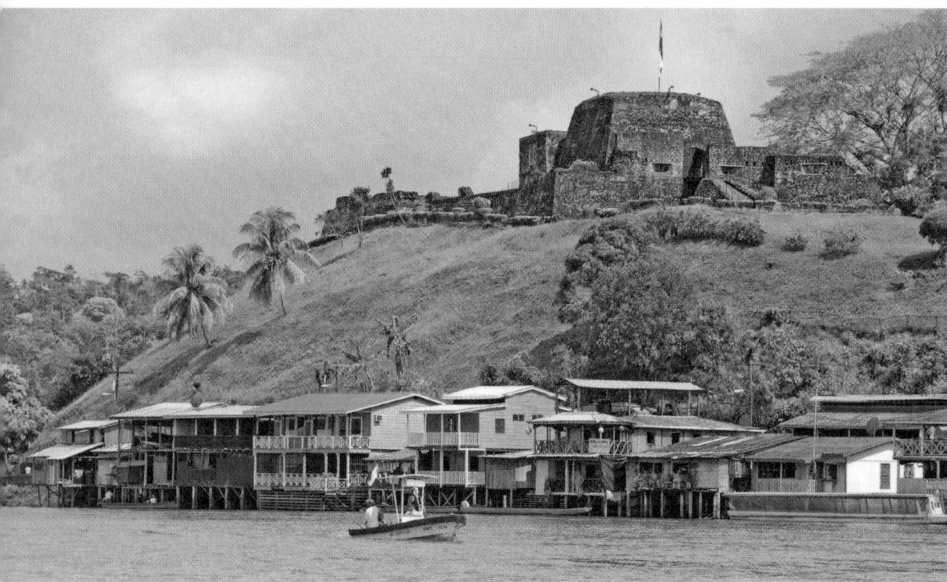

The stone fortress in El Castillo, overlooking the Río San Juan

23

Río San Juan

LOCATION Nicaragua **START/FINISH** San Carlos/San Juan de Nicaragua **DISTANCE** 119 miles (192 km) **TIME** 6 days **INFORMATION** www.visitnicaragua.us

Paddle past Nicaragua's largest biosphere reserve on a kayak trip along the historic San Juan River, once traversed by pirates and prospectors.

Accompanied by the meditative sounds of paddle splash and birdsong as you work your way down the Río San Juan, it is hard to imagine that the river saw bloody battles involving pirates like Sir Henry Morgan, who plundered the riches of colonial Granada in the 1600s. The most evocative reminder of its tumultuous past is evident at the town of El Castillo in Nicaragua, near the border with Costa Rica, where a squat stone fortress was built to take defensive advantage of the Devil's Rapids; a young Horatio Nelson took the fortress in 1780.

Paddling the Río San Juan blends history with modern-day life, the jungle communities along its banks little changed since the days when steamboats plied the waterway, carrying miners on the fastest route from the Caribbean to the Pacific during the California gold rush of the mid-19th century. The settlements are a constant presence on this journey, all the way to the swampy remnants of the British port of Greytown.

another way

At San Carlos de Nicaragua, where the Río San Juan opens into Lago Nicaragua, you can board a fast boat to whisk you across the lake to Islas Solentiname. It takes around two hours to reach the arts-and-craftsy archipelago.

24

Guna Yala

LOCATION Panama **START/FINISH** Corazón de Jesús (return) **DISTANCE** 37–50 miles (60–80 km) **TIME** 6–8 days **INFORMATION** www.sanblassailing.com; Dec–Feb rough seas can make the outer reefs inaccessible

Charter around Panama, a land of palm-topped cays and cane-and-thatch communities, and learn how the local Guna people live.

There are plenty of idyllic islands in the Caribbean, but what sets Guna Yala apart are the Guna themselves—Panama's most proudly independent Indigenous people, and residents of this island group for hundreds of years.

As you hop between the white-sand coconut isles on a catamaran, you can explore the island-villages' narrow sandy passageways, squeezed between densely packed cane-and-thatch huts; learn about *mola*-making, the traditional embroidered cloth for which the Guna are renowned; and join the locals in some informal afternoon beach volleyball.

Guna Yala is also home to swathes of luxuriant rainforest on the mainland it's part of, where on river trips you'll be shown medicinal plants and spectacular birdlife. A day's exploration by dugout is rounded off back on deck, with a chilled beer in hand as you watch the burnished sun sink behind the distant mountains.

THE 1925 REVOLUTION

Every February, the Guna celebrate the 1925 revolution against the Panamanian authorities, after which they gained a clearly defined region and a degree of political autonomy. Battle reenactments are carried out with enthusiasm, on land and at sea, accompanied by singing, dancing, and storytelling.

Boats moored off an island in Guna Yala

A boat passing under the Centennial Bridge on the Panama Canal

25

The Panama Canal

LOCATION Panama **START/FINISH** Panama City/Colón **DISTANCE** 52 miles (82 km) **TIME** 10–12 hours **INFORMATION** Panama Marine Tours (www.pmatours.net) offers partial and full transits of the canal year-round

Scything across Central America's isthmus, the Panama Canal is a remarkable feat of engineering and a magnificent encounter with nature. And the best way to appreciate both is from a boat.

Panama City's skyline glitters in the morning sun as the *Pacific Queen* slips out of the causeway harbor. Magnificent frigate birds wheel above, ushering the boat under the awe-inspiring Bridge of the Americas, stretching for 1 mile (1.6 km) across the canal. Yet it's only when you're confronted by the gargantuan Miraflores Locks that the sheer scale of the Panama Canal hits you. Position yourself on deck to catch the mighty 82 ft (25 m) gates opening, spewing forth a tumbling froth of water, and releasing a hulking container ship that dwarfs your triple-decked cruiser. Before you know it, you're enclosed within the towering lock chamber walls. Water spurts from both sides, propelling the boat upward in a matter

Position yourself on deck to catch the mighty 82 ft (25 m) gates opening

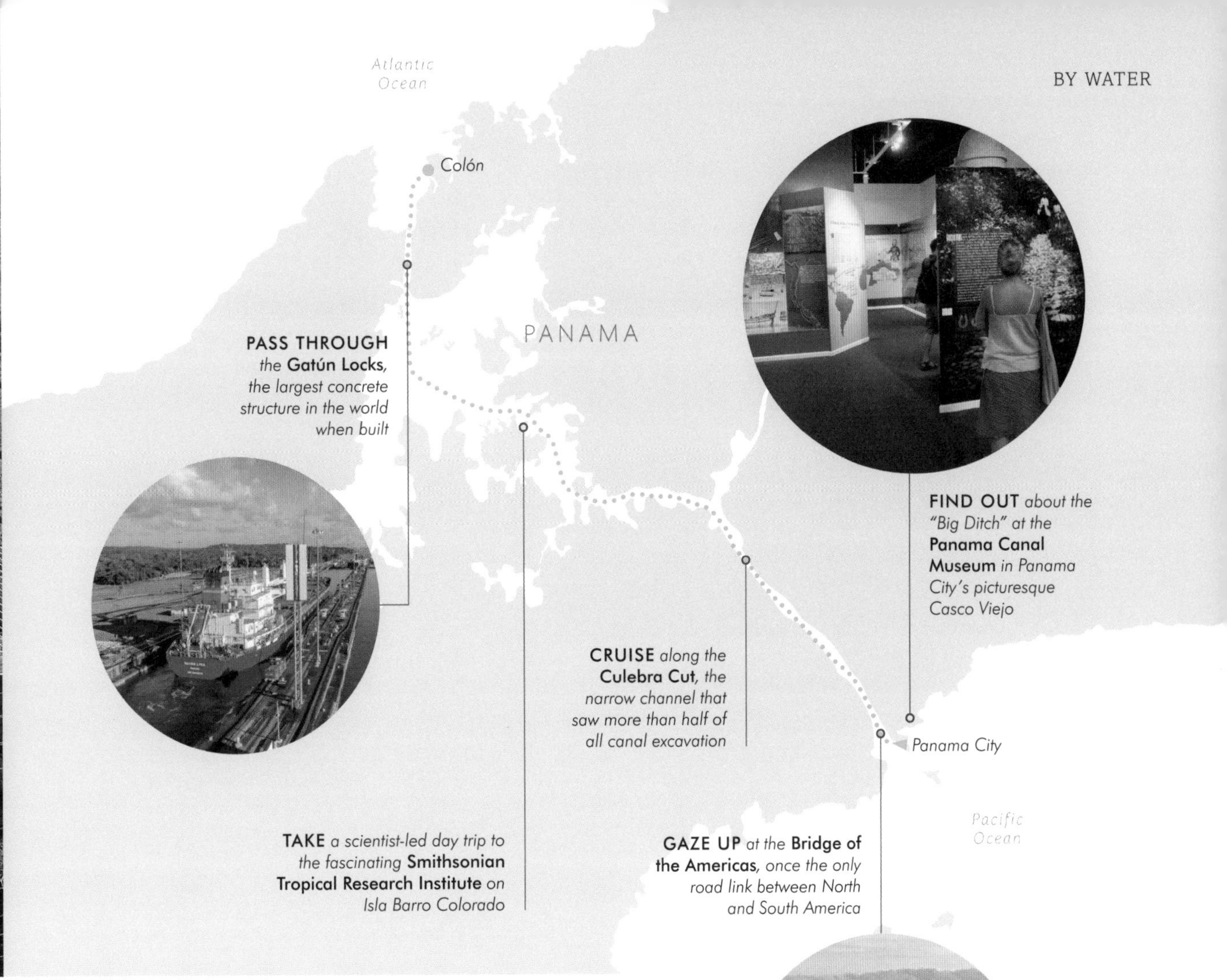

Atlantic Ocean

Colón

PANAMA

PASS THROUGH *the* **Gatún Locks,** *the largest concrete structure in the world when built*

FIND OUT *about the "Big Ditch" at the* **Panama Canal Museum** *in Panama City's picturesque Casco Viejo*

CRUISE *along the* **Culebra Cut,** *the narrow channel that saw more than half of all canal excavation*

Panama City

Pacific Ocean

TAKE *a scientist-led day trip to the fascinating* **Smithsonian Tropical Research Institute** *on Isla Barro Colorado*

GAZE UP *at the* **Bridge of the Americas,** *once the only road link between North and South America*

of minutes. Next thing, you're out the other side of the locks and ready to begin the process all over again.

As the boat works its way slowly along the canal—a full transit takes between 10 and 12 hours—the mood changes. After slicing through the rocky continental divide, the channel opens out into majestic Lago Gatún, a vast reservoir fed by the Río Chagres (this river has the unusual claim of draining into two oceans: the Pacific and the Atlantic). This is a magical wilderness, dotted with forested islands, its tentacled inlets lined with endless, lush rainforest. Keep your binoculars handy to catch toucans swooping from the canopy or playful monkeys chattering in the treetops; an expert eye might even spot watchful crocs basking in the shallows. Bathed in glowing afternoon light, you'll join a silent procession of ships traversing the millpond-still lake, bound for the final challenge: the immense Gatún Locks, the gateway to the Atlantic Ocean beyond.

another way

If cruising the whole canal seems too much, consider a five-hour partial transit. You still get to go through Miraflores and Pedro Miguel locks, and the Culebra Cut, before docking at the entrance to Lago Gatún.

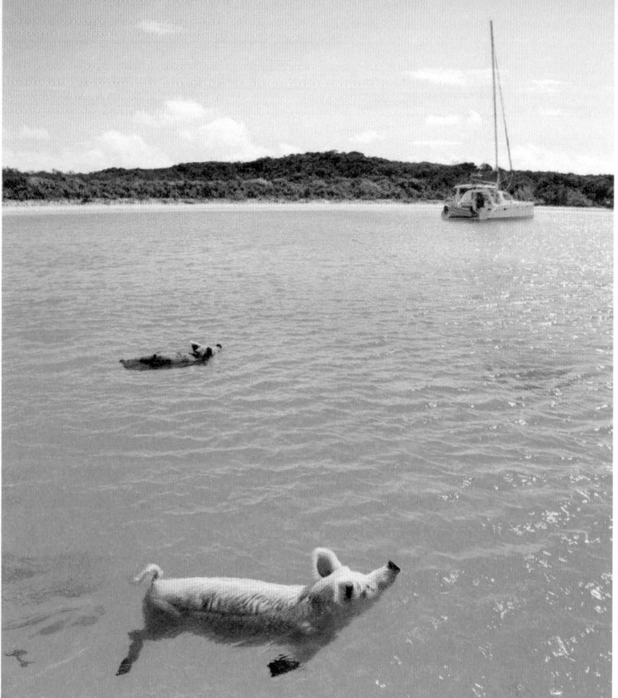

Swimming pigs, a curious sight in the Exumas' Big Major Cay

26

The Bahamas

LOCATION Bahamas **START/FINISH** George Town, Great Exuma (return) **DISTANCE** Up to 124 miles (200 km) **TIME** 7–10 days **INFORMATION** www.bahamas.com; avoid hurricane season (Jun–Nov)

The undisputed jewels of the Bahamas are the Exumas: 365 idyllic tropical islands and cays—one for every day of the year—sprinkled across 124 miles (200 km) of sparkling sapphire sea. Much of this pristine paradise lies within the protected waters of two national parks, best experienced on a catamaran cruise. Days are spent snorkeling among shoals of rainbow-colored fish and gazing at vibrant coral and grazing sea turtles. Alternatively, feel the powder-soft sand between your toes as you stroll along endless stretches of unspoiled pearl-white beach: Leaf Cay, maybe, where curious iguanas peer out of the scrub, or Big Major Cay, where water-loving hogs piggy-paddle through the shallows. Cocktails on deck at sunset are a must, followed by a beach barbecue of freshly caught seafood; miles from any city lights, flickering campfires illuminate a velvet night sky.

27

The British Virgin Islands

LOCATION British Virgin Islands **START/FINISH** Tortola (return) **DISTANCE** Various **TIME** 1 week **INFORMATION** www.bvitourism.com; avoid hurricane season (Jun–Nov)

There's nowhere better to hoist the mainsail and surge into the blue than the British Virgin Islands (BVIs), one of the best places to island-hop in the world. Conditions around this spectacular archipelago are just about flawless for sailors of all abilities: its 60-odd islands are close together, so navigation is generally possible by line-of-sight; the waters are well sheltered; and trade winds are warm and consistent. It's undeniably gorgeous, too, with plenty of white sand, swaying palms, and turquoise seas.

You can rent a boat with or without a captain and crew, depending on your skills. There's no one set itinerary to follow, although the marinas on Tortola, the main island, are good places to start. Highlights include sailing to (and swimming around) the unusual boulders of the Baths on Anegada, exploring the caves of Norman island, partying on lively Jost Van Dyke, and going to the Dogs, a handful of three paradisiacal islets.

another way

As well as the BVIs, you can also try Antigua, for Caribbean sailing at its most sociable. The island's Sailing Week (April/May) is one of the region's biggest maritime events and the après-sail bar scene is always buzzing.

28

"The Narrows"

LOCATION St. Kitts & Nevis **START/FINISH** Oualie Beach/Cockleshell Bay Beach **DISTANCE** 2.5 miles (4 km) **TIME** From 2 hours **INFORMATION** www.nevistostkittscrosschannelswim.com; event takes place in Mar or Apr

The Nevis to St. Kitts Cross Channel Swim is one of the world's most wonderful open-water events. The lush, laid-back sister isles are separated by the Narrows, and each year several hundred people come to splash across its sparkling waters.

The journey across is certainly a challenge. The sea can be choppy and is subject to variable conditions (an armada of safety boats keeps watch), but with training, most can manage it—past participants have ranged in age from eight to 80. The record is around 55 minutes, but many swimmers take two hours or more. While it is, of course, a race, the whole event has a party atmosphere, and the finish-line activities—music, a beach barbecue, a rum punch or two—are a huge part of the fun.

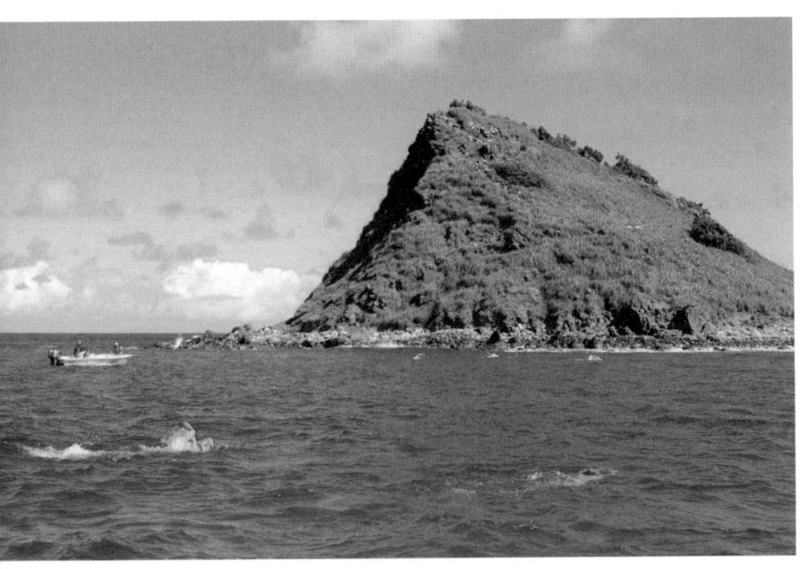

Swimmers crossing the Narrows between Nevis and St. Kitts

29

The Burro Burro River

LOCATION Guyana **START/FINISH** Surama (return) **DISTANCE** 50 miles (80 km) **TIME** 1 week **INFORMATION** www.suramaecolodge.com can help build an itinerary

To canoe the Burro Burro River is to pass through several lost worlds. One minute, it's a darkened River Styx, inky water lapping the tree trunks, black caimans stirring below the surface. The next, it's a kaleidoscope of color, yellow-banded poison-dart frogs flashing among the foliage and iridescent kingfishers flitting above the water. Everywhere is abuzz with life, thanks in part to conservation efforts funded by tourist dollars.

During a week in a wooden dugout canoe, Indigenous Makushi guides will show you the wildlife that lives here—otters, piranhas, jungle rats—and immerse you in the rainforest, building camps, making fires, and cooking campfire meals. Eco-tourism has changed the lives of the local people around here for the better—this is that rare trip where visitors give as well as take.

THE MAKUSHI

Petroglyphs in the Rupununi wetlands date back 7,000 years, but the Indigenous Makushi people have likely been here far longer—colonial contact with European settlers led to the gradual degradation of their traditions. Today, eco-tourism is helping the 9,000 Guyanese Makushi maintain their culture.

30

Around the Grenadines

The dazzling waters of Tobago Cays Marine Park

LOCATION St. Vincent and the Grenadines **START/FINISH** St. Vincent/ Union Island **DISTANCE** Around 50 miles (80 km) **TIME** 1–2 weeks **INFORMATION** www.discoversvg.com; check timetables

Take a slow, sociable tour by local ferry, for a wonderful way to link up the lovely little Grenadine islands of Bequia, Mayreau, Canouan, and Union.

The tadpole-shaped archipelago of St. Vincent and the Grenadines is a spectacular spot for a low-cost Caribbean adventure, with local ferries providing a cheap way to hop between the main island and the 30-odd smaller siblings that tail off to the south. Each island offers a different style of paradise. In beautiful Bequia, you can explore tiny Port Elizabeth and soak up the island's rich maritime history. Then catch the fast ferry on to Canouan, then Mayreau, and finally Union. Canouan is a mix of fancy resorts, a local village, and superb snorkeling, while walkable Mayreau is more laid back—and a good place to arrange a trip to the dazzling waters of Tobago Cayes Marine Park. Union is the adventure isle, with excellent opportunities for hill hikes, dive lessons, and kitesurfing classes. With so much trading and socializing centered on the country's decks and docks, the journey down to Union provides a colorful—and unforgettable—insight into St. Vincentian life.

> The archipelago is a spectacular spot for a low-cost Caribbean adventure

31

The Galápagos

LOCATION Ecuador **START/FINISH** Baltra or San Cristobal (return) **DISTANCE** Varies **TIME** 4–15 days **INFORMATION** www.galapagos.org; tourist card required

Board a boat to navigate this extraordinary South American archipelago, home to a curious cast of all creatures great and small.

The Galápagos: remote, minuscule, momentous. Lying 621 miles (1,000 km) off the coast of Ecuador, these 19 islands once shook the globe. Famously, in 1835, young naturalist Charles Darwin observed characteristics in the endemic wildlife here that influenced his groundbreaking evolutionary theories, changing the way we view the world in the process.

The wildlife remains just as inspiring today, a strange menagerie of land and marine iguanas, giant tortoises, flightless cormorants, seals and sea lions, equatorial penguins, and many types of booby and finch.

A range of vessels, from intimate yachts to 100-berth cruisers, offer trips around the islands from three to 14 nights. The itinerary of each one is strictly regulated, so there are never too many docked at the same landing site. Depending on which boat you choose, visits might include the Charles Darwin Research Station on Santa Cruz, the volcanic landscapes of Isabela, the flamingos of Rabida, or the waved albatross colonies of Española. But it might just be the snorkeling that you remember the most: an underwater window into this remarkable world.

another way

Isla de la Plata, 22 miles (35 km) off mainland Ecuador, is known as the "poor man's Galápagos." Depending on the season, you might see blue- and red-footed boobies, frigate birds, waved albatross, sea lions, and humpback whales.

Galápagos giant tortoises, cooling off in a pool, Santa Cruz island

32

Through the Amazon

LOCATION Peru **START/FINISH** Yurimaguas/Iquitos
DISTANCE 385 miles (620 km) **TIME** 3–5 days
INFORMATION Transportes Eduardo has cargo-ship departures to Iquitos from La Boca, Yurimaguas' main port

Pootle through the most biodiverse terrain on earth, stopping at remote jungle communities en route to the isolated Amazon town of Iquitos.

Reached after hours of bone-rattling bus travel, Yurimaguas is a languid town of dusty thoroughfares and a somnolent central square. Yet the end of one journey marks the beginning of another. Venture down to the riverbank, where—amid a clamor of vendors hawking cheap gadgetry, good-luck charms, manioc root, and jungle juices—you can eye up which of the vessels moored in the mud-hued water might best suit your next leg: through the Amazon to Iquitos.

And it's a boat you'll need. Barely halfway across Peru, the final furlong of road fizzles out at Yurimaguas, and the next few hundred miles of sticky jungle can be negotiated only by a two-hour flight or several days' drifting on a boat. Choose the river and you choose a slow, sweaty, sensory overload of a journey along the waterways of Loreto toward the rainforest metropolis of Iquitos, the world's largest city that's not connected by road.

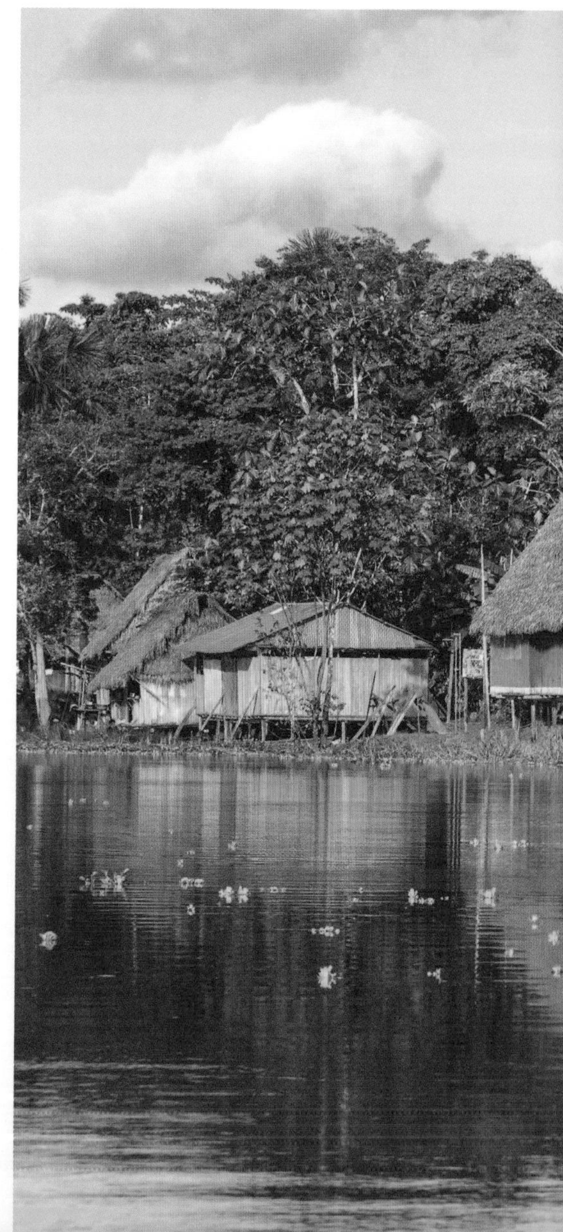

Choose the river and you choose a slow, sweaty, sensory overload of a journey

Right *Exploring a river tributary by kayak*
Below *Huts lining the riverbank on the outskirts of Iquitos*

Aboard a cargo boat, ungainly and often overloaded, you'll learn more about Peruvian Amazonian life, in all its color and cacophony, than you could hope to in a month on the road. It will be just you, perhaps a few other backpackers, and some locals, their animals, and their luggage, at close quarters for three, four, maybe five days—time blurs on the Huallaga and Marañon rivers. You'll tuck into hearty rainforest fare like *juanes* (chicken and rice steamed in jungle leaves) and share deck space with plantains and guinea pigs. Accompanying you will be a soundtrack of salsa or Peruvian folk music, conversations covering all aspects of Amazonian cargo logistics, and a fair few clucks and grunts from the nonhuman passengers. Your accommodations? The hammock you'll have no doubt recently purchased, idly swinging from the boat's wooden ceiling as a forested landscape astonishing in its vastness slides by.

another way

You can also catch cargo ships from Iquitos down the Amazon River to the tri-frontier with Brazil and Colombia, then continue toward Manaus in Brazil and, finally, Belém, where the second-longest river in the world meets the sea.

Left *A common woolly monkey feeding in the treetops in the Reserva Nacional Pacaya-Samiria*
Below *Passengers lazing away the day in hammocks on a cargo boat*

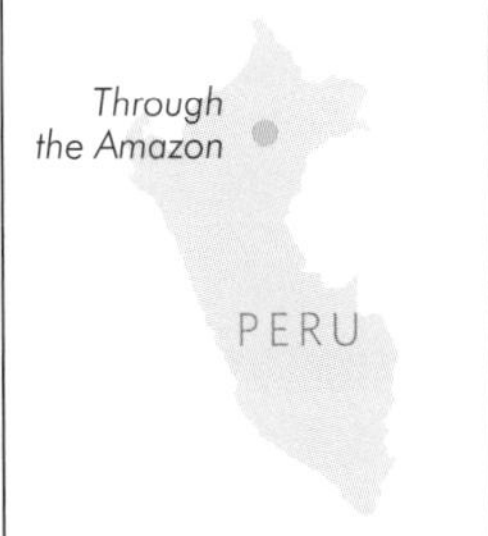

OBSERVE *the huge city of* **Iquitos** *rearing up surreally after hundreds of miles of tranquil jungle*

Iquitos

SWING *in your hammock during days of downtime, as the rainforest floats slowly past*

PERU

WATCH *an eclectic collection of cargo, from bananas to motorcycles, being loaded onto your vessel*

SPOT *one of the Amazon's pink river dolphins swimming alongside the boat*

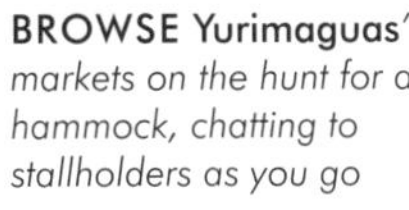

BROWSE Yurimaguas' *markets on the hunt for a hammock, chatting to stallholders as you go*

Yurimaguas

You'll chug across an area of Peru that's larger than Japan, and seemingly larger still due to your cargo boat's ponderousness. This is a place of scarcely penetrable foliage, populated mostly by a few scattered settlements at which you'll inevitably stop to load and unload sugar cane and construction materials and myriad more obscure items. The journey begins in secondary jungle, but soon primary, old-growth rainforest presses to the riverside in an entanglement of emerald green. Caiman bask on the banks and pink river dolphins occasionally cavort along the currents. You'll pass hours contemplating fauna-rich vistas as you forge through some of the planet's most biodiverse terrain, not least the enormous Reserva Nacional Pacaya-Samiria. And you'll spend almost as much time absorbed by life on board; this is one of the most captivating ways to slowly get from A to B.

PACAYA-SAMIRIA

The 8,030 sq mile (20,800 sq km) Reserva Nacional Pacaya-Samiria is Peru's largest protected space. You can stop off at the port of Lagunas en route for a guided tour into the heart of the reserve; you'll need several days to reach the areas with the most interesting flora and fauna. Other vessels (cargo boats or speedboats) can then take you on to Iquitos afterward.

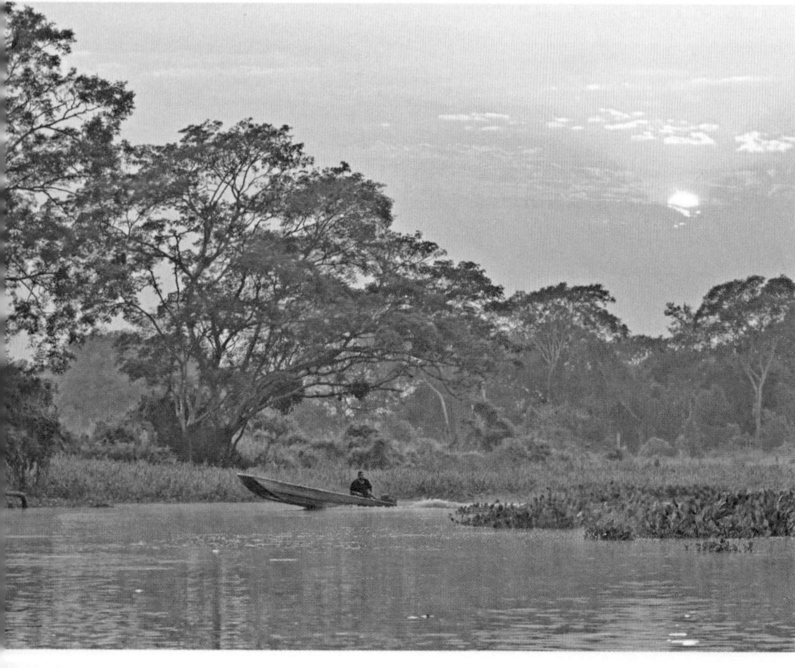

Above *A magnificent jaguar hunting in the Pantanal*
Left *Boating along a channel in the wetlands*

Floating fields of giant water lilies stretch as far as the eye can see

33

The Pantanal

LOCATION Brazil **START/FINISH** Porto Jofre (return) **DISTANCE** 87 miles (140 km) **TIME** 6 days **INFORMATION** www.brazilnaturetours.com

Cruise through the Pantanal wetlands on a traditional Brazilian houseboat, spotting tropical birdlife and perhaps a glimpse of an ever-elusive jaguar.

The Pantanal wetlands are home to some of the most remarkable wildlife in South America: floating fields of giant water lilies stretch as far as the eye can see; giant river otters drift along in the currents; giant anteaters root around in termite mounds; and hyacinth macaws squawk amid flashes of purple in the canopies above. During nearly a week spent on board, and with expert guides leading you on excursions down narrow river channels and on foot into the national park, you might even spot a jaguar, the most fearsome (and elusive) of the local residents.

On the water, you'll have plenty of chances to spot birdlife—it's hard to imagine a more relaxing afternoon than one spent sipping a caipirinha while looking out for technicolor toucans and red-throated jabiru storks. In fact, just relaxing on board is one of the most memorable experiences of taking a trip on the houseboats that ply this route, many of which combine traditional Brazilian style with modern levels of luxury—and, perhaps, a top-deck view of that charismatic big cat.

PROTECTING THE JAGUAR

The Pantanal is the best place in the world to see jaguars in the wild; the stronghold for an animal that once ranged from the US to Argentina. "Jaguar tourism" is helping protect the animals, by preserving their habitats and providing income for local people, deterring potential poachers.

Porto Jofre

ENJOY *some bird-watching from the deck of your boat, spotting storks and toucans*

MARVEL *at the giant water lily carpets and Amolar mountains of* **Pantanal National Park**

BRAZIL

RIDE *through narrow channels in small boats on the lookout for rare jaguars*

HIKE *the slopes of* **Caracara Hill,** *taking in sweeping views of the Pantanal from its summit*

BRAZIL

The Pantanal

34

To Tierra del Fuego

LOCATION Chile/Argentina **START/FINISH** Punta Arenas/Ushuaia **DISTANCE** 315 miles (583 km) **TIME** 4 days **INFORMATION** www.australis.com; visit Oct–Apr to see penguins

A cruise from Punta Arenas to Ushuaia transports passengers through fjords lined with mountains and creaking glaciers.

South of Patagonia, across the Strait of Magellan, Tierra del Fuego is a maze of channels, fjords, islands, and rocky outcrops. Home to Indigenous peoples, such as the canoe-based Yagán, for millennia, this spectacular, sparsely populated archipelago is unevenly split between Chile and Argentina.

The best way to explore the "Land of Fire" is by boat or ship. Luxury cruises travel between Punta Arenas and Ushuaia—both isolated port cities with fascinating histories—cutting across the gunboat-gray Strait of Magellan. They then travel the storied Beagle Channel, the shores of which are home to dense forests, ragged Andean peaks, and sweeping bays populated by flocks of marine birds.

En route, you'll visit pristine Parque Nacional Alberto de Agostini, an otherwise inaccessible realm of deep fjords, looming glaciers, and raucous colonies of elephant seals and penguins. And you'll also call in at Cape Horn, the most southerly tip of South America; overlooking the legendarily rough waters of the Drake Passage, the rocky promontory feels like the end of the world.

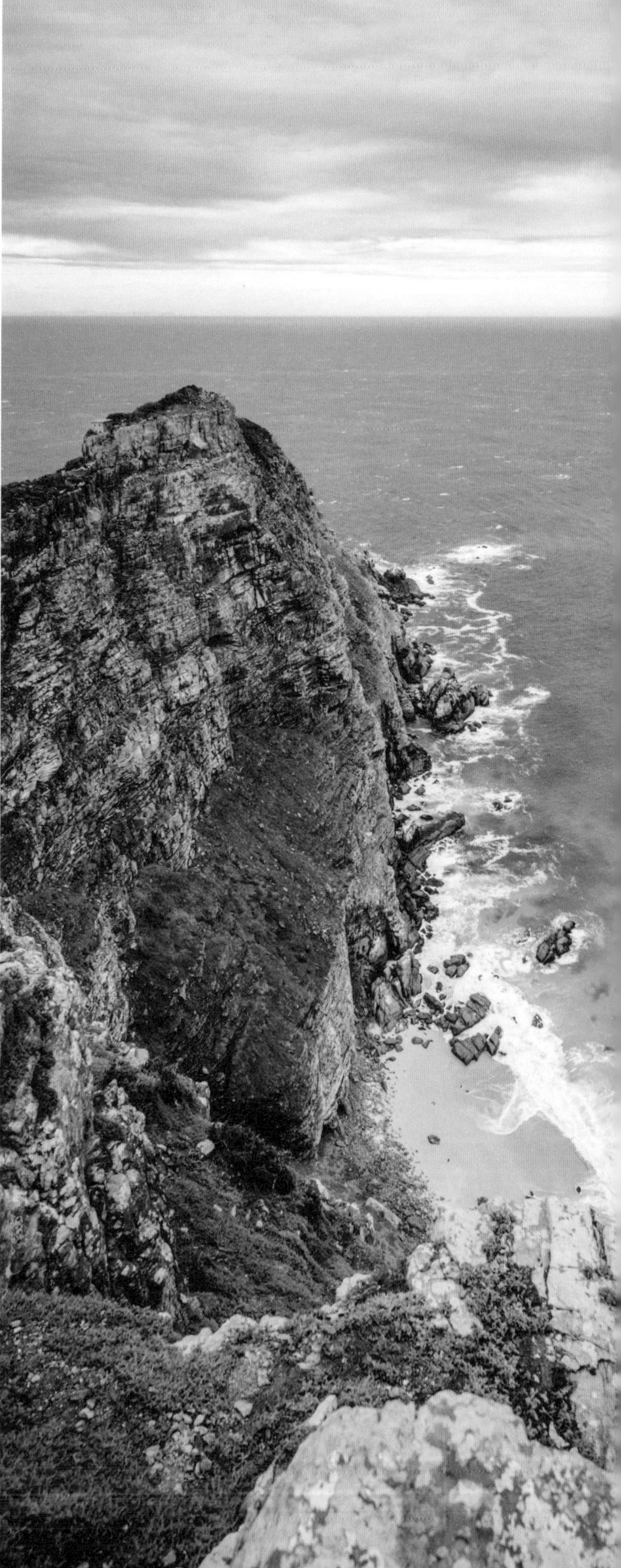

Cape Horn, the most southerly tip of South America

San Isidro lighthouse, Punta Arenas

35

Strait of Magellan: Cabo Froward

LOCATION Chile **START/FINISH** End of Ruta 9/Bahía Rosas **DISTANCE** 15.5–18.5 miles (25–30 km) **TIME** 3 days **INFORMATION** Patagonia's notoriously fierce winds can often delay kayaking trips, so allow some flexibility in your schedule

Paddle along a historic waterway, renowned for its wealth of marine life, to isolated Cabo Froward, the southernmost point on the mainland of South America.

At the tip of the Brunswick Peninsula, jutting into the Strait of Magellan, windswept Cabo Froward is a starkly beautiful spot that is accessible only by water or hiking trail. Guided kayaking trips are best, plowing through choppy waters patrolled by dolphins and humpback and minke whales. You'll explore a coastline that features an abandoned whaling station, a giant cross (erected to honor the 1987 visit to Chile of Pope John Paul II) and the lonely San Isidro lighthouse, at the foot of Monte Tarn; the latter was climbed by British naturalist Charles Darwin in 1834 during his groundbreaking voyage around South America.

At night, you'll wild camp in quiet bays sheltered by wind-sculpted beech forests, settings that provide a welcome sense of calm and solitude after an adrenaline-charged day paddling along the mighty Strait of Magellan.

another way

Swap your kayak for hiking boots and follow a 31-mile (50 km) trail along the windswept coastline from the end of Ruta 9 to Cabo Froward. It's a memorable, two-day trek along a little-trod route.

36

The South Shetland Islands

LOCATION Antarctica **START/FINISH** King George Island (return) **DISTANCE** 250–500 miles (400–800 km) **TIME** 2–4 days **INFORMATION** www.iaato.org; Nov–March only

A string of islands around 75 miles (120 km) north of the Antarctic Peninsula, the South Shetlands are more biodiverse than any other part of Antarctica and home to historic sites rich with stories.

For some first-time polar tourists, the prospect of setting foot on continental Antarctica overshadows every other experience the region can offer. However, a trip around the South Shetland Islands can be far more than just a prelude or coda to the big adventure; it can add real depth and breadth to your time on the Southern Ocean.

There are few places on earth where nature is so tangibly in charge, yet there are also noticeable traces of human activity, from the ruined remains of old whaling and research stations on Deception Island to the bust on Elephant Island that commemorates Luis Pardo, the Chilean mariner who helped rescue Shackleton's *Endurance* crew from this forbiddingly isolated spot.

Small-ship visitors can hop ashore several islands by rigid inflatable boat. Popular stops include Pendulum Cove, on Deception Island, where you can "swim" in the volcanically warmed water, and Hanah Point on Livingston Island, home to large penguin rookeries and elephant seals, who loll on the sands in defiance of the hostile conditions.

Cruising past snow-streaked Deception Island

Navigating the turbulent waters of the Drake Passage

37

Crossing the Drake Passage

LOCATION Between South America and Antarctica **START/ FINISH** Cape Horn/South Shetland Islands **DISTANCE** 500 miles (800 km) **TIME** 2 days **INFORMATION** www.iaato.org; crossings included in Antarctic expedition cruises; Nov–Mar only

The turbulent waters south of Cape Horn can test the hardiest of sailors, but for wildlife watchers, they offer ample reward—and Antarctica feels thrillingly close.

For most Antarctica-bound expedition cruise passengers, the adventure begins well over a day before the first icebergs appear on the horizon. Just beyond South America, the waves pick up and so does the excitement–the open ocean offers the chance to spot wildlife such as albatrosses, petrels, and humpback whales.

Before the advent of oceangoing ships, these waters were known only to Indigenous Fuegians, whose canoes couldn't make much headway against the raging waves. The scale of the sea remained a mystery until long-distance navigators began edging farther and farther south, searching for links between the Atlantic and Pacific. Eventually, in 1525 the Spanish mariner Francisco de Hoces deduced the existence of an open-water route around Cape Horn. In his honor, Spanish speakers call these waters Mar de Hoces. Seasoned cruisers of all nationalities, however, nickname it the Drake Shake–it's a common occurrence on the journey for the ship to start rolling–or, in moments of calm, the Drake Lake.

DRAKE'S VOYAGE

The Drake Passage is named after the Englishman Sir Francis Drake, who was perhaps the first European navigator to sail these waters. In 1578, beset by storms, he voyaged toward South America's southern tip in his ship *Pelican*, which he renamed *Golden Hind* en route.

A colony of gentoo penguins on the Antarctic Peninsula

38

The Antarctic Peninsula

LOCATION Antarctica **START/FINISH** Ushuaia (return) **DISTANCE** 500–1,500 miles (800–2,400 km) **TIME** 4–10 days **INFORMATION** www.iaato.org; most expedition ships traveling to the Antarctic Peninsula via the South Shetlands launch from Ushuaia (Argentina); a few launch from Punta Arenas (Chile); it's also possible to embark on King George Island (South Shetland Islands); Nov–Mar only

Compact and agile, small-scale expedition ships don't just show you Antarctica; they immerse you in its landscapes—and help make every trip an educational experience.

A voyage along the coast of the Antarctic Peninsula is a visual feast, rich in natural artistry, texture, and color. As your ship weaves between snowcapped rocky islands, through glacier-walled channels, and around icebergs of every size, you're wrapped in a multihued, ever-changing canvas. On some mornings, it glows apricot, coral, and gold. On others, the backdrop fades to black and white, with just the ice radiating blue.

There's more to expedition cruising than just gazing in wonder at the passing landscape, however. When conditions allow, there are at least two excursions a day, in carefully chosen locations. On ships carrying more than 100 passengers, those wishing to take part are split into groups to avoid overcrowding at the excursion sites, all of which are ecologically delicate and stringently protected. Dressed from head to toe in thermal waterproofs, you'll leave the ship by rigid inflatable boat to cruise around pristine bays or land on perfect little beaches, right in the thick of things. With crowds of penguins and herds of seals, none of whom pay much attention to the human visitors that putter or wander among them, these remote spots are among the most astonishing wildlife-watching destinations in the world.

The backdrop fades to black and white, with just the ice radiating blue

SEALS AND WHALES

Antarctica's marine mammals were ruthlessly exploited for much of the 20th century, but their populations are steadily recovering. There's a good chance of seeing humpback whales, minke whales, and orcas on a cruise; the more time you spend scanning the waters, the better the odds. Surprisingly, perhaps, Antarctica's seals can be just as impressive—particularly elephant seals, which can weigh more than a car, and leopard seals, which are ferocious predators.

WATCH *the fringes of a mighty glacier tumble into the water in* **Neko Harbour**

VISIT *the fascinating little museum at* **Port Lockroy**, *a former whaling station, military base, and research center*

GAZE *in awe at the spectacular snowscapes surrounding* **Paradise Bay**, *lapped by an ice-scattered sea*

WANDER *through the gentoo penguin colony at Port Charcot on* **Booth Island**

ENJOY *an otherworldly cruise through the* **Lemaire Channel**, *admiring the icy mountains reflected in its mirrorlike waters*

Left Kayakers paddling Neko Harbour, with a backdrop of glaciers and mountains
Below A leopard seal, resting on an ice floe

On some voyages, it's possible to go sea kayaking, snow-shoeing, or ice-camping, absorbing and interpreting the sights, sounds, and smells of your surroundings from a different perspective. To really get your heart racing, you may also be offered the chance to take a "Polar Plunge," jumping (under careful supervision) into the open water for a swift, bracing dip.

Typically, short voyages focus on the Gerlache Strait and Port Lockroy section of the Antarctic Peninsula's west coast, while longer trips cover a larger area, sometimes stretching from the northeast tip of the peninsula to a little south of the Antarctic Circle. However, with conditions prone to sudden change, the precise locations where activities take place are decided by the captain and expedition leader on a day-by-day basis, making every itinerary unique and adding an exciting element of spontaneity to the experience.

Between excursions, life on board revolves around gentle academic briefings, lectures, and screenings covering everything from zoology, ecology, and animal behavior to geology, history, and the impact of climate change. As well as naturalists and physical activity specialists, there's normally at least one professional photographer on the team, ready to offer inspiration and technical advice. Passengers are also usually welcome to head up to the bridge to watch the captain and officers at work—a particularly fascinating experience when there's some tricky navigation underway.

Friendly rivalries sometimes develop between passengers as each day's sightings are recorded on notice boards and word spreads of exceptional encounters. Special moments such as penguins porpoising, leopard seals hunting, and whales breaching or spy-hopping can occur in a blink of an eye. No two individuals will ever have exactly the same voyage.

another way

Bigger cruise ships also venture into these picturesque waters. While Antarctica's conservation guidelines don't allow their relatively large numbers of passengers to make shore landings, simply watching the passing scene from deck can be a superb experience.

INDEX

D

E

F

G

S

T

U

V

W

Y

Z

ACKNOWLEDGMENTS

DK Eyewitness would like to thank the following authors for their contribution to this book:

Jacqui Agate is a travel journalist and editor specializing in the US, with a keen interest in the southern states. She splits her time between the UK and the US, writing regular features for publications, including *The Times*, *The Telegraph*, *Wanderlust*, and *National Geographic Traveller*.

Rob Ainsley hasn't cycled all his life. Not yet anyway. He has five and a half bikes, all with rack and mudguards, and is collecting international End to Ends—some (e.g., Cuba) taking longer than others (e.g., the Faroes). He writes for cycling magazines about his native Yorkshire, Britain, the world and everywhere else, and blogs on e2e.bike.

Sarah Baxter is a travel journalist, author, hiker, and runner. She is a Contributing Editor of *Wanderlust* magazine and writes for many other publications, including *The Guardian*, *The Telegraph*, and *The Times*. She is the author of *A History of the World in 500 Walks* and several titles in the Inspired Traveller's Guide series, and has contributed to more than a dozen guidebooks.

Richard Franks is a freelance travel writer and journalist based in Birmingham, UK. Richard specializes in writing about adventure travel, the great outdoors, and music-based tourism across Scotland, the West Midlands, and the US. He writes articles for many publications, including BBC Travel, *National Geographic Traveller*, *The Telegraph*, *The Times* and *Sunday Times*, *The Independent*, and *The i*, as well as guide-books for DK Eyewitness, Rough Guides, and Lonely Planet. Richard enjoys photography, hiking, and wild camping in his spare time.

Zoey Goto is a journalist and author covering US travel, all things Americana, vintage style, musical icons, and midcentury pop culture. She has written books on Elvis Presley and retro fashion, while her editorial work has appeared in *National Geographic*, BBC Travel, *GQ*, *Esquire*, Lonely Planet, *Vogue*, and *Rolling Stone*. Zoey has a thing for celebrity sleepovers, having slept in Elvis's teenage bedroom and spent the night in Dolly Parton's dinky pink bed on her tour bus.

Emma Gregg is an award-winning travel journalist who has visited all seven continents. She specializes in responsible tourism, writing extensively about sustainable travel, including low-carbon, flight-free trips. Based in the UK, she loves forests, islands, and coral reefs, and is never happier than when embarking on a new adventure.

Sara Humphreys has journeyed around much of Latin America and the Caribbean—by dugout in the Darién, on a banana boat down the Amazon, and trekking in the Andes—and has written for DK Eyewitness and Rough Guides on Panama, Peru, Ecuador, and the Caribbean. When not exploring rainforests, mountains, or deserts, she can be found lolling in a hammock in Barbados.

Stephen Keeling has worked on several titles for DK Eyewitness, including the award-winning DK Eyewitness New York travel guide, plus guides to the US, California, Florida, Philadelphia, and Washington, DC. Born in the UK and based in New York City since 2006, he started his career as a financial journalist before writing his first travel guide in 2005.

Ben Lerwill is an award-winning freelance travel writer based in the English countryside. His specialist subjects include walking, wildlife, and rail travel, and his work appears everywhere from *National Geographic Traveller* to *BBC Countryfile Magazine*. He is also a children's author, focusing mainly on nonfiction books.

Mike MacEacheran is an award-winning freelance travel journalist who writes for many publications, including *The Telegraph*, *FT*, *The Guardian*, *National Geographic*, *The Washington Post*, *The Wall Street Journal*, *Conde Nast Traveller*, *Monocle*, *The Observer*, *The Independent*, and BBC Travel. He's reported from 115 countries and lives in Edinburgh.

Russell Maddicks is driven by a passion for venturing into parts unknown (to him) and polishing up his Spanish. Over the last 25 years, he has traveled all over Latin America, publishing his experiences in print, online, and on social media. He has written articles for BBC Travel, *National Geographic Traveller*, and *Songlines* and has authored guides to Cuba, Ecuador, Mexico, Nicaragua, and Venezuela. Join him on his travels on Instagram and X (formerly Twitter) @LatAmTravelist.

Shafik Meghji is an award-winning travel writer, journalist, and author of *Crossed off the Map: Travels in Bolivia*. Specializing in Latin America and South Asia, he has coauthored more than 40 guidebooks for DK Eyewitness, Lonely Planet, and Rough Guides, and writes for BBC Travel and *Wanderlust*, among others. He can be found at shafikmeghji.com and on Instagram and X @ShafikMeghji.

Dan Stables is a travel writer and journalist based in Manchester, UK. He writes for a variety of print and online publications and has authored or contributed to more than 30 travel books. He also hosts a podcast, Hungry Ghosts, about food and travel. Find his work at danielstables.co.uk, on Instagram @DanStabs, or on X @DanStables.

Charles Usher is an American writer and editor whose work focuses on travel and culture, particularly in the American Midwest and South Korea. He's the author of the book *Seoul Sub-urban* and has written for *The Guardian*, DK Eyewitness, and Lonely Planet, and other outlets. He lives in Milwaukee, Wisconsin, with his wife and their dog, Bono.

Lisa Voormeij is originally from the Netherlands and now resides both in the mountainous West Kootenay region of British Columbia and along the Pacific shores of Mexico. She's been writing about adventurous sightseeing since 2006 and has contributed to more than 60 travel books.

Kerry Walker is an award-winning travel writer and photographer based in the wild Cambrian Mountains in mid Wales. Never happier than when hoofing up a mountain or diving into the sea or snow, she has traveled all seven continents, contributing to dozens of travel guides, books, and articles for publishers, including *National Geographic Traveller*, *The Times*, and *The Independent*. Her website is kerryawalker.com and she can be found on X @kerryawalker.

Luke Waterson is a Wales-based adventure/culinary travel writer and novelist with a penchant for the UK outdoors, Scandinavia, and Latin America, about which he writes for the BBC, Lonely Planet, *The Telegraph*, Adventure.com, *The Sunday Times*, and many others. Read about his latest writing projects and travels at lukeandhiswords.com.

DK Eyewitness would like to thank the following for their kind permission to reproduce their photographs:

(Key: a-above; b-below/bottom; c-center; f-far; l-left; r-right; t-top)

123RF.com: chuyu 146tl, Panoramic Images 207t, Sean Pavone 92tr, phbcz 111tr

4Corners: Massimo Ripani 229tr

Alamy Stock Photo: AFF / Curtis Hilbun 85, agefotostock 50tr, All Canada Photos 38bl, 105, All Canada Photos / Chris Cheadle 222tr, All Canada Photos / Rolf Hicker 104, All Canada Photos / Ryan Creary 139br, All Canada Photos / Steve Ogle 162bl, Cedric Angeles 230tl, Al Argueta 50tl, Associated Press / Kent Sievers 90, Mary Liz Austin 17, Biosphoto / Jack Chapman 221bl, Maciej Bledowski 181bl, Paul Brady 219crb, Dominique Braud / Dembinsky Photo Associates 137tr, BRUSINI Aurlien / hemis.fr 56, Marc Bruxelle 148br, Cavan Images 114, Cavan Images / Michael Wilson 15b, Mike Cavaroc 23tr, Pravine Chester 113t, Thornton Cohen 79crb, Colouria Media / Thomas Haltner 246crb, Peter Conner 82cr, Hemis / CORDIER Sylvain 238t, Ian Dagnall 83t, Danita Delimont 136-137, 142, 154br, Design Pics Inc 165clb, Design Pics Inc / Robert Postma 223, Wolfgang Diederich 196bl, 205cla, Don Johnston_WC 219cl, Stephen Dorey 218tl, Douglas Peebles Photography 18, Johannes Elze 31, Clint Farlinger 135, Jerry Fornarotto 5tl, 122-123, Jon G. Fuller 19cr, Roberto Fumagalli 46cl, GARDEL Bertrand / hemis.fr 46tc, Jorge Garrido 191t, Ken Gillespie / Design Pics 188bl, Diego Grandi 58-59, Jeffrey Isaac Greenberg 9+ 133b, GUIZIOU Franck / hemis.fr 155, Robert Haasmann 172, Russ Heinl 45, hemis.fr / HEINTZ Jean 5bl, 168-169, Dan Herrick 49, Image Professionals GmbH / LOOK-foto 67clb, imageBROKER.com GmbH 35tl, 35c, imageBROKER.com GmbH & Co. KG / Peter Giovannini 115cb, imageBROKER.com GmbH & Co. KG / Schoening 108cl, imageBROKER.com GmbH & Co. KG / Stefan Wackerhagen 35, Florida Images 55tr, Images By T.O.K. 15t, 176clb, Rebecca Jackrel 243, Karol Kozlowski Premium RM Collection 157tl, Ton Koene 186br, Larry Larsen 226, Chon Kit Leong 191c, Yadid Levy 167tr, William Manning 132tl, mauritius images GmbH 156b, Robert McGouey / Industry 184-185, Ann Moore 128-129tc, Tim Moore 147t, Nature Picture Library / Kirkendall-Spring 22fcla, Ron Niebrugge 101tr, M. Timothy O'Keefe 229cla, Douglas H. Orton 99tr, Brian Overcast 190t, Panoramic Images 152, Kevin Parsons 132cr, Peter Phipp / Travelshots.com 232tl, Graham Prentice 64tr, Prisma by Dukas Presseagentur GmbH / Heeb Christian 118bl, 192, Pulsar Imagens 60cl, Wasin Pummarin 64tl, Francesco Puntiroli 62tl, Sergi Reboredo 247tr, Edwin Remsberg 83br, robertharding / Bhaskar Krishnamurthy 188tr, robertharding / Richard Maschmeyer 47br, Pep Roig 34, Roussel Photography 194clb, Susan Rydberg 87, Jekaterina Sahmanova 63t, James Schwabel 213crb, scott sady / tahoelight.com 145tl, Witold Skrypczak 26-27, 143tr, 153cb, SOPA Images Limited 175tr, Spring Images 30, Stacy Walsh Rosenstock 126, 127br, dave stamboulis 119cl, Stephen Saks Photography 138bl, Stockimo / hippsdesign 215, Stan Tess 78c, The British Columbia Collection 222cla, TMI 32tr, Gary Tognoni 25b, Morgan Trimble 218b, Richard Uhlhorn 29cra, Rohan Van Twest 225, Greg Vaughn / VWPics 153tr, Frank Vetere 78t, vicy 153br, Margaret Welby 157cr, Michael Wheatley 187tl, Daniel Wilson 82bl

AWL Images: Walter Bibikow 43tr, ClickAlps 37cra, Danita Delimont Stock 121, Michele Falzone 216-217l, Francesco Riccardo Iacomino 217br

Cass Scenic Railroad: Walter Scriptunas II 179t

Depositphotos Inc: hecke06 219tl, kamchatka 119tl, 187cl, Vitor Marigo 61br, naticastillog 89tl, rjv101@charter.net 96tr, sepavone 89cra, zrfphoto 75tr

Dreamstime.com: 139bl, Christopher Babcock 41tr, Linda Bair 183br, Juergen Bochynek 109t, Darryl Brooks 100, Rafa Cichawa 52, 63b, Santiago Cornejo 165ca, Jim Cottingham 29tl, David Crane 173bc, Simon Dannhauer 108cr, Dianabahrin 180tl, Leandro Dures 60cr, Elovkoff 191crb, Emicristea 68, F11photo 204-205tl, Aqnus Febriyant 4bl, 8-9, Kirk Fisher 144, Jonas Friard 102, Filip Fuxa 158, Roberto Galan 14tl, Alexander Garaev 108c, Ggw1962 40ca, Erik Gonzalez 194br, Ben Graham 176cr, Henryturner 97c, Svitlana Imnadze 99bc, Ritu Jethani 127cl, Bill Kennedy 96tl, Ivan Kokoulin 54, Kwiktor 22tc, 29cl, Larry Gevert 145tr, Martinmark 44tr, Sergey Mayorov 166bl, Vadim Nefedov 57, Marketa Novakova 224, Pancaketom 241tr, Paulbuhr 205cr, Nancy Pauwels 131tl, Vadim Petrov 2-3, Photosimo 164tr, Ronniechua 37tc, Jekaterina Sahmanova 62cr, Saintdags_Photography 51, Faustino Sanchez 228tl, Curtis Smith 220, Kalyan V. Srinivas 24t, John Stager 40crb, Aleksandar Todorovic 110tl, Christopher Venus 173tr, Michael Ver Sprill 128tl, Wirestock 115cla, 134

Getty Images: 500px Plus 101tl, Per Breiehagen 206b, Daniel Vi photograhy 21br, Jeff Foott 153cla, Getty Images News / Mario Tama 236br, Jeff Hutchens 91br, Martin Zwick / REDA&CO / Universal Images Group 120, Photography by Deb Snelson 207cr, Piriya Photography 6-7, RiverNorthPhotography 143cra, Jean Surprenant 44tl

Getty Images / iStock: 12MN 237tr, 2016 Danaan Andrew-Pacleb. All Rights Reserved. 112b, adamkaz 74, ademyan 32bl, aiisha5 178, benedek 28br, 140, Marc Bruxelle 146br, brytta 244-245, btrenkel 240, CampPhoto 150-151, Harry Collins 37cl, Raphael Comber 61bl, Gerald Corsi 138tr, 238b, DC_Colombia 234-235b, DenisTangneyJr 16, 182, dennisvdw 55tl, diegograndi 198tl, evenfh 69, Shunyu Fan 40-41, FilippoBacci 130, filrom 161br, franckreporter 14tr, GlowingEarth 36, grandriver 177, HaizhanZheng 99cl, haydukepdx 47t, helovi 233b, Hsa_Htaw 127tl, Francesco Ricca Iacomino 20, imagoDens 81, jarcosa 67b, JaySi 119br, JeffGoulden 93bl, jimfeng 38-39, jon chica parada 237cla, kanonsky 97tl, KenWiedemann 208tl, kickstand 129b, IRYNA KURILOVYCH 163t, 165bc, Davis Ladd 75tl, Daniel Lange 229crb, marktucan 115tr, Meinzahn 131cr, Nikada 156t, Henrique Nishimura 174-175tl, Maciej Noskowski 110-111, Onfokus 148bl, Andrew Peacock 116-117, 246bl, David Peloquin 76-77, Arturo Pea Romano Medina 48, James Perilli 79t, Pgiam 43cl, Fred Pinheiro 60bl, Edsel Querini 167tl, RichardSeeley 80, Robert DelVecchio - OcuDrone 212t, RollingEarth 197, Nuthawut Somsuk 4r, 70-71, Sportstock 141, stockstudioX 103, tomwachs 92bl, Michel VIARD 237cr, Jennifer Wan 19t, wanderluster 21clb, WerksMedia 12-13, Westhoff 210, Wirestock 205tr, Serge Yatunin 53

Tourism Nova Scotia: Patrick Rojo 187tr

Shutterstock.com: Mihai Andritoiu 84, Olesya Baron 149t, Joe Belanger 91bl, Jefferson Bernardes 199, Francisco Blanco 213tl, Tony Campbell 13br, canadastock 94-95, Janice Chen 33, Larissa Chilanti 59r, Rob Crandall 214, JC Cuellar 154bl, Danita Delimont 236bl, evenfh 242, f11photo 23b, 86, FCG 239clb, Tim Fleming 239cr, Mark Green 195, Paul Harrison 212b, Deborah Housten 138c, 143cla, Daniel Huebner 40bc, Judyta Jastrzebska 66, K_Boonnitrod 65, Khanh Le 177tr, Kit Leong 97br, Elisa Locci 164tl, lunamarina 109br, Jim Mallouk 211, MarinaaaaniraM 193, Maritxu 106-107, robert c. mosher 14cr,

Stefan Neumann 227br, Henrique Nishimura 159, Nowaczyk 235tr, Alexey Olenchenko 28bl, Paulbuhr 209, Sean Pavone 133t, Anton Rodionov 246cl, Eddy Savage 189t, Eleanor Scriven 247tl, SCStock 35cra, Alexey Seafarer 189, Oksana Shturo 98, StompingGirl 176tr, SurangaLK 186bl, T photography 191bl, TierneyMJ 75br, Willem Tims 5tr, 200-201, uniquephotography 221tr, Nadia Yong 99crb, Brett Zimmerman 42-43

All artwork by Clyfford Still, © City and County of Denver / ARS, NY: Brien Hollowell 75cl

SwimTrek: 231bl

Unsplash: Benjamn Gremler 160, Thomas Griggs 118-119bc

Cover images: *Front, Back, and Spine*: **Niaz Uddin**; *Back*: **Getty Images:** Cavan Images RF cr; **Getty Images / iStock:** DenisTangneyJr cl, filrom bc

All other images © Dorling Kindersley

This book was made with Forest Stewardship Council™ certified paper–one small step in DK's commitment to a sustainable future.
For more information go to www.dk.com/our-green-pledge

The rate at which the world is changing is constantly keeping the DK Eyewitness team on our toes. While we've worked hard to ensure that *Unforgettable Journeys The Americas* is accurate and up-to-date, we know that roads close, routes are altered, places shut, and new ones pop up in their stead. If you notice we've got something wrong or left something out, we want to hear about it. Please get in touch at travelguides@dk.co.uk

Project Editor Keith Drew
Senior Designer Vinita Venugopal
Senior Editor Zoë Rutland
US Senior Editor Jennette ElNaggar
Project Designer Ankita Sharma
Designer Donna-Marie Scrase
Proofreader Kathryn Glendenning
Indexer Hilary Bird
Picture Researcher Marta Bescos
Senior Cartographic Editor Casper Morris
Cartography Manager Suresh Kumar
Cartographer Ashif
Jacket Designer Laura O'Brien
Jacket Picture Researcher Laura O'Brien
Senior Production Controller Jason Little
Production Controller Kariss Ainsworth
Managing Editor Hollie Teague
Managing Art Editors Sarah Snelling, Priyanka Thakur
Art Director Maxine Pedliham
Publishing Director Georgina Dee

First American Edition, 2024
Published in the United States by DK Publishing
1745 Broadway, 20th Floor, New York, NY 10019

24 25 26 27 28 10 9 8 7 6 5 4 3 2 1
001-340101-Mar/2024

Published in Great Britain by Dorling Kindersley Limited

A catalog record for this book is available from the Library of Congress.
ISBN 978-0-7440-9512-8

Printed and bound in China
www.dk.com